"*Voices from the Confederacy: True Civil War Stories from the Men and Women of the Old South* is full of wonderful firsthand stories and accounts. It is well documented and the stories flow smoothly and give a true glimpse into the life and minds of Southerners through their eyes and the eyes of others. Samuel Mitcham's writing style glides from telling the tale to providing personal insight and thoughts. It was a learning read and the footnotes lead me to other great reads and great sources. It is a wonderful collection of anecdotes from those who were there."

—Jason Boshears, Lieutenant Commander-in-Chief, Sons of Confederate Veterans

"The human element of the War offers both inspiration and tragedy. The stories from those who fought, served, and suffered in this tremendous struggle will make you laugh and cry, but more importantly, they will earn your respect. Samuel Mitcham's books is essential reading to understand not only how men fought, but why they fought and why so many Southerners were willing to lose everything for the cause."

—Dr. Brion McClanahan, Author of *The Politically Incorrect Guide to the Founding Fathers* and several other books

VOICES *from the* CONFEDERACY

VOICES *from the* CONFEDERACY

True Civil War Stories from the
Men and Women of the Old South

SAMUEL W. MITCHAM, JR.

A KNOX PRESS BOOK
An Imprint of Permuted Press
ISBN: 978-1-63758-517-7
ISBN (eBook): 978-1-63758-518-4

Voices from the Confederacy:
True Civil War Stories from the Men and Women of the Old South

Permuted Press, LLC
New York • Nashville
permutedpress.com

Published in the United States of America
1 2 3 4 5 6 7 8 9 10

CONTENTS

CHAPTER I

THE START

The Civil War, to a large extent, was a clash of cultures. If culture is defined as "the total way of life of a people," Northerners and Southerners definitely took different paths since early colonial times. Dr. John Codman Ropes of Boston, the founder of the prestigious Military Historical of Massachusetts and one of the premier military historians of the period immediately after the Civil War, gives us some insight into why the South fought so hard and the Confederate Army performed so well.[1] In 1894, he wrote of the antebellum South: "The population [of the Southern States], almost wholly occupied in agricultural pursuits, was necessarily accustomed to life in the open air, to horses, to hunting and fishing, to exposure, to unusual physical exertion from time to time. Such conditions of life naturally foster a martial spirit. Then the aristocratic *régime* that prevailed in the slave-holding States was conducive to the preference

---

[1] Ropes (1836–1899) a Harvard graduate, a Boston lawyer, philosopher, and military historian, was physically unfit for military service, although he rendered all the assistance he could for the Union, especially for the men of his brother's regiment, the 20th Massachusetts Infantry. His brother, Henry Ropes, was killed at Gettysburg. One of his books, *The Army under Pope*, focused public attention on General Fitz John Porter (1822–1901), who was unjustly court-martialed and condemned for the Union defeat at the Second Manassas. Porter was vindicated by a special commission in 1878 and by a special act of Congress in 1886. See John Fiske, *Proceedings of the American Academy of Arts and Sciences*, Vol. XXXV (1899–1900), pp. 641–646, for an excellent summary of Ropes's life and career.

of military over civil pursuits that has generally been characteristic of aristocracies. The young men of the better classes eagerly embraced the profession of arms as offering by far the noblest opportunities for the exercise of the higher virtues, and for allowing the greatest distinction in the State. They made excellent officers, while those below them in the social scale, sharing as they did largely in the same feelings, and possessed by the same ideas of life and duty, made admirable private soldiers and warrant officers. Endowed with a marvelous capacity of endurance, whether of physical exertion or lack of food, uncomplaining, ever ready for a fight, the soldiers of the South were first-rate material in the hands of the able officers who so generally commanded them...They loved fighting for its own sake, and no more willing troops ever responded to the call of their leaders.

"...it cannot be doubted that the Southern volunteers frequently scored successes over their Northern adversaries for the simple and sole reason that to them, the game of war, was not only a perfectly legitimate pursuit, but one of the noblest, if not the noblest that could claim the devotion of brave and free men. They went into it *con amore*; they gave to its duties their most zealous attention; and they reaped a full measure of the success which those who throw themselves with all their hearts into any career deserve and generally attain."[2]

Eliza Frances Andrews (called "Fanny") put it another way. She was the daughter of a strongly antisecessionist Georgia judge and went on to become an internationally acclaimed botanist and author. In 1908, reflecting on her life, she wrote: "The Old South, with its stately feudal regime, was not the monstrosity that some would have us believe, but merely a case of belated survival, like those giant sequoias of the Pacific slope... It had outlived its day...the last representative of an economic system that had served the purposes of the [human] race since the days when man first emerged from his prehuman state until the rise of the modern

---

[2]   John Codman Ropes, *Story of the Civil War*, Vol. I (New York: 1894), pp. 126–129.

industrial system made wage slavery a more efficient agent of production than chattel slavery."[3]

Even today, despite the leveling and degrading influence of television and other media, the South is different. It has its own cuisine, dialect, value system, and social mores. Southerners also tend to be more religious, and the South is often referred to as "the Bible Belt." Southern hospitality, which is famous today, was even more pronounced antebellum. Fanny Andrews dubbed it "Our chief extravagance." Before the war, it was virtually unlimited. "Anybody respectable was welcome to come as often as they liked and stay as long as they pleased," she recalled. Her own family consisted of her father, his wife, their seven children, her brother's wife and daughter, an aunt, and a niece. But, she recalled, "I remember very few occasions during my father's life when there were no guests in the house."[4] The family even built two cottages—one on either side of "the Big House," to handle the overflow.

The war divided many families. Eliza's father, Judge Garnett Andrews, would not allow it to divide his. Andrews owned about two hundred slaves but was a fervent supporter of the Union. He would not allow the secession crisis to be discussed in his house. His daughter, Eliza, was a firm Confederate, and three of her four brothers joined the Confederate Army; the other was twelve. Judge Andrews was elected to the legislature, despite the fact that the county was strongly pro-secession, and his pro-Union views were well known. He managed to convince the legislature it should hold a secession convention and popular referendum on the issue instead

---

[3] Eliza Frances Andrews, *The War-Time Journal of a Georgia Girl, 1864–1865* (New York: 1908), p. 11 (hereafter cited as "Andrews"). Her father was a superior court judge, a plantation owner, and a strong Unionist, although three of his sons fought in the Confederate army. "Fanny" Andrews was well educated at LaGrange Female College, where she graduated in 1857. She was fluent in French and conversant in Latin. She became a popular writer and penned novels and dozens of articles for national magazines. Financial difficulties after the war and her parents' deaths forced her into a teaching career. She became an internationally acclaimed botanist and wrote two books on the subject, one of which was a standard college and university text for years. She was the first woman invited into the prestigious International Academy of Literature and Science. Fanny Andrews died in Rome, Georgia, in 1931, at age ninety.

[4] Andrews, pp. 177–178.

of simply voting to leave the Union on its own authority, as Louisiana did. Perhaps he hoped the people would vote against secession. His hopes were dashed. The pro-secessionist delegates won 50,143 votes, as opposed to 37,123 for those who voted to try to cooperate with the Lincoln regime. The convention voted to leave the Union, 208 to 89, on January 19, 1861. Incidentally, the antisecessionists received the derogatory nickname "submissionists."

Eliza Frances Andrews

Although attitudes varied from place to place and even from plantation to plantation, black-white relations in the South were generally good prewar. Mary Polk Branch wrote about master-slave relations in her book, *Memoirs of a Southern Woman*. She was the daughter of Dr. William Julius, longtime president of the First Bank of Columbia, Tennessee, and a cousin of James K. Polk. Her brother was Confederate Brigadier General Lucius E. Polk. She was educated at Madam Canda's French School in New York and in Philadelphia. She returned to her family's plantation in Tennessee. She recalled: "There was such a kindly feeling on both sides between the owners and their slaves—inherited kindly feelings. How could it be otherwise? Many were descendants of those who had served in the same family for generations—for instance, the nurse who nursed my children was the daughter of my nurse, and her grandmother had nursed my mother. My maid Virginia (I can not recall the time when she was not my maid) was a very handsome young mulatto to whom I was especially attached. When she was married in her white dress and long veil flowing to her feet, the ceremony was performed in our back parlor, and Bishop Otey, the first bishop of Tennessee, officiated."[5]

"Our nurses we always called 'Mammy' and it was not considered good manners to address any old negro man or woman otherwise than as 'uncle' or 'aunt,' adding the name whatever that might be—the surname was always the master's. We were taught to treat them with respect."[6]

Confederate veteran Thornton Hardie Bowman also wrote about master-slave relations after the war. Bowman was born in the Feliciana country of southeast Louisiana. His ancestors were from South Carolina, fought with Francis Marion ("the Swamp Fox") during the Revolutionary War, and were with Andrew Jackson at New Orleans in 1815. His father started out with little material wealth but moved to the lands west of the Tensas (northeast Louisiana) and cleared a large tract of land out of the dense canebrakes. He built a plantation he called Alphenia on the banks of the river and became wealthy. He recalled his "free and happy boyhood which sounds now to my children as unreal as a dream. Pecans, walnuts, grapes and muscadines grew everywhere in great profusion. Fish of all kinds, from the red-sided perch to the fifty-pound cat[fish], abounded in the lakes and bayous. Squirrels, turkeys, deer, bear and wildcat roamed the woods undisturbed. The lakes in the winter were literally covered with ducks and geese...I was provided with boat and fishing tackle, gun and pony. About twelve little negro boys, too small to go to the fields, were my constant attendants and playmates. Together we rowed the boat; together we fished and went swimming." Bowman liked to climb trees and shake the limbs, causing the nuts to fall. The little African Americans would pick them up and they divided the proceeds. If a hunt was successful, they ate together in the big house. "I loved these black friends and they loved me..." he

---

[5]   Mary Polk Branch, *Memoirs of a Southern Woman "Within the Lines"* (Chicago: 1912), p. 12 (hereafter cited as "Branch").

[6]   Branch, p. 11.

recalled. "Is it any wonder, then, that kindly feelings, which have had so much to interrupt them, still exist between the old master and his former slaves?"

"So much has been said and written by uninformed persons about the unkind and even brutal treatment of the negroes…They, of course, had to work, and many of them to work hard; but not so hard as many white laborers at the North…. They were happy at their work. Think you that if they had been driven like galley slaves, the coon songs, some of which we find in print, would ever have rung out on the morning air in delightful melody as these contented servants went and returned to the fields? They were well fed on good, wholesome food. It was the master's interest so to do. I remember how the dinner buckets, well filled with bread and bacon, hominy and potatoes, were sent out to the fields by water cart. Molasses, milk and vegetables were freely furnished." Many plantation owners did not require the servants to keep themselves clean, but Bowman's father required them to bathe every Saturday night.[7]

Most of the African Americans had a "patch" on which they could grow what they pleased and sell the proceeds for small sums of cash. "They were well cared for when sick. On many plantations the physician was paid an annual salary. Many, many time have I been called up in the midnight hours to carry medicine to the quarters," Bowman recalled.

Preaching was handled by Daddy Billy, an African American Methodist circuit rider, who impressed young Bowman with his eloquence. He preached the gospel at several surrounding plantations. When the war broke out, Bowman recalled tears streaming down Daddy Billy's face as he threw his arms around Bowman's father's neck.

Bowman Sr. left Daddy Billy in charge of the plantation during the war. Neither Billy's color nor profession saved him when the Yankees came. He recalled: "Them poor white trash, dressed in blue, come here. I axed 'em in and told 'em I was a minister of the gospel; but law, chile, dat never done

---

[7]   Thornton H. Bowman, *Reminiscences of an Ex-Confederate Soldier or Forty Years on Crutches* (Austin, Texas: 1904), pp. 9–10 (hereafter referred to as "Bowman").

a bit er good. They stole Mary's chickens and one of my pigs...and dem blasted rascals broke down de do' of de smokehouse and tuk my pony."[8]

None of this is meant to imply that the slaves did not want to be free— most of them did. But this does not mean they necessarily hated their master or his white family—most of them did not. Many of them worked for Confederate victory, and without their skill and labor, the Southern armies could not have held out as long as they did. Some of them went to war with "Massa" or the master's son. Quite a few recovered his body and took it home for burial after he was killed. It will no doubt surprise some readers, but of thousands of African Americans fought for the Confederacy. Private James G. Bates of the 13th Iowa Volunteers was certainly surprised when an African American Confederate sniper shot some of his comrades. He wrote to his father: "I can assure you of a certainty, that the rebels have negro soldiers in their army. One of their best sharp shooters, and the boldest of them all here is a negro.... You can see him plain enough with the naked eye"[9] In fact, the first Union officer killed in battle in the Civil War was Major Theodore Winthrop, a member of a prominent New England abolitionist family. He was shot down in the Battle of Big Bethel by an African American Confederate sniper.[10]

The Federals had been warned. Famous Abolitionist Frederick Douglass, himself a former slave, told Abraham Lincoln to his face that, unless he guaranteed the slaves freedom, "they would take up arms for the rebels." The president would not listen—at least not yet. As a result, Douglass wrote in September 1861, "There are at the present moment, many colored men in the Confederate Army doing duty not as cooks,

8   Bowman, pp. 11–13.

9   https://scv-kirby-smith.org/Black%confederate.htm. Accessed 2012.

10   Frank Moore, *The Civil War in Song and Story* (New York: 1865), p. 481. Also see Richard Rollins, "Black Southerners in Gray," in Richard Rollins, ed., *Black Southerners in Gray: Essays on Afro-Americans in Confederate Armies* (Redondo Beach, California: 1994), p. 16 (hereafter cited as "Rollins").

servants and laborers, but as real soldiers, having muskets on their shoulders and bullets in their pockets ready to shoot down loyal troops and do all that soldiers may do to destroy the Federal government."[11]

Horace Greeley essentially agreed in 1863 when he wrote: "For more than two years, Negroes have been extensively employed in belligerent operations by the Confederacy. They have been embodied and drilled as rebel soldiers and had paraded with white troops at a time when this would not have been tolerated in the armies of the Union."[12]

In September 1862, Robert E. Lee ordered a staff officer to determine for him how many armed slaves were serving in the ranks of the Army of Northern Virginia. There were more than three thousand under arms, carrying "rifles, muskets, sabers, Bowie knives, dirks" and all sorts of other weapons.[13] This report was delivered shortly after the Battle of Sharpsburg (Antietam). Three thousand men would equal more than 7 percent of his army. Lee later commented that "When you eliminate the black Confederate soldier, you eliminate the history of the South."[14]

Other generals would agree with Lee. "There is no better soldier anywhere in the world than the black Confederate soldier." These words were spoken by Nathan Bedford Forrest, a slave trader before the war, a Confederate lieutenant general during the war, and the head of the Ku Klux Klan after the war. He also said of his black soldiers: "These boys stayed with me...and better Confederates never lived."[15] Even today, there is a significant African American membership in the Sons of Confederate Veterans.

---

[11]   Frederick Douglass, *Douglass' Monthly*, Vol. IV (September 1861), p. 516.

[12]   Walter E. Williams, "It's Too Bad War's Victors Get to Write Its History, Often with Bias," Deseret News, November 3, 2010, https://www.deseret.com/2010/11/3/20150347/walter-e-williams-it-s-too-bad-war-s-victors-get-to-write-its-history-often-with-bias.

[13]   Thomas C. Mendes, "Blacks, Jews Fight on the Side of the South," *Washington Times*, June 15, 2002.

[14]   See Rollins.

[15]   "Papers," Old City Courthouse Museum, Vicksburg, Mississippi.

A squad of Confederate combat infantrymen. They were part of the 5th Georgia Infantry Regiment, which spent three years on the western front. Note the third man from the left is African American (Old City Courthouse Museum, Vicksburg, Mississippi)

How many African Americans fought for the South? Confederate records are, as usual, too inadequate to give us precise numbers. Estimates of the number of African American combat soldiers vary from a few thousand to one hundred thousand, with eighty thousand to ninety-six thousand being the best estimates, in my view, based on the report to General Lee. Ed Kennedy, a historian, graduate of Command and General Staff College, and a retired colonel, seems to agree. He estimated that 7–8 percent of the Confederate forces were black.[16] Incidentally, the black Rebels were much better led than their Union counterparts because they had the same officers as the white Rebels. African Americans who fought for the North were often (but certainly not always) commanded by "duds."

The election of 1860 gave a Northern sectional party control of much of the government. The influential *Southern Literary Messenger* editorialized

---

[16] See J. H. Segars and Charles K. Barrow, *Black Southerners in Confederate Armies* (Gretna, Louisiana: 2001), p. 203ff.

in January 1861: "…we are obliged to say, that a free government cannot be long administered by a sectional party…So that, in the opinion of the writer, the time has come when the strongest dictates of prudence—nay, the very sense and duty of self-preservation, demand that the South should set up for herself and leave the country."[17] It included a popular lyric:

> "Yankee Doodle undertook
> With patriot devotion
> To trim the tree of liberty
> According to his notion.
> "Yankee Doodle on a limb,
> Like any other noodle,
> Cut between the tree and him
> And down came Yankee Doodle.
> "Yankee Doodle broke his neck
> And every limb about him,
> And then the tree of liberty
> Did very well without him."[18]

The advent of the Republican Party also changed society in Washington, D.C. Writing in 1904, a New York correspondent recognized that Southern women controlled Washington society before the arrival of Lincoln. Sara Pryor, the biographer of Martha Washington and the wife of Virginia congressman Roger Pryor, recalled: "With their natural and acquired graces, with their inherited taste and ability in social affairs, it was natural that the reins should fall to them. They represented a clique of aristocracy; they were recognized leaders who could afford to smile good-naturedly at the awkward and perplexed attempts of the women from the other sections— Mrs. Senator This, Mrs. Congressman That—to thread the ins and outs of Washington's social labyrinth. To none of these ladies was the thought

---

17   George S. Bernard, comp. and ed., *War Talks of Confederate Veterans* (Petersburg, Virginia: 1892), p. 3 (hereafter cited as "Bernard").

18   Bernard, p. 3, citing *Southern Literary Messenger* (January 1861).

pleasant of secession from the Union and consequent giving up whatever of social dominion she had acquired." But politics in 1860 was a man's world. Mrs. Pryor added, "…we [women] dared not express opinions in public (and not freely in private), such was the time. Conversation had been always, in the South, an art carefully cultivated. Conversation suffered at a time when we were forced to ignore subjects that possessed us with absorbing interest and to confine ourselves to trivialities."[19]

Mrs. Pryor is a fine example of the truth of this statement. Her own husband, Roger A. Pryor, was a "fire-eater"—a rabid secessionist who helped lead Virginia out of the Union. He was even offered the opportunity of firing the first shot on Fort Sumter and starting the war on April 12, 1861. At least he had sense enough to decline this "honor."

Lincoln called for seventy-five thousand volunteers to "suppress the rebellion" in the cotton states on April 15, 1861. This one act doubled the size of the Confederacy's military potential because it led directly to the succession of Arkansas, Tennessee, North Carolina, and Virginia. The Virginia State Convention, which twice voted against succession and by wide margins, voted eighty-eight to fifty-five to leave the Union on April 17. The convention did, however, provide for a plebiscite on May 23. "Perhaps the people will not vote us out of the Union after all," one Washington insider exclaimed hopefully to Robert M. T. Hunter.

"My dear lady," the U.S. senator from Virginia replied, "you may place your little hand against Niagara [Falls] with more certainty of staying the torrent than you can oppose this movement. It was written long ago in the everlasting stars that the South would be driven out of the Union by the North."[20]

---

19 Mrs. Roger Pryor [Sara Agnes Rice Pryor], *Reminiscences of Peace and War* (New York: 1905), pp. 81–82 (hereafter cited as "Pryor"); *New York Herald*, February 7, 1904.

20 Pryor, p. 124.

Hunter was right: Virginia voted to secede 124,896 to 20,390.[21] The next day, May 24, the U.S. army crossed the Potomac and occupied Arlington Heights and Alexandria.

When the legislature voted to secede, many of Virginia's citizens were still opposed, or at least lukewarm, to the war. Then, on the night of April 20, 1861, the Gosport naval yard (just south of Portsmouth, Virginia) was evacuated by U.S. forces. "[T]he yard with all its shipping and buildings, and vast stores of ammunition, went up in flames," Lieutenant John H. Lewis recalled. The old battleship *Pennsylvania* was burned. Its guns were still loaded, and when the flames reached them, discarded toward Norfolk. The Federal fleet went down the river, with its gun ports opened and its heavy naval artillery aimed at Southern towns. From that moment, Lewis recalled, "the whole state was firmly cemented to the cause of the South."[22]

Jubal A. Early voted against Virginia's Ordinance of Secession, but he "regarded Abraham Lincoln, his counsellors and supporters, as the real traitors who had overthrown the constitution and government of the United States, and established in lieu thereof an odious despotism...I recognized the right of resistance and revolution as exercised by our fathers in 1776, and, without cavil as to the name by which it was called, I entered the military service of my State, willingly, cheerfully, and zealously."[23]

21 "Virginia County Vote on the Secession Ordinance, May 23, 1861," New River Notes, https://www.newrivernotes.com/historical_antebellum_1861_virginia_votefor secession.htm. Also see Nelson Lankford, "Virginia Convention of 1861," Encyclopedia Virginia, February 1, 2021. https://encyclopediavirginia.org/entries/virginia-convention-of-1861.

22 John H. Lewis, *A Rebel in Pickett's Charge*, (1895; digital ed., Byte Books: 2016), p. 55. All page numbers from this book are from the Kindle edition.

23 Jubal A. Early, *A Memoir of the Last Year of the War for Independence in the Confederate States of America* (Lynchburg: 1867), p. v (hereafter cited as "Early").

When Virginia joined the Confederacy, he embraced its cause with the same ardor. "I fought through the entire war, without once regretting the course I had pursued..."[24]

Militia companies were forming throughout the South since John Brown's terrorist attack on Harpers Ferry in October 1859. After the South fired on Fort Sumter on April 12, 1861, the Southerners organized these companies into regiments and brigades under the supervision of the state governments.

"The Confederate soldier," McCarthy wrote, "was a venerable old man, a youth, a child, a preacher, a farmer, merchant, student, statesman, orator, father, brother, husband, son—the wonder of the world, the terror of his foes." The Rebel soldiers faced staggering odds. The North had every advantage. The population of the United States in 1860 was 31,443,321. Of this, nine million people resided in the Southern states. This included three million five hundred thousand slaves, giving the South five million five hundred fifty thousand white people from which to field their armies. According to historians John H. and David S. Eicher, the "Military Population" of the North (white males aged eighteen through forty-five) was 3,954.776, as opposed to 1,064,193 for the South.[25] These figures do not include roughly one hundred ninety-one thousand black men who served in the Union Army, as well as 489,920 foreign mercenaries from

---

[24] Early, p. vi.
[25] John H. Eicher and David J. Eicher, *Civil War High Commands* (Stanford, California: 2001), p. 6. These figures exclude 516,085 from the border states of Missouri, Kentucky, and Maryland and 89,011 from the territories and the District of Columbia, most of whom adhered to the Union.

fifteen different countries.[26] At their maximum extent, the Northern armies fielded more than one million men. During the 1861 to 1865 period, 2,898,304 men served in the Union army.[27] That was 1,812,121 more troops than served in all of America's other wars combined up until that point. We do not know exactly how many men served in the Confederate Army because many Southern records were lost or destroyed at the end of the conflict. Estimates vary between six hundred thousand to slightly over a million, with eight hundred thousand to eight hundred fifty thousand being commonly cited figures. General Cooper, the Southern Historical Society, and Thornton H. Bowman, however, put the number at six hundred thousand.[28] It is unlikely that President Davis and his generals ever fielded more than three hundred thousand men at any one time.[29]

The 24th Virginia Infantry Regiment was somewhat typical. It formed under Colonel Jubal Early in Lynchburg in May and June 1861. During the course of the war, 1,303 men served in this regiment. One hundred six of them were killed in action, 202 died from disease, 509 were wounded, and 325 were captured. The regiment suffered 1,142 casualties during the war. It surrendered twenty-two enlisted men at Appomattox Court House on April 9, 1865. Not one officer was left standing.

The experiences of and casualties suffered by the 24th Virginia were not unusual in the Confederate Army.

---

[26] Many Southern blacks were conscripted into the Union army against their will. See James Ronald Kennedy and Walter Donald Kennedy, *The South Was Right!*, 3rd ed. (Columbia, South Carolina, 2021). Also see "Report of U.S. Brigadier General Rufus Saxton to Secretary of War Edwin M. Stanton, December 30, 1864," in United States War Department, *The War of the Rebellion: A Compilation of the Official Records of the Union and Confederate Armies*, Fred C. Ainsworth and Joseph W. Kirkley, comp. (Washington, D.C.: 1900), Series 3, Vol. IV, Sec. 2, pp. 1022–1042 (hereafter cited as "O.R.") for an eye-opening account of conditions among black people in South Carolina. All O.R. entries are from Series 1 unless otherwise noted.

[27] Thomas L. Livermore, *Numbers and Losses in the Civil War in America* (Boston and New York: 1900), p. 1 (after cited as "Livermore").

[28] Bowman, p. 35. A lieutenant during the war, Bowman was later Texas secretary of state.

[29] All the figures cited above include state and militia units.

The Confederate volunteer of 1861 bore little resemblance to the veteran of 1865. When the war began, he made extensive preparations for life in the field. He wore heavy boots with thick soles, a heavy, often double-breasted coat with a long skirt, a small, stiff cap with a narrow brim, and a huge, long, heavy overcoat, frequently with a cape.

On his back was a knapsack, which contained a full load of underwear, soap, towels, a comb, brush, looking-glass, toothbrush, writing paper, envelopes, pens, ink, pencils, boot polish, smoking tobacco, chewing tobacco, pipes, cotton strips in case he was wounded, needles, thread, buttons, a table knife, fork, and spoon, as well as anything else an individual soldier thought might be necessary. On the outside were two tightly folded blankets and a rubber oilcloth. The knapsacks weighed fifteen to twenty-five pounds and occasionally more.

Typically, the soldier had a haversack, in addition to the knapsack. It was loaded down with provisions. He also carried a canteen full of water, which increased its weight. He carried revolvers and Bowie knives, as well as his rifle and bayonet. Flannel and wool shirts were at first considered necessary, as were gloves. All three were soon eliminated.

Besides each soldier's private luggage, each mess (five to ten men) had a large camp chest, containing skillet, frying pan, coffee boiler, coffee box, lard bucket, salt box, sugar box, meal box, flour box, and plates, cups, and the like. The chests were so large that eight or ten of them filled up the typical army wagon, and it took two strong men to load one into a wagon. Each mess owned an axe and water bucket. Each company had several tents and small sheet-iron stoves with stove pipes. Officers had valises and their own trunks. McCarthy recalled the result was "an immense pile of stuff, so that each company had a small wagon train of its own."[30] Early in the war, many messes had a "boy"—a body servant to black boots, and fetch water, cook cornbread, fetch wood, and take care of other such tasks. "Never was there fonder admiration than these darkies displayed for their

---

[30] Carlton McCarthy, *Detailed Minutiae of Soldier Life in the Army of Northern Virginia, 1861–1865* (Richmond, Virginia: 1899), pp. 17–19 (hereafter cited as "McCarthy").

masters," McCarthy recalled. As the war wore on and rations got short, many of the servants were sent home.

Incidentally, Southerners of that era generally called their chattels "servants" rather than slaves.

The volunteers were so loaded down with all manner of things that a march was torture. There were also so many wagon trains that it was impossible to guard them in hostile territory. "The change came rapidly," McCarthy recalled. The Confederate Army applied the principle of less luggage equals less labor. Heavy boots were discarded in favor of strong brogues (brogans) with big, fat heels. Short-waisted, single-breasted jackets replaced long-tailed coats, and soft slouch hats succeeded caps. Overcoats proved to be great inconveniences and were discarded; it was thought that the trouble of carrying them in hot weather outweighed the comfort of wearing them on cold days. Many Rebels discarded their overcoats in summer because they were confident they could capture one from the enemy in cold weather. Often, they were right.

The knapsack disappeared early in the conflict. Clean clothes and underwear were too much trouble to carry. "Certainly it did not pay to carry around clean clothes while waiting for the time to use them." The men also found that one blanket was sufficient. It (and the oil cloth) was rolled up and carried across the chest, over the left shoulder, with the ends tied under the right arm. Tents became a rarity. The men slept on the ground. Usually, two men slept together. One oilcloth was placed on the ground, the men covered themselves with two blankets, and the second oilcloth was placed on top. They slept with reasonable comfort in all kinds of weather.

The immensely practical haversack was used throughout the war, but as the war wore on, it rarely contained rations. Many men discarded it as well and carried nothing but what they had in their pockets. Some infantrymen even discarded their cartridge boxes and carried their ammunition caps and cartridges in their pockets.

Canteens were often replaced by strong tin cups because they were lighter and easier to fill. They were also useful in making coffee or ersatz coffee. Some men kept their canteens, but they frequently carried cider or buttermilk instead of water.

The enlisted men found revolvers were heavy and fairly useless, so they sent them home; therefore, their women could protect themselves and their children from ruffians, who were numerous in many sectors. The wool and flannel shirts were replaced by cotton shirts, which were easier to wash. It was also found that vermin did not multiply so rapidly in cotton as in wool. Usually, the cotton shirts were white.

Gloves were soon discarded as useless because one could not buckle a harness, load a musket, handle a ramrod, or wield an axe with them on. Most of the men also threw away their bayonets. The camp chests were also scrapped, even by the generals, except in the rear area service support units. One skillet and a couple of frying pans became adequate for several messes. The water bucket was never replaced.

At the start of the war, artillerymen were issued heavy sabers. They proved to be of little use. They frequently stuck them in the mud so the ordnance officers could pick them up and give them to the cavalry.

"Reduced to the minimum, the private soldier consisted of one man, one hat, one jacket, one shirt, one pair of pants, one pair of drawers, one pair of shoes, and one pair of socks," one of the veterans recalled. "His baggage was one blanket, one rubber blanket, and one haversack. The haversack generally contained smoking tobacco and a pipe, and a small piece of soap, with temporary additions of apples, persimmons, blackberries, and such other commodities as he could pick up on the march."[31]

Sometimes the wagon trains would carry the company's property, which usually consisted of three frying pans and skillets, although these were more frequently carried by the soldiers. The wagons carried ammunition and commissary and quartermaster stores. Any baggage the men had was carried by the men themselves.

Initially, the typical Confederate was not well armed. "When our Company was formed at San Antonio we were notified that we must furnish our own accouterments," Private Alfred J. Wilson of Company K, 1st

---

[31]   McCarthy, p. 26.

Texas Infantry recalled, "so each got him an old squirrel rifle and a double barrel shot gun and big six-shooter. Then we gathered up all the old mill saw files and had them made into butcher knives a foot long, and so made that they could be used for bayonets. C. C. Johnson, who ran a saddle shop, and I made each of the boys a leather belt, pistol and knife scabbard and cap box."

"The shotguns did the best execution as they were loaded with a charge called 'Buck and Ball,' which consisted of one ball and a number of buckshot and was wrapped in a paper and tied up so that they were convenient to carry and load and when fired always found something. It was like a charge of grape and canister on a small scale."[32]

During the last three years of the war, the Rebel soldier had little to weigh him down, and this fact certainly had an impact on several campaigns. "No soldiers ever marched with less to encumber them, and none marched faster or held out longer," McCarthy recalled.

"The courage and devotion of the men rose equal to every hardship and privation, and the very intensity of their sufferings became a source of merriment…they laughed at their own bare feet, ragged clothes and pinched faces; and weak, hungry, cold, wet, worried with vermin and itch, dirty, with no hope of reward or rest, marched cheerfully to meet the well-fed and warmly clad hosts of the enemy."[33]

---

[32]   Mamie Yeary, *Reminiscences of the Boys in Gray, 1861–1865*, Volume II, (Dallas: 1912), pp. 803–804, referred to hereafter as "Yeary").

[33]   McCarthy, p. 28.

CHAPTER II

THE WOMEN

The women of the South were the Confederacy's strongest and most uncompromising supporters. Phoebe Levy Pember, the daughter of a highly respected Jewish family from Charleston, South Carolina, recalled: "The women of the South had been openly and violently rebellious from the moment they thought their States' right touched. They incited the men to struggle in support of their views, and whether right or wrong, sustained them nobly to the end. They were the first to rebel—the last to succumb...feeling a passion of interest in every man in the gray uniform of the Confederate service, they were doubly anxious to give comfort and assistance to the sick and wounded."[34]

Pember had no idea what she was in for. Despite the fact that she had no medical background whatsoever, she became the matron (administrator) of Richmond's Chimborazo Hospital in December 1862 and served in this post until after Appomattox. She and her staff treated seventy-six thousand sick and wounded patients during the war, and she became perhaps the most famous hospital administrator in the conflict. She was honored by the U.S. Postal Service in 1955, when a stamp bearing her likeness was issued.

---

[34] Phoebe Yates Pember, *A Southern Woman's Story* (New York: 1879), p. 13 (hereafter cited as "Pember").

Phoebe Levy Pember

At the start of the war, one young man, Ben Shepard, proposed to a young lady named Helen. She promised him an answer on a particular night. When he appeared at the appointed time, she was noncommittal because he had not enlisted in the army.

"You promised me my answer to-night," he pressed her.

"Well, you can't have it, Ben, until you have fought the Yankees," she responded.

"What heart will I have for fighting if you give me no promise?" he asked.

"I'll not be engaged to any man until he has fought the Yankees," she said firmly. "You distinguish yourself in the war, and then see what I'll have to say."

"But suppose I don't come back at all!"

"Oh, then I'll acknowledge an engagement and be good to your mother—and wear mourning all the same—provided—your wounds are all in the front."

This answer was not the one Ben wanted to hear, but it was that way throughout the South. "Engagements were postponed until they could find of what mettle a lover was," Sara Pryor recalled.[35]

---

[35] Pryor, pp. 129–130.

Ben Shepard enlisted in a Virginia infantry regiment. Helen and practically every young wife or sweetheart, father, mother, matron, or third cousin twice removed, was present when the regiment marched to the train depot while the band played "Dixie." When the train began to move, Shepard leaned out the window and asked Helen, who was just below him, "Can't I have the promise now, Helen?"

"Yes, yes, Ben—dear Ben, I promise!" As the cars rolled away, she turned to her friends and calmly announced: "Girls, I'm engaged to Ben Shepard."

"I'm engaged to half a dozen of them," one of the young ladies retorted.

"That's nothing," another replied. "I'm engaged to the whole regiment."

There was a depressed pall over the crowd after the train rolled out of sight. What were they to do next? "We will hold a prayer meeting in each other's houses, at four o'clock every afternoon," one of the women declared. "We can pray, if we cannot fight."

The prayer meetings continued every day until the end of the war.[36]

"To be idle was torture," Sara Pryor recalled. "We women resolved ourselves into a sewing society—resting not on Sundays. Sewing machines were put into the churches, which became depots for flannel, muslin, strong linen, and even uniform cloth. When the hour of meeting arrived, the sewing class would be summoned by the ringing of the church bell."

Mrs. Pryor was a woman of the upper class and had little or no experience in sewing. "We instituted a monster sewing class, which we hugely enjoyed, to meet daily at my home on Market Street."[37] By the end of the war, General Pryor's wife was an expert couturiere. So were all the others.

Most of the volunteers of 1861 had no idea what they were in for. They thought their principal occupation would be actual combat with the

---

[36] Pryor, pp. 133–136
[37] Pryor, p. 131.

Yankees. They didn't realize that they would sometimes camp for months without firing a shot, or march and countermarch twenty miles just to deceive—rather than fight—the enemy. Guard duty and picket duty were necessary but so was drudgery. They built bridges, repaired roads, drove wagons or ambulances, and performed myriad other mundane duties.[38]

Confederate soldiers were almost always willing to fight but only begrudgingly submitted to routine duty or camp discipline.

Private soldiers were willing to fight and needed no urging to do their duty; in fact, just the opposite was true. Initially, Confederate soldiers were outraged when they were held in reserve. They regarded such an order as a deliberate insult, administered because colonel or general so-and-so had a grudge against their company, regiment, or battery. The purpose of the order, they averred, was to humiliate them by denying them a place in the battle. "How soon," McCarthy recalled, "did they learn the sweetness of a day's repose in the rear!"[39]

Company D, 24th Virginia Infantry, was organized in Pearisburg, Giles County, on April 25, 1861. It had a strength of 122 men and James H. French was elected captain. Private David E. Johnston, then sixteen years old, recalled his company leaving home:

"It was a lovely May morning; the sun shone in all his splendor, the birds sang, all nature seemed to smile, and there was nothing to indicate that this should be the last farewell for many noble Giles County boys to home, friends, and loved ones. We seemed to be going on a holiday journey, to return in a few days. But alas! when the time of departure arrived, what a change of scene! The town was being filled with people,—the fathers,

---

[38] Picket or guard duty usually consisted of two hours on, followed by a relief and four hours off.

[39] McCarthy, p. 30.

mothers, brothers, sisters, wives, relatives, friends and lovers of the men and boys who were starting on the errand of war. Here was a fond and loving mother clinging to her baby boy, weeping, sobbing, praying the Father of all Mercies to protect and preserve the life of her darling child, amid the fury and storm of battle. There stood the patriotic, gray haired father, the tears trickling down his cheeks, giving to his beloved son words of comfort, begging that he act the man, be brave, do his duty, refrain from bad habits, and to shun all appearance of evil. A loving sister might be seen with her arms around a brother's neck, reminding him of her love and attachment, and her grief and sorrow at parting from one with whom she had been associated from childhood's days, upon whom she had leaned for protection, and upon whom her fondest hopes for the future rested, and whose face she was, in all probability, gazing upon for the last time. Ears were not deaf to the mutual promises and plighted faith of lovers, of what they hoped one day should be realized. Nor were eyes dim to the parting glances and silent tears, for scarcely could be found an eye that was not bathed in tears on this occasion. It was weeping, shaking of hands, 'goodbye,' and 'God bless you;' and thus the scene continued until the long train of wagons drove us away."[40]

Private David E. Johnston (1861) from his book, *The Story of a Confederate Boy in the Civil War*, published in 1914

---

[40] David E. Johnston, *Confederate Boy in the Civil War* (Portland, Oregon: 1914), (hereafter cited as "Johnston") from Project Gutenberg, https://www.gutenberg.org/files/44889/44889-h/44889-h.htm.

Congressman David E. Johnston, circa 1906

The company marched to a railroad station twenty-one miles away and took the train to Lynchburg, where they were quartered in "rude plank sheds," which were part of Camp Davis. Their beds consisted of a little straw and blankets. They were issued a tin cup, camp kettle, and frying pan, and were forced to learn how to cook. (None of them knew how.)

A few days later, they were issued Springfield muskets, bayonets, scabbards, and cartridge boxes but no ammunition. They learned the basics of handling arms, standing guard, and so forth. After eight days at Camp Davis, however, they left for Manassas Junction on May 31. After an all-night train ride, they reached Camp Pickens, as the post at Manassas was called. Two or three days later, they marched to Davis Ford on the Occoquan River, where they pitched their tents and occasionally performed outpost or picket duty. They had company drill every day and religious devotionals every night.

"First the order is given: 'Prepare to march!'" Private McCarthy recalled. "The soldiers rolled their blankets and threw away unneeded items. They weighed the benefit of having something against the trouble of carrying it five to 20 miles. For example, a man with a collection of four or five blankets might decide to leave three of them. Often, items discarded by one soldier were picked up by another.

"The orderly sergeant yelled 'Fall in!' and called the roll. The troops assembled and marched off in an orderly fashion. They typically marched in step for about an hour, after which somebody started a song, and 'route step' replaced marching 'in step.' Laughter and joking then broke out. They often poked good-natured fun of passers-by, such as an officer on horseback. 'Come out of that hat!' they would yell. 'You can't hide in there!' They usually appeared to the onlooker to be cheerful and happy on the march, even though they might be suffering. In the summer, the dust filled their nostrils and they felt 'grit' between their teeth. Dust got into their eyes, mouth, ears, beards, hair, and shoes—if they had any. Often soldiers would take their shoes off and march barefooted, to conserve shoe leather. The heat caused perspiration, which mixed with the dust and became most uncomfortable. The sun also gave the men deep tans so that they were often barely recognizable when they secured leave and visited home.

"Mud, rain, snow, ice, and wind also presented problems. Rain was the worst natural enemy to their comfort. It got into everything, and when the march ended there was no dry wood to burn. Clothes, etc., could not be dried and food could not be cooked. Ammunition might be wet, and they had to sleep on wet ground. Most of the roads over which they marched were dirt, and they became mud when it rained.

"Halts on the march," one soldier recalled, "were pleasant, but perhaps not worth it. As soon as a man got situated and comfortable, the march was resumed, and his limbs were stiff and sore.

"Brass bands accompanied the columns early in the war and the music was quite good. They became very rare in the last years of the conflict, and the quality of the music deteriorated considerably, but the men still cheered them.

"Typically, an infantry column would be given an hour's rest between noon and 1 p.m. Sometimes they napped. If water was available, they would bathe their tired feet, and nothing was more enjoyable.

"As the men grew tired, there would be less talking, and the whole mass of men became quiet and more serious. Each soldier was lost in his own thoughts. The best time in a march was usually when they entered a friendly village or town, where they were met by friendly women, whose husband, brother, uncle, etc., were often in the army. They emptied their meager stores of food for the dusty troops."

Sometimes, enterprising African Americans would approach the column with a cart load of pies—sort of. They did not resemble the pies of antebellum days because they had no sugar. They tasted like a combination of rancid lard and crab apples, but "they filled up a hungry man wonderfully."

Straggling was frequent. Most stragglers were actually suffering, but some were merely ingenious liars.

A man who was lost got no sympathy from Confederate soldiers. If he asked where he was, every man within hearing would give a different answer. Then they would roar with laughter and ask the lost man: "Does your mother know you are out?"[41]

Early in the war, rations were good and plentiful. The men got plenty of sleep. If their rest was disturbed by guard duty, picket duty, or the like, they typically took a nap the next day—if the flies, gnats, and mosquitos allowed it. There were plenty of all three. In the beginning, however, the war was not hard. That would come later.

---

[41]   McCarthy, pp. 49–50.

Mutual recognition of friends from the old army was fairly common during the Civil War. In the summer of 1861, Confederate Colonel Jeb Stuart was on a reconnaissance mission with two or three of his men. He saw Captain Perkins, an old friend from West Point, coming to meet him.

"Hello, Perk!" he exclaimed. "Glad to see you. What are you doing here?"

"Why, Beauty," Perkins replied, using Stuart's nickname at West Point, "how are you? I didn't know you were with us."

"And I didn't know you were on our side!" Stuart retorted. "What is your command?"

"That is my command," he said, pointing to a battery just coming into sight.

"Oh, the devil!" Stuart exclaimed and burst into laughter. It was a Union battery. "Good-bye, Perk!" he cried as he wheeled rapidly and galloped away, much to the amusement of the Federal captain.[42]

General Fitz Lee

---

[42] William C. King and W. P. Derby, comp., *Camp-Fire Sketches and Battle-Field Echoes* (Springfield, Mass.: 1886), p. 555 (hereafter referred to as "King and Derby").

In June 1862, Confederate General Fitz Lee captured a company of Union cavalry on the Chickahominy. They were escorting the prisoners to the rear when Lee stopped and suddenly cried: "How are you, Brown? Are you down here? How's Robinson and the rest of my old people?"

Lee had captured his old company from the frontier army. The prisoner looked intently at Fitz Lee and suddenly his face lit up. "Why, how are you, lieutenant?" he exclaimed. A moment later, the Confederate general and Union private were enthusiastically shaking hands.[43]

In camp, comical incidents occurred frequently, especially early in the war. Most of the men of Captain French's company, 7th Virginia, were asleep one night when Private Blondeau, a Frenchman, caused a stir. He fired on the "enemy," which turned out to be a cow wandering in the brush near him. The long roll (the signal to rush into battle formation) was sounded and confusion reigned supreme. In the uproar, sleeping men were jolted awake. One man lost his boots, another could not find his trousers, another lost his musket, and so forth. The entire regiment turned out, but it was a false alarm.[44]

Reverend John Atkinson, the president of Hampden-Sidney College, rushed to the colors with his students, most of whom were underage. They were ordered to the front in western Virginia before they had an opportunity to learn even basic drills. Governor John Letcher considered sending them back to school, but a committee from the company persuaded him to allow them to proceed.

The beardless boys fought in several minor engagements until July 12, 1861, when U.S. General McClellan outflanked them at Rich Mountain and captured the entire command. The depressed young men were visited by McClellan, who asked them: "Why in the world are you here?"

---

[43] King and Derby, p. 556.

[44] Johnston, n.p.

"We are here to fight!" the boys answered. "What do you suppose we came for?"

McClellan smiled and said, "Well, boys, make yourselves easy. I'll send you home to your mothers in a few days."

And he did. The company was paroled but was not exchanged for a year—an unusually long delay in 1861. They always suspected that George McClellan was behind this delay. He gave them an extra year at school.

Eventually, all the boys returned to the front but as individuals, not as a company.

As the enemy approached, things became grimmer. The Federals staged major amphibious landings on the coast of North Carolina. Lieutenant John H. Lewis saw his first dead men at South Mills, North Carolina. He was not impressed "as to the glories of war." He went to find a bookstore from which to buy a prayer book.[45]

The war of a typical private was (is) about a hundred yards wide. As the Union Army of the Potomac advanced on Manassas, the 7th Virginia did not know anything was afoot until they were ordered to cook three days' rations, pack their haversacks, and be ready to move at a moment's notice. They were in high spirits when they broke camp at noon on July 17. They spent the night in a pasture. The next day, they were placed behind Bull Run. As they marched, they saw General P. G. T. Beauregard, who appeared calm and collected. "Keep cool, men," he said, "and fire low, shoot them in the legs."[46] He said this because excited, inexperienced troops tended to fire high.

---

[45]   Lewis, p. 132.
[46]   Johnston, n.p.

After the war, Confederate veteran J. M. Hough wrote of the "incomparable heroism and devotion" of Southern women. "In many respects she did more for the cause and complained less than the boys with their muskets."[47] This was a common theme in virtually every account of the war by a Southern warrior.

When the war began, the Confederate States Army had no medical services branch and never had much of one. Surgery was considered a man's job in 1861. Other than that, medical services, including nursing and often hospital administration, were left to women, and there was never a shortage of volunteers. In the summer of 1861, women formed an ad hoc medical facility at Bristow, not far from the front lines. On July 20, General Beauregard sent word to the women and children at Bristow that a battle was impending, and the result was impossible to predict. He placed a railroad engine and a car at their disposal so they could immediately leave for safer parts. The women, who were sewing flannel shirts and making bandages as rapidly as they could, sent their thanks, but they preferred to stay.[48] And they did. The First Battle of Manassas (Bull Run) was fought the next day.

[47] J. M. Hough, "The Last Days of the Confederacy," in U. R. Brooks, *Stories of the Confederacy* (Columbia, South Carolina: 1912), p. 304 (hereafter cited as "Brooks").

[48] Mrs. Burton Harrison (nee Constance Cary), *Recollections Grave and Gay* (New York: 1911), pp. 50—51 (hereafter cited as "Harrison").

CHAPTER III

FIRST BLOOD

Colonel Egbert Jones and his 4th Alabama Infantry were eating break-fast near Manassas Junction when "we saw for the first time the little sphere of white vapor produced by the burst of a shell," Lieutenant William A. Robbins recalled after the war.[49] The regiment double-timed (ran) to the Confederate left but barely arrived when they were ordered further upstream, to Sudley's Ford. The brigade commander, Bernard Bee, saw that Henry Hill was the key position, and he needed to delay the Federal advance before it reached the high ground; accordingly, he ordered his brigade (the 4th Alabama, 2nd Mississippi, and 11th Mississippi) forward. "Down the slope we rushed," Robbins recalled, "panting and breathless, but still eager, because ignorant of the desperate crisis which doomed us to probable destruction, to save the whole army."

They heard the firing between the Federals and Brigadier General Shanks Evans's brigade (which included the "Louisiana Tigers" of Major Roberdeau Wheat's 1st Louisiana Battalion) and the invaders on Matthews Hill. Bee's brigade joined the battle after the Northerners

---

[49] Originally from North Carolina, Major Robbins (1828–1905) was a lawyer in Eufaula, Alabama, when the war started. He rose to the rank of major and was seriously wounded in the Wilderness Campaign but was present at Appomattox. Later, he returned to North Carolina and served in the North Carolina Senate (1869–1873) and the U.S. House of Representatives from 1873 to 1879. An outspoken prohibitionist, he was defeated for reelection in 1878. He was the Southern commissioner of the Gettysburg Battlefield Commission from 1894 until his death.

took the crest. When the 4th Alabama exited the woods just south of Matthews Hill, they saw a long, advancing line of Federals eighty yards in front of them. The Yankees stopped and fired a volley, but the Southerners threw themselves on the ground, and the Unionists' aim was high (typical for green troops). It went over their heads. The Rebels then fired a more effective volley, and the enemy fell back to the crest of the hill. They advanced again and were checked once more. The third time, however, they extended their line well beyond the Southern line and "their fire hurt us badly" and "now the conflict became bloody and terrible." Colonel Jones was among the casualties.[50]

"Then War began to show us his wrinkled front. It seemed our safest course to hug the ground and pepper away at them; and so from sheer desperation, as much as anything, we kept at it, until, to our great joy, the enemy fell back once more behind the crest." But General Bee, who saw that they would be overwhelmed if the Yankees attacked again, ordered a withdrawal. They left behind nearly a third of the regiment, killed or wounded.

As they fell back, a regiment approached to within a hundred yards of them at right angles. It was wearing blue, but the Alabamians thought it was the 6th North Carolina, which was also part of Bee's brigade—until it opened fire. It was a New York regiment. Several men were wounded or killed, including both surviving field grade officers (Lieutenant Colonel Evander Law and Major Charles L. Scott [both wounded]), leaving the 4th Alabama without a field-grade officer. "We didn't stay there," Robbins recalled. "It is frank to say that we got back to the main Confederate line in the shortest time possible." It rallied and was placed on the right flank of the Rebels defending Henry Hill. Meanwhile, the 6th North Carolina was overwhelmed, and its colonel, Charles F. Fisher, was killed. But the Union tide was broken on Henry Hill by General Thomas J. Jackson and his 1st Virginia Brigade.

---

[50] King and Derby, pp. 19–20. Jones was shot through both hips and died of his wounds on September 21. An attorney in Huntsville and a state legislator, Jones was a captain in the 13th U.S. Infantry during the Mexican War. Bruce S. Allardice, *Confederate Colonels* (Columbia, Mssouri: 2008), p. 218 (hereafter cited as "Allardice, *Colonels*").

There was a lull on the Confederate right flank. General Bee galloped up to the 4th Alabama and cried: "My brigade is scattered over the field and you are all of it I can find. Men, can you make a charge of bayonets?"

"Yes, General," someone replied. "We will go wherever you lead and do whatever you say."

Bee pointed to the 1st Virginia. "Over yonder stands Jackson, like a stone wall! Let us go to his assistance." He then dismounted and led the regiment to Jackson's position. The struggle was fierce. Bee was mortally wounded shortly after, and another brigade commander, Colonel Francis S. Bartow, was killed a stone's throw away.[51]

The battle raged on until about 5:30 p.m., when the Union army panicked and precipitously fled the field. "The battle ended so suddenly that the Confederates could neither understand nor scarcely believe it," Robbins recalled.[52]

On July 21, Jubal Early's brigade marched from behind the Confederate right flank to its far left. It arrived just in time. Private David Johnston of the 7th Virginia recalled: "Approaching the scene of action, a wild cheer was heard, following which a man on horseback at full speed, hatless, face flushed, covered with perspiration and dust, brandishing his sword over his head, and shouting, 'Glory! Glory! Glory!' rode rapidly by. In answer to inquiry as to what was the matter, he said, 'We have captured Rickett's battery and the day is ours.' This was the first glad news we had received, and all were thrilled with new courage. Cheering wildly, the men pressed forward at double quick. Passing in rear and beyond a wood into which [Edmund Kirby] Smith's Confederate brigade had just entered, we encountered the fire of the enemy, mostly United States Regulars. The 7th Virginia here formed quickly, the 7th Louisiana and 13th Mississippi forming on

---

[51] Bartow was a former Georgia superior court judge and a member of the Confederate congress from February to May 1861. He resigned to join the Confederate army. Bartow helped pick gray as the color of the Confederate uniforms.

[52] King and Derby, pp. 20–22.

the left, thus completing the battle line with three regiments front. Nor had we arrived a moment too soon, for the enemy was pressing our left flank sorely. There they were, in full view on our front, and to the left of us on the higher ground. Here Colonel Early ordered us not to fire, saying that they were our friends: a grievous blunder upon his part, the result of misinformation not easily explained. Captain [Thomas B.] Massie, whose company was armed with rifles, called out, 'Colonel, they may be your friends, but they are none of ours. Fire, men!' and fire they did.[53]

"As we formed, the enemy at long range kept up an irregular fire, inflicting upon our men considerable loss in killed and wounded, and all this while we were too far away from them to pay them back in their own coin. As we pushed forward towards the enemy, they retreated pell-mell, we chasing them over the hill towards Bull Run, considerably in advance of the general Confederate battle line forming across a peninsula created by a sharp curve on Bull Run between Stone Bridge and the mouth of Catharpin creek [sic].

"Up to this time we had little realization of the utter defeat of the Federal army, the evidence of which we saw a few days after, when, following his line of retreat, we found guns, caissons, muskets, ambulances, spades, picks and knapsacks abandoned in his flight. The only reason seemingly the enemy had for running as he did was because he could not fly."[54]

After the Battle of First Manassas, McCarthy wrote, "The newspaper men delighted in telling the soldiers that the Yankees were a diminutive race, of feeble constitution, timid as hares, with no enthusiasm, and that they would perish in short order under the glow of our southern sun." He recalled that no one who faced a regiment from Ohio or Maine believed this. "And besides," he continued, "the newspapers did not mention the English, Irish, German, French, Italian, Spanish, Swiss, Portuguese, and negroes [sic], who were to swell the numbers of the enemy…True, there

---

53   O.R., Vol. II, pp. 555–556.
54   Johnston, n.p.

was not much fight in all this rubbish, but they answered well enough for drivers of wagons and ambulances, guarding stores and lines of communication, and doing all sorts of duty, while the good material was doing the fighting."[55]

Many soldiers on both sides did not hold the newspapers in high esteem. They thought—and not without reason—that nineteenth-century fake news—and especially abolitionist fake news and "fire-eating" editors—were major contributing causes for the war. Jefferson Davis certainly had a low opinion of most of them.

After the First Battle of Manassas, the women invented the "Wayside Hospital." Lilla Carroll of Aiken, South Carolina, worked in one such facility, where ladies and doctors met the trains, gave refreshments to wounded soldiers, dressed wounds, and provided resting places for them to sleep until time for a train to run again. Some of the nurses were African Americans. These wayside hospitals were adopted by the Prussians during the Franco-Prussian War in 1870. "What sacrifices our dear people made!" Carroll exclaimed. "And how faithful our servants were!"

Mrs. Bartow, Lilla's aunt, worked at the "Ladies Hospital" in Columbia. It was a former railroad shed converted into a medical facility. "The cots were white and neat," Lilla recalled. "The lady visitors came with offerings of eggs, fruit, flowers, and sometimes money."[56]

When the war began, the term "enemies" was not used, even in private. They were called "Federals." Before long, gentlemen called them "enemies"

---

55 McCarthy, p. 34.

56 Lilla Carroll, "Recollections of a Confederate School Girl—1861–1865," manuscript printed in Brooks, *Stories*, pp. 22–24. Carroll was the niece of Mrs. Louisa Bartow, the wife of Colonel Francis S. Bartow, who resigned his seat in Congress to command a brigade in the Confederate army. He was killed in action at the First Manassas.

with considerable venom. When scornfully disposed, they became "Yankees." The term "Yanks" was considered deliberately insulting.[57]

When a man fought his first battle, of course, depended on the unit to which he was assigned. Ben Martin, a private in the 15th Alabama, first saw action in the Battle of Cross Keys, Virginia, on June 8, 1862.[58] He recalled: "I can see now just how funny we looked. A lot of farmer boys who had never been out of sight of home before, with heavy knapsacks strapped on their backs, looking more like a lot of old-time foot peddlers than soldiers. Soon we began skirmishing and falling back, and the bullets began popping the fence rails near us. I know that we did look funny going over that rail fence with those big knapsacks on our back. Away we went, every fellow for himself, through the wheat field, the bullets cutting the wheat all around us. The most of those knapsacks were left in that field; at least, I left mine there."

"...Our Colonel [James Cantey], having been in the Mexican War, had some idea of what was coming, and had us all to lie down behind an old fence. Our Colonel kept saying: 'Hold your fire, boys, until you can see the whites of their eyes.' So we held it until he gave the order to fire, and when we did fire we came near killing and wounding the whole force."[59]

The "Texas Invincibles" were sent to Richmond, where it seemed the whole city turned out to welcome them. They first saw action in the retreat from Yorktown in May 1862. Covering General Joseph Johnston's rear, they retreated through rain and mud to near Eltham's Landing on the York River, where they took up a line of battle in breastworks originally

---

[57]   Pryor, p. 152.
[58]   This battle, a Confederate victory, was part of Stonewall Jackson's famous Valley Campaign.
[59]   Yeary II, p. 463.

constructed by George Washington's men. Colonel Alexis Rainey, the regimental commander, instructed them to be quiet and not to fire until they saw the whites of the enemy's eyes. He added that they should aim low, so they would cripple those they did not kill.[60]

"When the blue line came in sight and as they drew nearer," Private Alfred Wilson remembered, "we became so amazed at the beauty and grandeur of the scene that some of us would have forgotten what we were there for, but for the ringing command of our officers which brought us to realize that this splendid array meant death and destruction, and I frankly admit that some of us would rather have been somewhere else, but rallying to the situation we took deliberate aim and fired with such telling effect that it became their turn to fall into consternation and those who were not killed threw down their guns and ran for dear life, we following, shooting and giving vent to wild Texas yells. We pursued them to their gunboats and when night became on we quietly fell back out of range."

Private Wilson noted that "This little affair was only child's play compared to what we were to see later on." The Texas Invincibles fought throughout the war, mainly as part of Robert E. Lee's Army of Northern Virginia.[61]

Because his father was in poor health, James B. Wilson of Allons did not enlist in the 24th Tennessee until November 22, 1862. Six weeks later, he first saw combat in the Second Battle of Murfreesboro. Soon "we were in the thickest of the fight and my company was making a desperate charge," he recalled, "and in the excitement I got a little in advance of my company and was enjoying the protection of a friendly tree trunk. From this position I was firing into the ranks of the enemy with much precision and as rapidly as possible. After loading and firing several times, and as I was taking aim my attention was called to a wounded Federal soldier who was lying

---

[60]   Alexis T. Rainey (1822–1891), a lawyer from Palestine, Texas, was disabled at Gaines Mill. He returned to Texas, where he was a staff officer. He was a state legislator postwar. Allardice, *Colonels*, p. 316.

[61]   Yeary, II, pp. 803–804.

near the root of a tree. Seeing my canteen he called on me for some water. I wanted to give him the water but wanted to first finish my shot. Just then the other was given to retreat and I lost my opportunity to relieve him. I have always regretted that I did not respond to his call for water at once."[62]

When the war began, Ephraim Anderson joined a Missouri State Guard (militia) company. Like many such companies, it lacked weapons. This one had only eight firearms, and they were old-fashioned rifles and shotguns. It was ordered to Boonville, where there were said to be guns. It arrived in Fayette, Missouri, about sixteen miles from Boonville, when it received word that there were no arms in Boonville. The officers met and considered returning home to get more squirrel rifles and shotguns but decided to proceed to Boonville. They arrived at Franklin, across the Missouri River from Boonville, on June 17, 1861—just as the defeated pro-Southern Missouri State Guard (MSG) forces retreated. It was a minor affair with light casualties: nineteen Northerners and twenty-eight Southerners were killed or wounded.

Anderson arrived at the main Rebel camp after the Battle of Wilson's Creek was fought. He got a three-day pass to visit his father's home. It took him a day to get there and a day to return, so he had only a one-day visit. It was his last for four years. When the MSG forces were reorganized, he became part of the 6th Missouri Infantry Regiment. It was armed with shotguns and rifles; some of its men had no firearms at all.

After the Confederate victory at Wilson's Creek, the Union government enacted strict measures to prevent men from "going south." Anderson recalled, "…arrests were made every day." Guards were placed along the roads and the prisons and jails were filled to overflowing. "Men knew not

---

[62]   Yeary II, p. 807.

what offences they were charged with, and asked in vain to know the cause of their imprisonment; their demands for trial were treated with neglect, perhaps with greater rigor in their confinement, and any interference of the courts was derided and defied."[63]

---

[63] Ephraim McD. Anderson, *Memoirs, Including the Campaigns of the First Missouri Confederate Brigade* (St. Louis: 1868), p. 31 (hereafter cited as "Anderson, *Missouri*").

CHAPTER IV

THE AWAKENING

Food was always an issue in the Confederacy. Its subsistence branch was the weakest department in its army and was notoriously badly run. As the blockade tightened, ports fell, and rich agricultural regions were lost, things became progressively worse. Wear and the lack of spare parts for locomotives also retarded the delivery of vital supplies to the armies.

The supply of food varied from time to time and often from day to day. Sometimes there was plenty of meat but no flour or cornmeal to cook bread; other times, there was an abundance of bread but no meat. Another day, there was plenty of sugar but no coffee. On rare occasions, there was coffee and no sugar. They often received salt pork "without intermission." They usually had a preserved concoction called "blue bacon," which was edible but just barely. A joke in the Rebel army went: "Our bacon outranks General Lee."

To go one day without food was common. Two days of fasting was not uncommon, and sometimes no rations arrived for three or four days. On the march from Petersburg to Appomattox, Lieutenant Colonel Wilfred E.

Cutshaw's artillery battalion[64] received no rations for a week. They lived on corn intended for the horses and raw bacon captured from the Yankees.

Typically, the Rebels cooked bacon until the pan was half full of boiling grease. Then the flour (mixed with water) was poured into the grease and stirred rapidly until it was a dirty brown mix. Then it was ready to serve. If any sugar was available, it was added.

"The inability of the government to furnish supplies forced the men to depend largely upon their own energy and ingenuity to obtain them," Private McCarthy recalled. "…It was not uncommon sight to see a brigade or division, which was but a moment before marching in solid column along a road, scattered over an immense field searching for luscious blackberries. And it was wonderful to see how promptly and cheerfully all returned to the ranks when the field was gleaned. In the fall of the year a persimmon tree on the roadside would halt a column and detain it till the last persimmon disappeared."

When corn ears were mature enough, they were thrown into the ashes of the campfire with the shucks on and made a good meal. Turnip and onion fields also produced food, cooked or raw.

Crackers or "hardtack" were eaten much of the time, and it was poor eating indeed. When time and resources allowed, the hardtack was soaked in water and then fried in bacon grease. A piece of solid pork fat helped. Liquid sorghum replaced the molasses of antebellum days and was much treasured.

Unlike the Northern army, the sutler's wagon was unknown in the Army of Northern Virginia because the men had no money to buy sutlers' wares, and the potential sutlers were drafted into the army. It did have "cider carts," usually owned by an old African American, or someone with a basket of pies and cakes for sale on the side of the road. The Southerner

---

64 Wilfred E. Cutshaw (1838–1907) graduated from V.M.I. in 1858 and served under Generals John B. Magruder, Stonewall Jackson, and Jubal Early. He was successively promoted from lieutenant to lieutenant colonel, despite being shot in the knee at the First Winchester and spending months in Union prisons. On April 6, 1865, he lost a leg at Sayler's Creek. His battalion, now under Captain C. W. Fry, surrendered at Appomattox three days later. After the war, Cutshaw was city engineer of Richmond for thirty-four years.

also counted on the Yankee to supply him with food when they overran a Union camp. These included coffee, fine cooked beef, peaches, lobsters, milk, barrels of ground and roasted coffee, salt, liquors, wine, cigars (including imported Havanas), tobacco, and luxuries from the sutlers' wagons.[65] Sometimes, the Rebels would loot the haversacks of dead Federals.

In December 1861, Sergeant Harry Gilmor of Ashby's cavalry captured the Baltimore and Ohio depot at Alpine. It was full of supplies for the Union army. "Such quantities of stores at one view I had never seen. There was case after case loaded with shoes, and clothing of all kinds; sugar, coffee, whisky, molasses, and stores of every description, besides haversacks, knapsacks, canteens, and two cases of Enfield rifles—the aggregate value not less than half a million dollars."[66]

Meanwhile, the women quietly continued with their self-appointed duties without the slightest complaint. Constance Cary later wrote of her mother, Monimia Fairfax Cary: "My dearest mother was by now well launched in her hospital nursing at Culpeper Court House, first, among the many soldiers ill in the Methodist church, and, later, among the wounded. Her life from this time forward (afterward at Camp Winder, near Richmond) was of the hardest and most heroic kind. I have never known any woman possessed of better qualifications for her task. With a splendid physique, almost unbroken good health, a tireless hand, and a spirit of tender sympathy, she was the ideal attendant upon homesick boys from the far South, disheartened by illness at the outset of their campaign, as well as those cruelly mangled and wounded in the first fights. Almost every comfort we have nowadays in nursing was absent from the beginning, and toward the last the hospitals were unspeakably lacking in needfuls. Sleeping on a soldier's bunk, rising at dawn, laboring till midnight, my mother faced death and suffering with the stout spirit that was

---

[65]   McCarthy, pp. 56–64.
[66]   Harry Gilmor, *Four Years in the Saddle* (New York: 1866), p. 17 (hereafter cited as "Gilmor").

a rock of refuge to all around her. Her record, in short, was that of a thousand other saintly women during that terrible strife. How many dying eyes looked wistfully into hers; how many anguished hands clung to hers during operations or upon death-beds! What poor lonely spirits far from home and kin took courage from her lips, to flutter feebly out into the vast unknown! What words of Christian cheer she whispered! What faith, hope, love were embodied in that tall, noble figure and sweet, sad face moving tirelessly upon her rounds!"[67]

Constance followed in her mother's footsteps and became a volunteer nurse in a hospital near Richmond. She recalled: "My whole heart passed into the work. I could hardly sleep for wishing to be back in those miserable cheerless wards, where dim eyes would kindle feebly at sight of me and trembling lips gave me last messages to transmit to those they would never see again. Once, going into one of my mother's wards, I found my way blocked by an arm lying on the floor, and the surgeons who had just amputated it still at work on Cavanagh, one of our favorite patients, a big, gentle Irishman, always courteous and considerate. The blood was gushing profusely from the flaps they were sewing together, and for a moment I paused uncertain. 'Can you stand it?' asked one of the doctors kindly. 'If so, there's a little help needed, as we're short-handed this morning.' I stayed, and in a moment I saw clear and all seemed easier. When they hurried off, leaving Cavanagh to me, he came out of chloroform looking me full in the eyes, as I stood sponging his forehead. 'So it's gone at last, the poor old arm we worked so hard to save,' I said, trying to speak lightly. 'Yes, miss, but it's not meself you should be thinkin' about,' he answered, 'an' you standin' by, dirtyin' your dress with the blood o' me.' Cavanagh, I am glad to say, got well and left the hospital, swearing eternal fealty to his nurse."[68]

The winter of 1861–62 in Virginia was cold and dreary. The Confederates constructed log huts with wooden chimneys for winter quarters. Supplies

---

[67]   Harrison, pp. 54–55.
[68]   Harrison, pp. 184–185.

became a problem for the first time. Transporting them was also an issue. They had to be carried six miles by wagon over a dirt road through deep mud.

"Again we were on picket," Johnston recalled, "Crawford on outpost, with instructions to keep a sharp lookout, as the enemy was near, but not to shoot without calling 'halt' the usual three times, and if no halt made, to shoot. Shortly after Crawford took post, his cries of 'Halt! Halt! Halt!' were heard, and bang! went his gun. The corporal ran to see what was the matter: he found Crawford standing quietly at his post as if nothing had happened—a stray fat hog had wandered to the post and had not halted at Crawford's command, consequently was dead. Crawford's only explanation was, 'I obeyed orders.' The hog was roasted, with many compliments for Crawford, and all had a feast."[69]

It only gradually dawned on the men in the ranks that the South was in deep trouble. "The Confederate soldier opposed immense odds," Carlton McCarthy recounted. In the Seven Days Battles, he recalled, it was outnumbered eighty thousand to one hundred fifteen thousand. At Fredericksburg, it fielded seventy-eight thousand men against one hundred ten thousand. At Chancellorsville, fifty-seven thousand Rebels whipped a Union army of one hundred thirty-two thousand. At the Wilderness, sixty-three thousand Confederates checked one hundred forty-one thousand enemy soldiers.[70] "If the Confederate soldier had then had only this disparity of numbers to contend with, he would have driven every invader from the soil of Virginia," McCarthy asserted. But, in addition to these odds, the South had poorer transportation facilities, especially in terms of railroads; and the North was backed by a treasury "which was turning out money by the ton, one dollar of which was equal to sixty Confederate dollars."

---

[69] Johnston, n.p.

[70] Numbers vary slightly from source to source; I believe, for example, that McCarthy's figures on Lee's strength at Fredericksburg are high.

Also, the South was "restricted to its own territory for supplies, and its own people for men, while the North could draw upon the entire world for material and upon many nations for men. Union arms and ammunition were so abundant and good that it, in effect, supplied both armies. The North's manufacturing facilities "were simply unlimited."

Confederate medical supplies were extremely finite, especially in terms of chloroform and morphia, which were subject to the blockade. The Rebels, McCarthy stated, fought "good wagons, fat horses, tons of quartermaster's stores; pontoon trains by the mile, gunboats and men-of-war; and United States' commerce, which traded with the world. The Rebel also fought the distress from home—tales of want, insult, robbery, and rape.[71]

For many of the Southern soldiers, the awakening came at Shiloh. The Orleans Guards Battalion is a typical example. It consisted of six companies under the command of Major (later Lieutenant Colonel) Leon Queyrouze. It was a Louisiana militia unit formed in New Orleans in December 1861. It was outfitted in blue uniforms. At one time, General Beauregard was a member of its predecessor unit, and his name was always called at roll call. He was listed as "Absent, on special assignment."

The Guards (411 men) were mustered into Confederate service as a ninety-day regiment on March 6, 1862, and were sent to Corinth, Mississippi. The battalion included an artillery battery of four six-pounder smoothbore howitzers and two twelve-pounders under Captain Henry Ducatel. The battalion was part of Colonel Preston Pond's brigade, Ruggles's division, Braxton Bragg's II Corps. Pond's command included the 16th Louisiana, 18th Louisiana, and Crescent regiments, as well as the 38th Tennessee Infantry.

On April 4, 1862, these men set out for Shiloh. The next day it rained heavily. Around 2 p.m., they abandoned their light baggage and loaded their muskets. They camped in the woods near the Tennessee River about 4 p.m. The next day, they reached Shiloh about 8 a.m. and passed through the camp of the 6th Iowa, where they found an "abundant

---

[71] McCarthy, pp. 4–7.

supply of delicacies for ten regiments." Shortly after, they were fired on by a "friendly" Kentucky and Tennessee regiment because the Guards were still wearing blue uniforms. Two Louisianans were killed. They watched Alfred Mouton's 18th Louisiana disappear as it charged up a hill. Its ranks were well-dressed as it advanced; it was "mutilated, cut to pieces, leaving behind a trail of blood" when it came back down. Mouton was seriously wounded and replaced by Colonel Alfred Roman. At this point, Colonel Queyrouze gave the order to fix bayonets and charge.

In the War for Southern Independence, battle flags were not decorative. The men in the ranks guided on and followed the color-bearers, who thus naturally became special targets for the enemy riflemen. It was not unusual for several color-bearers to be killed or wounded in a single battle. This happened to the Orleans Guards at Shiloh. Bankston recalled: "The battle-flag fell from the hands of G. Poree, the color-bearer, who was shot dead. Before touching the ground it was caught by Gallot, who was shot through the head. Then it was seized by Coiron, whose arm was shattered while holding it. The fourth standard-bearer was Percy, who was also wounded. The fifth time it was seized without ever having touched the ground, and upheld by an unknown private soldier."

They opened fire at forty paces and drove the enemy from the field. During a pause, the men were ordered to turn their uniforms wrong side out, so they would not appear to be Yankees to Confederate sharpshooters. One soldier noted this gave them the "appearance of going to a masquerade ball." The Orleans battalion lost seventeen men killed at Shiloh, fifty-five wounded, and eighteen missing. Colonel Queyrouze was seriously wounded and replaced by Captain Charles Roman. Among those who distinguished themselves that day was Father Turgis, who went with the men into the thickest of the battle and administered religious rites to the fallen on both sides. Known for his goodness and his happy, genial nature, he fought throughout the war. When he finally died, his body was followed to the grave by the largest funeral procession ever seen in New Orleans.

The next day, April 7, the second day of the Battle of Shiloh, the battalion fell back. It was a hard retreat. The men were largely barefoot and their feet were swollen. They were not issued food during the retreat.

One historian wrote that, after Shiloh, the South never smiled.

The defeated Confederate Army retreated into Mississippi, and the Guards fought in the Battle of Farmington and the Siege (First Battle) of Corinth. It also took part in the retreat to Tupelo. Meanwhile, New Orleans fell on April 29. When its enlistments expired, the battalion was disbanded on June 6, 1862. Many of the men returned home. Those who remained in the service were transferred to other Louisiana units. Some of them became Company F, 30th Louisiana Infantry. Its artillery was merged into the 10th Missouri Battery and fought in South Carolina, at Chickamauga, Chattanooga, the Siege of Charleston, and the Carolinas Campaign. It surrendered with the Army of Tennessee on April 26, 1865. Its infantry fought as part of the Army of Mississippi and surrendered at Port Hudson on July 9, 1863. After being exchanged, some of them joined the Army of Tennessee and surrendered after the fall of Mobile.[72]

General Beauregard was the second-in-command of the Army of Mississippi when the Battle of Shiloh began. He was a flashy officer and had a magnificent coach, *a la* Napoleon, and it was flanked by the general and his rather large staff. He was not afraid to risk his life on the front lines. As the Rebels advanced, Beauregard and his entourage got in the way of Captain Dewberry, the commander of Company C of Colonel Andrew K. Blythe's Mississippi regiment. The company halted in confusion, much to the displeasure of Blythe. "Move forward, Captain Dewberry!" the colonel shouted. Dewberry turned to one of Beauregard's aides and roared: "Take that damned old stage out o' the way or I'll tumble it down the hill!" The general and his people removed themselves immediately.

The regiment overran General McClernand's tents and fought throughout the day. Colonel Blythe was among those killed, as was Captain Dewberry. Lieutenant Colonel Herron, the regiment's second-in-command, was also

---

[72] Marie Louise Benton Bankston, *Camp-Fire Stories of the Mississippi Valley Campaign* (New Orleans: 1914), pp. 107–110 (hereafter cited as "Bankston").

slain. The regiment lost two hundred men (including eighty killed) out of 330 engaged.

B. F. Sawyer was among the wounded. Meanwhile, the regiment over-ran the 14th Ohio Battery. The men threw Sawyer, shot through the knee, onto the gun. He recalled it made "an excellent ambulance" and "I rode out of that terrible fight as proudly as ever rode a Roman conqueror of old."[73]

Henry Meyer, a native of Germany, was also at Shiloh. He joined the 2nd Texas Infantry regiment at Houston in 1861. "We left singing 'The Girl I Left Behind Me,' and were as fine a body of patriotic young men as ever took up their country's cause," he recalled.

During the night of April 5/6, "We slept with gun in hand," he recalled, as they neared Shiloh Church, "...and Sunday morning were formed in line of battle. The spring day was fine but we were gloomy. Just then we heard a cannon boom and the Colonel rode up and said, 'boys, we have no time to cook so we will eat breakfast in the Yankee camp.' Then came the command, 'Shoulder arms, guide right, double quick,' and we were in the fight. The first blood that we saw was a milk-white horse, charging through the lines all spattered with blood, but with no rider. Next a cannon ball took off my side man's head...This young man had a presentiment that morning that he would be killed and told me to inform his dear mother. By this time our artillery took part and the Yankee's first line was broken. We were ordered forward and soon got up to the line of the Blue Coats when one man called out, 'We can not stand to be fired at.' Then we raised a yell like wild Indians, fixed our bayonets and charged. This was too much for them and they ran. It was not 6 o'clock when we entered the Yankee camps and

---

[73] King and Derby, pp. 53–55. Colonel Blythe was killed on April 6, 1862, while leading an attack. He was a prewar lawyer from Columbus, a captain in the Mexican War, a Mississippi state representative, and U.S. consul to Hawaii. He was called "a perfectly courageous man...soft-hearted as a girl." His regiment was later designated the 44th Mississippi. Allardice, *Colonels*, pp. 64–65. Sawyer later commanded the 24th Alabama.

we followed them and had several hot scraps that day, but they always ran. On we went till 3 or 4 o'clock when [Union] Gen. Prentiss surrendered."[74]

Blythe's regiment and the Orleans Guards were not the only units to be severely battered at Shiloh. Most regiments on both sides lost heavily and some were decimated. The North suffered 13,047 casualties at Shiloh, of whom 1,754 were killed. The South lost 10,699 men, of whom 1,728 were killed. Total casualties on both sides stood at 23,746. The United States lost 1,733 killed and 4,152 wounded (5,885 total) during the entire Mexican War. The North and South suffered four times as many casualties at Shiloh as the U.S.A. lost in the entire Mexican War. A Union soldier spoke for both sides when he declared that no one who was at Shiloh ever spoiled for a fight again. Among the dead was General Albert Sidney Johnston, the highest-ranking officer on either side killed in action during the war.

The casualties appalled the North, whose newspapers demanded to know why so many men had been lost. Abraham Lincoln felt compelled to ask the Union commander, General Grant, why the losses were so high. Grant reportedly replied: "Because of the Rebel generals and their men." This answer seemed to satisfy the president.

The Union pursuit after Shiloh was halted by Nathan Bedford Forrest, who launched a surprise attack on Sherman's vanguard in the Battle of Fallen Timbers on April 8. Thomas H. Bowman was among the casualties.

Prior to the war, Bowman lost his mother and four of his seven siblings within a week to a plague. The Bowman plantation was a house of prayer, however, and "I remember how my dying mother's face was lighted by a blaze of glory." His sister Anna was seven years old when she died. Her last

---

[74] Yeary, Vol. II, pp. 513–514

words were: "Tell cousin Lizzie I will be at the beautiful gate waiting and watching for her."[75]

Thomas survived and went to boarding school, then Southern University at Greensboro, Alabama, a Methodist institution. When the war began, he joined Company A of Wirt Adams's Mississippi Cavalry regiment. His company was a Louisiana unit. He served with Sidney Johnston in Kentucky and Tennessee and rode with Forrest in the Battle of Fallen Timbers. He was crippled when his horse fell; he lost the use of his right leg and was captured. After his exchange, he joined a horse artillery battery and became a lieutenant. Eventually, his health forced him to leave the service in the summer of 1864.

---

[75]   Bowman, pp. 14–15.

CHAPTER V

UGLY TURNS

Three weeks after Shiloh, the war took an ugly turn.

Like many places in northern Alabama, Athens was a largely pro-Union town but certainly not entirely. It voted for Stephen Douglas, a Northern Democrat, in 1860 and burned fire-eating secessionist William Lowndes Yancey in effigy during the secession debate. It flew the Union flag over the courthouse two months after Alabama left the Union. But there were also Confederate sympathizers in the town, which had a population of nine hundred.

On April 27, 1862, Ohio units took Athens. Their occupation was peaceful, and their soldiers were orderly. On May 1, the 1st Louisiana Cavalry Regiment launched a surprise attack, routed the 18th Ohio, and retook the town. As the Yankees fled, some of the pro-Confederate townspeople spat at them, waved white handkerchiefs, and greeted the Rebels with cheers. The Bayou State horsemen almost immediately left Athens and headed for Huntsville. Athens was reoccupied by Turchin's brigade on May 2. It faced no opposition.

Colonel Ivan Vasilovitch Turchinoff, using the alias John Basil Turchin, was a former Cossack officer in Russia. In February 1862, he became a brigade commander in the Army of the Ohio. He believed in the European system of plunder and pillage, as opposed to the American tradition of chivalry, forbearance, and Christian soldiering. He promised his men he would turn a blind eye toward their behavior for two hours. This was all the excuse they needed. They immediately went on a crime spree and looted and sacked the town. They broke into private homes, smashed store windows, stole gold watches, ripped open trunks, robbed citizens of jewelry, pocketed silverware, appropriated molasses, adult beverages, tobacco, and other items, and looted a drug store and other businesses. Their violence caused one lady to suffer a miscarriage, and both she and the fetus died. They also raped a fourteen-year-old slave girl.

General Ormsby Mitchell, Turchin's divisional commander, was upset when he learned what happened. He rushed to Athens, met with some of the victims, urged them to submit claims for damages against the U.S. government, and encouraged them to gather evidence against Turchin and his men. They submitted claims for $54,689 ($1,439,136 in 2020 money).

Like Mitchell, Don Carlos Buell, the commander of the Army of the Ohio, was a gentleman. He relieved Turchin of his command and ordered him court-martialed, with Brigadier General James A. Garfield (a Church of Christ elder and a future U.S. president) presiding. Turchin's offer to resign was rejected. He was found guilty, and it was recommended that he be cashiered (i.e., dishonorably discharged). Lincoln set aside the verdict and promoted Turchin to brigadier general. Athens's claims for damages were denied.

Turchin later died in a lunatic asylum in 1901, but his actions in Athens were seen as a signal from the Lincoln régime for how Southern civilians could be treated. After Athens, destruction of private property and abuse of civilians—including African Americans—became the norm.

Compare Turchin's behavior with that of Robert E. Lee. In June 1863, he invaded the North. On June 27, he issued General Orders No. 73. It read:

> *The Commanding General [Lee] has observed with marked satisfaction the conduct of the troops on the march and confidently anticipates results commensurate with the high spirit they have manifested.*
>
> *No troops could have displayed better fortitude, or better performed the arduous marches of the past ten days.*

Their conduct in other respects has, with a few exceptions, been in keeping with their character as soldiers and entitles them to approbation and praise.

There have, however, been instances of forgetfulness on the part of some, that they have in keeping the yet unsullied reputation of the army, and that the duties exacted of us by civilization and Christianity are not less obligatory in the country of the enemy than in our own.

The Commanding General considers that no greater disgrace could befall the army, and through it our whole people than the perpetration of the barbarous outrages upon the unarmed and defenceless [sic], and the wanton destruction of private property, that have marked the course of the enemy in our country.

Such proceedings not only degrade the perpetrators and all connected with them, but are subversive of the discipline and efficiency of the army, and destructive of the end of our present movement.

It must be remembered that we make war only upon armed men, and that we cannot take vengeance for the wrongs that our people have suffered without lowering ourselves in the eyes of all those abhorrence has been excited by the atrocities of our enemies, and offending against Him to whom vengeance belongeth, without whose favor, and support our efforts must all prove in vain.

The Commanding General, therefore, earnestly exhorts the troops to abstain with most scrupulous care from unnecessary or wanton injury to private property, and he enjoins upon all officers to arrest and bring to summary punishment all who shall in any way offend against the orders on this subject.

R. E. LEE, General

In September 1862, Confederate Colonel Joseph C. Porter (who was on recruiting mission in northeast Missouri) raided the town of Palmyra.[76] His men captured Andrew Alsman, a Union informer who caused several of his neighbors to be arrested for being Confederate sympathizers. Porter subsequently released Alsman and ordered six of his men to escort Alsman to a place of safety specified by himself. Alsman personally selected three of his escorts. They reported that they released him at the appointed place, but the snitch vanished, never to be seen again. It was (is) believed that some members of the families of Alsman's victims made him "disappear," and there is no evidence that Colonel Porter had anything to do with it. Union Colonel John McNeil nevertheless ordered William R. Strachan, his provost-marshal for Northeast Missouri, to execute ten Confederate military or civilian political prisoners if Alsman were not returned. He placed an ad in the local newspaper, demanding Porter return Alsman within ten days, or he would execute ten prisoners. Apparently, the Rebel colonel never saw the ad. In any case, ten soldiers, civilians, guerillas, and/or Southern sympathizers were incarcerated and marked for death.

Strachan, Joseph A. Mudd of Porter's command recalled, was "maddened by three demons, liquor, lust and human hate." William T. Humphrey of Lewis County was on the original list to be executed. On the morning he was to face the firing squad, his wife, Mary Humphrey, met with Strachan. She fell on her knees and begged for her husband's life. Strachan agreed to spare him—if she would pay him $500 and have sexual

---

76   Colonel Porter was a farmer in Lewis County before the war. A man of natural charisma, he commanded a division in the Missouri State Guard (1861–1862) and was wounded at Lexington. He was commissioned as a colonel in the Confederate army in December 1861 and commanded the 1st Northeast Missouri Cavalry. In the autumn of 1862, he returned home to recruit and raised several thousand men. His unit, however, was dispersed while trying to reach Confederate lines. Porter was given command of a brigade in Marmaduke's cavalry division in late 1862 but was mortally wounded in an attack on Hartsville, Missouri, on January 11, 1863. He died on February 19. Allardice, *Colonels*, pp. 310–311.

intercourse with him. She paid the prices, but only after putting her two-year-old daughter outside on the doorstep.

Two Union soldiers were drawn to the house by the sobs of the little girl. They peered inside and saw Strachan having his way with Mrs. Humphrey. One can only call this rape. Filled with indignation, the two Northern soldiers informed Colonel McNeil of what they witnessed. McNeil did everything in his power to cover up the incident.

One of those slated to die was Willis Baker. Shortly before his appointment with the firing squad, Hiram Smith—who was just a boy and certainly not a Confederate soldier—went to comfort his friend Baker, who was related to him by marriage. After he finished using Mrs. Humphrey, Provost Marshal Strachan went to the jail, removed Humphrey from the list, and told Hiram that he had two hours to live. He simply replaced Humphrey with the first available male.

The prisoners were shot on October 18. Thirty pro-Union militiamen composed the firing squad. Several of them deliberately fired high, but enough shot to kill to get the job done.

The condemned men faced death so bravely that it "robbed Strachan of half his pleasure in the deed," Mudd recalled. Nineteen-year-old Tom Humston literally laughed at the firing squad and declared: "Why not death now as well as any other time?" Several prominent pro-Unionists called for McNeil and Strachan to show mercy to the prisoners. These included Mrs. Alsman. They were ignored.

One of the two ministers present with the prisoners called upon the victims to forgive McNeil and Strachan. He asked them to forgive Strachan and to shake his hand. (McNeil found a pretext not to attend the execution.) Most of them did but not Willis Baker. He said Strachan and his men were murderers, and murderers deserved hell, and he would not forgive anything pertaining to Satan.

The legal murder of ten innocent men caused a wave of indignation to sweep throughout the South. On November 17, President Davis ordered Lieutenant General Theophilius H. Holmes, the commander of the Trans-Mississippi Department, to communicate with U.S. General Samuel R. Curtis—his Federal counterpart—and demand the immediate surrender of Colonel McNeil, who was now known as the "Butcher of Palmyra." If he failed to deliver the murderer, Davis instructed Holmes to execute ten Union officers then in Confederate custody.[77]

General Holmes would not retaliate against innocent prisoners, and the matter was quietly dropped. Abraham Lincoln promoted John McNeil to brigadier general on November 29. This sent another message to the Union army in the West as to what the Lincoln régime would tolerate vis-à-vis Southern civilians. The war in Missouri, which was already growing brutal, took an even nastier turn.

Mrs. Humphrey did not tell her husband of her rape for three months. Eventually, the truth came out. Strachan was court-martialed but was found innocent of rape. He was found guilty of embezzlement and other crimes and was sent to prison, but General William S. Rosecrans, who became commander of the Department of Missouri in December 1864, ordered him released. After the war he briefly fled to Mexico. He died in New Orleans in 1866, as Mudd wrote, "of a horrible disease, friendless and alone."[78]

U.S. Major General Alfred Pleasonton later arrested and court-martialed McNeil for cowardice in the Battle of Westport, but he escaped conviction. He resigned his commission on April 12, 1865. Later he was nominated for United States marshal in Missouri but the Senate refused to confirm him.

One of the more infamous military occupations in U.S. history was the Union occupation of New Orleans under General Benjamin Butler. A Lincoln political appointee, he was once a delegate to a deadlocked Democratic convention, where he voted to nominate Jefferson Davis for president of the United States on fifty-six straight ballots. He was totally unable to deal with the ladies of New Orleans, who refused to speak to Union soldiers and would walk across the street to avoid even coming in

---

[77]   Joseph A. Mudd, *With Porter in North Missouri* (Washington, D.C.: 1909), pp. 294–309 (hereafter cited as "Mudd").

[78]   Mudd, p. 308.

contract with the shadow of a U.S. flag. After a woman dumped the contents of a chamber pot onto Admiral Farragut's head, Butler issued General Order No. 28, which stated that any female who insulted or showed contempt for a Union soldier should be treated as a "woman of the town plying her avocation." He was nicknamed "Spoons" because he frequently changed the location of his headquarters. When he left and the rightful owners returned, all their silverware was missing. When he was informed that Father Murphy refused to even hold funeral services for Yankee soldiers, Butler sent for him and lambasted him for his un-Christian attitude.

"General, you have been misinformed," the priest declared when he could get a word in edgewise. "Nothing would afford me greater pleasure than to perform the funeral service over you and all your soldiers."[79]

Butler was also a notorious anti-Semitic. A prominent Jew, Eugenia Levy Phillips, the sister of the famous hospital Matron, Phoebe Levy Pender, was accused of laughing when the funeral procession of a Union officer passed her home. She stated that she laughed because a child's birthday party was in progress and something humorous had occurred, but Butler did not believe her. Although there was no trial (probably because there was no crime), the general sentenced her to imprisonment on the isolated and desolate Ship Island. She told Butler: "It [the island] has one advantage over the city, sir. You will not be there." Her remark became famous both at home and abroad.[80]

Father Mullen was accused of refusing to bury Federal soldiers. He also denied the charges. "I will bury them all, with pleasure!" he told General Butler.

Episcopal clergymen Dr. Leacock, Dr. Fulton, Dr. Goodrich, and Dr. Hedges were all exiled from New Orleans. All had large congregations.

---

79 United Confederate Veterans, *Confederate Women of Arkansas in the Civil War, 1861–1865* (Little Rock: 1907), pp. 41–42 (hereafter cited as "CWA").

80 Sullivan, p. xv. Eugenia (1819–1902) was a friend of Rose Greenhow and was arrested as a suspected Rebel spy in 1861. Unlike her husband, Philip Phillips, who was a strong Unionist, Eugenia was a fervent secessionist. Their son Eugene was a midshipman in the Confederate navy. Eugenia remained on the desolate island until her health began to fail and she was released to her family.

Hedges's church was converted into a school for young "contrabands." It was "accidentally" burned to the ground one night.

Dr. Markham, a noted Presbyterian pastor, joined the Army of Tennessee. Father Hubert, a Jesuit priest, left the Crescent City and joined Lee's Army of Northern Virginia.

Father Mullen, the pastor of St. Patrick's Church in New Orleans, always prayed for Jefferson Davis. General Butler ordered that this practice cease and posted guards at the church to see that it did. The reverend father, at the appointed time, instructed his congregation to bow their heads in silence for ten minutes.[81]

Meanwhile, back at the front lines, four main Confederate armies formed to defend four fronts. West to east, they were: the Trans-Mississippi; the Army of Mississippi, defending the Mississippi River Valley, especially Vicksburg; the Army of Tennessee (formerly the Army of Mississippi), operating in Tennessee and, for a time, in Kentucky; and the Army of Northern Virginia.

In 1862, Generals Grant, Sherman, and Rosecrans, among others, hammered unsuccessfully at Vicksburg. Lieutenant General John C. Pemberton, the commander of the Army of Mississippi, has been treated harshly by historians, but he repulsed five major attempts by Grant to take Vicksburg before he was finally defeated. One of his victories occurred in Grant's Central Mississippi Offensive. Here, in the Battle of Oakland, Mississippi, J. J. Silvey was wounded in the hand.

Silvey was a private in Whitfield's legion. He had previously been wounded at Iuka and the Second Battle of Corinth, but the Oakland wound kept him out of action for the rest of the war. He was sent home to Texas on medical furlough. On the way, he stopped for the night at the home of a rich planter, "whose hospitality could not be excelled," he recalled. The planter had two beautiful and talented daughters. When they

---

81   Bankston, p. 91.

saw he was wounded, they washed and dressed his hand, washed his face, combed his hair, and "brush[ed] me up so nice I hardly knew myself."[82]

It took Silvey a year to recover from his wounds. Still in fragile health, he was assigned to the Quartermaster Bureau of the Trans-Mississippi Department, where he remained until the end of the war.

A Texas soldier walked alone one day and ran into a preacher, who asked him to what regiment he belonged.

"The ____ Texas regiment of Van Dorn's army," came the reply. "What army do you belong to?"

"I belong to the army of the Lord," the minister responded.

"Well, then, my friend, you are a long way from headquarters," the old soldier responded.[83]

Samuel P. Moore was named surgeon general of the Confederacy with the rank of colonel on March 16, 1861. Although brusque and a stern disciplinarian—perhaps because he was a Regular army surgeon since 1835—he was a highly capable organizer and administrator, noted for his brilliance, quick comprehension, and energy.[84]

Moore was never promoted to general officer—probably because of difficulties with Jefferson Davis—although he should have been. He was directly responsible for the barracks hospital design, which is still in use today. He improved the ambulance corps, established the *Confederate States Medical and Surgical Journal*, and directed the successful efforts

---

[82] Yeary, Vol. II, pp. 689–690.

[83] CWA, p. 61.

[84] Samuel P. Moore (1813–1889) held his position throughout the war. He practiced medicine in Richmond after the war and his buried in Hollywood Cemetery, Richmond. Allardice, *Colonels*, p. 279.

to develop substitutes for scarce pharmaceuticals from plants grown in the South.

Initially, many small hospitals were hastily set up in the South. This was necessary at first, but they were expensive and difficult to operate efficiently. Moore responded by gradually incorporating them into larger hospitals. He organized five immense medical facilities in the Richmond area: Camp Jackson, Camp Winder, Chimborazo Hospital, Stuart Hospital, and Howard Grove. Each hospital had wards each of which accommodated thirty to forty patients. Thirty to forty wards formed a division, and generally speaking, five divisions formed a hospital. Each hospital included a carpenter's shop; blacksmith shops; apothecary facilities (pharmacies); bakers' facilities; an ice house; and commissary and quartermaster's departments. There were also mess halls and offices for surgeons, stewards, ambulance drivers, nurses, baggage masters, clerks, and even cobblers. There were also what Mrs. Pember called "hospital rats": men who resisted being cured because of a disinclination to engage in field service.

By the autumn of 1862, Colonel Moore and the Confederate congress realized the hospitals could be run more efficiently. In September 1862, the Confederate congress passed the Matron Law, allowing women who were not physicians to administer and run hospitals. It was designed to free men to fight and free doctors from administration, so they could actually practice medicine. Although the law worked beautifully for the South, the U.S. army did not adopt similar regulations for more than one hundred years.

Phoebe Yates Levy was born in Charleston, South Carolina, in 1823, the child of a wealthy and respected Jewish family. They were prominent in the Kahal Kadosh Beth Elohim Synagogue, which is still extant today. Phoebe married Thomas Pember, a gentile from Boston. They relocated to Marietta, Georgia, when the war began. Thomas died of tuberculosis on July 9, 1861, and is buried in Savannah. Afterward, Phoebe relocated to Richmond to help the Southern war effort. After the Matron Law was passed, she was approached by Mary Elizabeth Randolph, the wife of Secretary of War George W. Randolph. She and her husband wanted Pember to direct the Chimborazo Hospital in Richmond. Phoebe was startled. This was one of the largest military hospitals in the Confederacy. But after an interview with Colonel Moore, she accepted the position.

Pember faced opposition from those who derisively called her administration "petticoat government." Many men in 1862 objected to being supervised by a woman, even one of high social status. Pember certainly had her challenges—especially vis-à-vis the whiskey ration—but under her leadership, Chimborazo became one of the premier military hospitals in the South. She continued to administer the hospital brilliantly, despite ever dwindling resources, until well after the surrender. By the end of the war, it had treated an estimated seventy-six thousand patients.

An account of the loyalty of some slaves to their masters will no doubt surprise some people, but it happened frequently. Sallie Phillips, the wife of Dr. James M. Keller, the future medical director of the Trans-Mississippi Department,[85] worked as a nurse and an administrator at the Overton Hotel Hospital in Memphis early in the war. She then organized the Old State Hospital, where she worked with the Dominican sisters of the Catholic Church. She was instrumental in the establishment of other medical facilities and was prominent in Confederate medical circles. For this reason, after they captured Memphis, the Federals exiled her and her two small children to a swampy area south of the city. It was believed she would die there of malaria. One of her former slaves, however, rescued her and her children and helped them escape. She rejoined her husband. After the war, she was busy organizing chapters of the Daughters of the Confederacy, was frequently president of the Arkansas State organization, and was honorary president of the United Daughters of the Confederacy at the time of her death.[86]

---

[85] Dr. and Mrs. Keller celebrated their golden (fiftieth) wedding anniversary in Hot Springs in 1901. She died in 1906.

[86] CWA, pp. 113–114.

Meanwhile, women continued to provide the medical services the government could not. After the Battle of Prairie Grove, Arkansas, Confederate surgeon Dr. Joel H. Blake lavished praise on the women who help care for the wounded soldiers. Mrs. N. J. Morton's home was between the two armies. It was filled with wounded men of both sides, as was its porch. About sundown, several women went out onto the battle-field and carried the wounded of both sides to the house. They worked all night, tore up sheets and pillow cases for bandages, nursed the wounded, and made and served herbal drinks. The next morning, those who were still alive were transported to a nearby Presbyterian church, which was converted into a hospital.[87]

---

[87]   CWA, p. 158.

CHAPTER VI

VICTORIES

"Lee's Light Horse" company was formed on May 23, 1861. It included sixty-one men, with Thomas Stuart Garnett, M.D., as captain and R. L. T. Beale as first lieutenant. "There was nothing very martial in the appearance of the company," Beale wrote later. "The officers and men were clad in their citizens' dress, and their horses caparisoned with saddles and bridles of every description used in the country. Their only arms were sabers and double-barrelled shotguns..."[88]

Lee's Light Horse became part of the 1st Virginia Cavalry Battalion and then Company C, 9th Virginia Cavalry, when it was formed in January 1862. Garnett, meanwhile, joined the 48th Virginia as the regiment's lieutenant colonel. He became colonel and commander of the 48th in October 1862. On May 3, 1863, Brigadier General Elisha F. "Bull" Paxton, the commander of the Stonewall brigade, was killed in action at Chancellorsville. Garnett assumed command of the brigade but was shot through the throat within hours. He died the next day.[89]

John E. Johnson, the commander of the 1st battalion, became commander of the 9th Virginia when it was formed in January 1862. It was

---

[88] R. L. T. Beale, *History of the 9th Virginia Cavalry* (Richmond: 1899), p. 9 (hereafter cited as "Beale").

[89] Garnett was born in Westmoreland County, Virginia, in 1825 and fought in the Mexican War, where he was wounded twice. Antebellum, he served as a medical doctor and a judge. Allardice, *Colonels*, p. 158.

reorganized on April 18 and William H. F. "Rooney" Lee defeated Johnson in the election for colonel. Beale moved up to lieutenant colonel, and Meriwether Lewis was promoted to major.

The Virginia cavalrymen spent the winter of 1861–1862 on patrol on the Potomac and in northern Virginia. They had to spend several days in the rain and snow without any kind of shelter, resulting in severe illnesses and several deaths.

In April 1862, Rooney Lee's cavalry was driven back to the heights above Falmouth, where it was reinforced by a detachment from the 40th Virginia Infantry under Major Taliaferro. Not realizing the Rebels were reinforced, the Union cavalry charged. The Southern infantry allowed them to get very close before they delivered a devastating volley. A second Union attack also failed.

The next day, the 9th Virginia was involved in the evacuation of the Northern Neck, as the peninsula between the Potomac and Rappahannock Rivers is called.[90] The infantry set the bridges on fire and the cavalry was left to make sure the enemy did not put out the fire and save the bridges. Here it was brought under artillery fire and suffered several casualties. One man was accidently killed when a gun discharged. The bullet entered the lower part of his head and passed out the top, hurling his hat several feet in the process.

"Our route was through Fredericksburg," Major Beale recalled, "and here all was hurry and confusion, army wagons rattling away, steam engines hissing, women lamenting, and bodies of troops moving toward… Richmond."[91] The 9th, however, remained in the hills overlooking Fredericksburg, on picket duty.

Like many Confederate regiments early in the war, the 9th was in poor condition. Most of its ten companies were armed with such sporting guns as was available in their respective counties of origin. Three companies were partially armed with inferior carbines and pistols. The equipment of the horses was "of the most inferior kind," and there was no standardization

---

[90]   Virginia's four large peninsulas are (north to south): the Northern Neck; the Middle Peninsula; the Peninsula (aka the Virginia Peninsula); and the Eastern Shore.

[91]   Beale, p. 13.

of anything. There was no regular squad, company, or regimental drill, and the supply of books on tactics was "wholly inadequate."[92]

On March 17, 1862, U.S. General John B. McClellan began embarking the huge Army of the Potomac to the Virginia Peninsula, between the James and York Rivers. Joseph E. Johnston followed suit and brought his Confederate army to Yorktown, beginning the Peninsula Campaign. They fought the Siege of Yorktown (April 5–May 4), after which Johnston retreated up the Peninsula. There was a major rearguard action at Williamsburg on May 5, and Norfolk was evacuated on May 9. A Federal attempt to capture Richmond via naval action was checked at Drewry's Bluff on May 15, and the Southern retreat ended that same day, after the army crossed the Chickahominy. In places, McClellan's forces were within six miles of Richmond.[93]

During the Battle of Williamsburg, Johnston's thirty-one thousand men faced forty thousand Yankees. The Confederates suffered 1,565 casualties, the Federals 2,288—heavy losses for a rearguard action. Sergeant Tapley P. Mays, the color-bearer of the 7th Virginia, particularly distinguished himself. The staff of his flag was severed three times by Union fire, and the flag itself was pierced twenty-three times by enemy shot and shell. Remarkably, Mays was not hurt. Virginia Governor John Letcher wrote him a letter of commendation, complimented his astonishing bravery, and promised him a fine sword as a reward for his gallantry.

---

[92] Beale, pp. 15–16.
[93] E. B. Long, *The Civil War Day by Day* (New York: 1971), May 16, 1862 (hereafter cited as "Long").

Mays probably never received his sword. Carrying his flag with his customary courage, he was killed in action at Turner's Gap on September 14.

On June 12, 1862, Jeb Stuart began his famous "Ride around McClellan." His first step was to defeat the Union cavalry screen near Hanover Court House. He struck them at daybreak with twenty-five hundred men. Captain von Borcke recalled: "...we surprised a picket of the enemy's cavalry, every man of which fell into our hands from the suddenness of our attack...The Yankees were not able to withstand the impetuous onset of the Virginia horsemen, and, after a *melee* of a very few minutes, there commenced a most exciting chase, which was continued for nearly three miles. Friend and foe were soon enveloped in blinding clouds of dust, through which pistol and carbine shots were seen darting to and fro like flashes of lightning."[94] The Federals fled in confusion, but most of them escaped because they had fresher horses, although several prisoners were taken. Only one Rebel was killed: Captain Latane of the 1st Virginia Cavalry was struck by five bullets.

Stuart and his men passed within two and a half miles of McClellan's headquarters. Advancing rapidly, they captured a great many men who were simply walking along the road with no idea the Rebels were anywhere close. They also captured dozens of loaded wagons, which they burned because they could not carry them with them. They did, however, liberate some champagne, pickles, oysters, preserved fruits, oranges, cigars, lemons, and other luxuries. They also captured three transport ships on the Pamunkey and burned them. They were loaded with corn, wheat, and other provisions.[95]

Stuart knew his command's safety—and even its survival—lay in speed. He and his men rode all night, only stopping for an hour to rest and feed the horses. They reached the Chickahominy River at 5 a.m.

---

[94] Heros von Borcke, *Memories of the War for Confederate Independence* (Philadelphia: 1867), p. 27 (hereafter cited as "Borcke").

[95] Borcke, pp. 27–29.

and to their astonishment, found it was unfordable. It was normally a shallow stream, but the rain in the mountains over the last twenty-four hours swelled it to a depth of fifteen feet. And a division of enemy cavalry was on their tail. Coolly, Stuart posted two regiments with two guns as his rearguard, while he used the rest of his command to construct a foot bridge. The men crossed, carrying their saddles, as did about five hundred prisoners. The Rebels who could swim crossed the stream with the horses. The men pushed the two cannons across. General Stuart was the last man to cross. His cavalry was almost constantly in the saddle for two days and two nights.[96]

Lieutenant Colonel Beale, who was on the ride, recalled that they traveled 260 miles and captured 165 prisoners from June 12 to 15. "The country, denude of fences, offered no obstacle, and our line of march was through the fields bordering the road," he remembered. "Sutlers' wagons loaded with varieties of fruits and confectioneries, and heavier wagons filled with quartermaster and commissary supplies in quantities and variety such as we had not seen before, were standing in the road, deserted by their drivers, and in some cases without teams. This temptation proved too strong for resistance, and many troopers broke from the ranks to seize and appropriate the rich spoil. In some instances these became laden with more than could be carried."[97]

Shortly after the Battle of Secessionville, South Carolina,[98] 1st Lieutenant Adolphus E. Morse of John T. Wheaton's artillery battery was attached to the Confederate States Balloon Corps under Major E. Porter Alexander. They had a railroad engine and flat car at their disposal, inflated the balloon at night, and with the flat car in front, were driven to about five miles

---

96   Borcke, pp. 27–31.

97   Beale, p. 19.

98   The Battle of Secessionville (June 16, 1862) was fought on James Island, south of Charleston. A Rebel victory, the sixty-six hundred Yankees suffered 683 casualties. The South lost 204 killed, wounded and missing out of twenty-five hundred engaged.

from the Union front lines before daylight, stopping on a hill. They sent back reports on Federal movements throughout the Seven Days battles. Then the balloon was attached to a tugboat, but it ran aground on July 4, and the enemy was able to capture both the boat and the balloon. Morse and his men, however, escaped. They were ordered to return to Savannah, where they built a new balloon, using more than one thousand yards of silk. Sent to Charleston, the second balloon was attached to vessels, where Morse's men observed Union positions and movements on Morris Island and determined the location and number of guns on U.S. gunboats.

Morse was transferred back to his company after eighteen months and fought until the end of the war.[99]

Reenlistment became a problem in the spring of 1862. The men of many regiments enlisted for twelve months, and their term of service was ending. Enthusiasm for the war (war fever) declined. The government initially dealt with the problem by offering a fifty-dollar bonus and a thirty-day furlough to anyone who would reenlist. Some did. A few accepted the bonus and never returned (i.e., they deserted). The issue, however, was finally settled by the Confederate congress. With some exceptions, it drafted everyone between the ages of eighteen and thirty-five into the army for three years or until the end of the war. Men already in the army were retained. Officers at the company and regimental levels were to be elected.

Many authors denounced the process of electing officers, and I am opposed to the idea on principle, but I also do not believe it hurt the Confederacy to the degree that some writers have suggested. As Private John Franklin of Company E, 32nd Texas Cavalry, wrote later: "It might seem that the necessity to be elected by the men could give rise to a group of officers who would be subservient to the men, but this was not the case. The men elected the officers to lead them, and any officer who failed to lead would have been deposed." He added: "I never wanted any man

---

[99]   Yeary, II, pp. 546–547.

over me, but if I had to have one, I wanted the hair on his chest as thick as pencil lead."[100]

From May 7 to June 9, Stonewall Jackson launched his famous Valley Campaign of 1862. Despite being outnumbered fifty-four thousand to seventeen thousand, he outmarched and outwitted five separated Union armies, smashed them one after another, won victories at McDowell, Front Royal, Winchester, Cross Keys, and Port Republic, cleared the Shenandoah Valley of invaders, threatened Washington, D.C., froze another fifty thousand Federals in place, and joined Lee in front of Richmond for the Seven Days Campaign. It was one of the most brilliant campaigns in world military history.

Jackson's cavalry was commanded by Colonel Turner Ashby (later brigadier general), the "Black Knight of the Confederacy." He was a great warrior and personally killed several Yankees in hand-to-hand combat. A great fighter, however, does not often make a great commander. Ashby had a laissez-faire attitude toward the war and had little interest in imposing discipline on his wild band.

Captain Harry Gilmor, for example, was organizing his company in Winchester, Virginia, in March 1862, when Stonewall Jackson evacuated the place. Ashby commanded the rearguard and told the captain: "Gilmor, you had better move away as soon as possible; the enemy are coming into town at the other end."

Instead of leaving, however, Gilmor and his brother, a sergeant, dismounted and went into the saloon of the Taylor House hotel to write some letters. When they emerged, Jackson's army was gone and the Gilmors and Private McAleese were the only Rebels in Winchester. They looked down Main Street and saw an enemy column passing by the Virginia House, only two blocks away. Still, they were in no hurry. They remounted and slowly rode out of town, conversing with young ladies along the way. They even

---

[100] Carl I. Duaine, *The Dead Men Wore Boots: An Account of the 32ⁿᵈ Texas Volunteer Cavalry, C.S.A.* (Austin, Texas: 1966), p. 26 (hereafter cited as "Duaine").

stopped to eat cake with some of them, although they did post one of the belles as a lookout. When they finally left, some of the Yankees shot at them but did no damage.

Once out of town, they engaged in scouting. Jackson, they knew, would want to know what Union formation had entered Winchester and its approximate strength. The enemy pursued them more rapidly than they anticipated, and they found themselves cut off from the turnpike and were forced to jump a stone wall to escape. The Gilmors managed to clear the wall, but McAleese's horse was shot through the shoulders as he leaped and landed on top of the wall, hurling his rider over the fence in the process. Captain Gilmor quickly picked him up, even though he took a Yankee bullet in the process. They rode double; the horse leaped another stone wall and despite carrying two men, carried them all the way to Strasburg, about eighteen miles, where they rejoined their comrades. Gilmor later remarked that he suffered intensely from his wound.[101]

Harry Gilmor's adventures continued the following month—April 1862—when he clashed with the enemy cavalry near Harrisonburg. "... we had just wheeled about, when the enemy broke forth from the woods about a quarter of a mile from our rear, and charged in splendid style, yelling like demons," the captain recalled. He got his men across a stream and linked up with Captain Fletcher's company and "knowing that all the fun would be there, I wheeled about and went in by his side."

"When the two forces met, the shock was tremendous, and several men and horses rolled on the ground. It was then that I captured Adjutant Hasbrouck. The adjutant had on, as I afterward found, a steel breastplate underneath his clothing, rendering him bullet-proof to some extent. I fired twice at him, and he three or four times at me. At length I got close to him and fired. Great was my astonishment that he did not fall. This was my last load; so, drawing sabers, we closed for a hand-to-hand fight." Gilmor

---

[101]   Gilmor, pp. 21–22.

knocked the saber from the lieutenant's hand, and as the Rebel drew back his saber to cut him down, Hasbrouck surrendered.[102]

The battle continued. Gilmor managed to rally his company and repulsed two charges. Meanwhile, four of his men were badly wounded and captured. Gilmor determined to rescue them and, in the process, was cut off from his command. Seven Union soldiers called upon him to surrender but did not cease firing. There was a fence behind him and "I determined to make my horse jump it or break it down...I struck him severely with the spurs, and he cleared the fence without touching a hair."

While Gilmor reloaded, the Yankees tore down the fence. When they resumed the attack, the captain shot and wounded two of them. The Northerners decided not to pursue further. Gilmor, however, was unable to save his wounded. When he returned to the scene of the battle the next day, they were all removed. He found eight badly wounded horses, all of which he shot. He then rejoined his command, which had assumed he was captured. When he rode into camp, "they almost hugged me with joy—all very gratifying to me."[103]

Clarence Payne of the 2nd Virginia Cavalry had a Yankee sweetheart, Miss Ann Goodheart. He was sure of her beauty but not of her loyalty to the Confederacy. She invited him to tea. When he arrived, she received him cordially and introduced him to a Northern lieutenant and two friendly Union soldiers. They were very nice and all had an enjoyable time. At the end of the evening, the lieutenant told Payne that he was very sorry, but he was going to have to arrest him and carry him to Washington. They chatted a little longer, until Payne gave the signal and two armed Confederates burst into the parlor and got the drop on the Yankees. "I am very sorry, Lieutenant," Payne said, "but I will have to take you all to Richmond," which he did.[104]

---

[102] Gilmor, p. 25–26.
[103] Gilmor, pp. 25–26.
[104] Yeary, II, p. 645.

A Texas infantrymen asked Stonewall Jackson: "General, where are we going?"

Jackson stared at him and finally said: "Are you a good hand to keep a secret?"

"Yes, sir."

"Well, so am I," Jackson replied and rode off.[105]

Colonel Bradley Johnson of the 1st Maryland, C.S.A., attacked the 1st Maryland, U.S.A., in the Battle of Front Royal (May 23, 1862). The battle started when the Confederate cavalry drove in the Union picket line. A short pause in the fighting ensued, during which Johnson saw one of his men sitting beside the road, at the foot of a tree. "Come on!" Johnson shouted at him. "We are going into action."

"I can't go, General," he replied, sorrowfully.[106]

---

[105] Yeary, II, p. 616.

[106] Johnson was nominated for the rank of brigadier general by Stonewall Jackson. His recommendation was not approved because there were not enough Maryland troops. Johnson did not become a brigadier general until 1864.

"What do you mean?" the officer retorted.

"General," he sobbed, "I have just killed my brother! And I don't feel as if I could fight any more today!"

The soldier explained that during the charge on the picket line, he had cut down a Union cavalryman. As the man fell, the Rebel realized it was his own brother, who was fighting for the North.[107]

---

[107] King and Derby, pp. 556–557.

CHAPTER VII

MORE VICTORIES

In 1857, the United States Supreme Court ruled that black African slaves and their descendants were property and had no rights the white man was bound to respect.[108] In 1862, a captain in Colonel Roger Pryor's command owned a black boy named Caesar. One day, the captain went into a skirmish and ordered Caesar to watch his tent and its contents.

"Mayn't I go he'p de cook?" Caesar asked. He was not enthusiastic about being brought under enemy fire.

"Stay there, sir, and protect my property!" the captain ordered sternly.

An unhappy Caesar did so—for a while. Then shot and shell began to fall around the tent, so he fled and hid in the bushes. The captain returned to camp before Caesar did.

"You rascal!" the officer barked. "Didn't I leave you here to protect my property? It might have been all stolen."

"I knows it, sah," the slave responded, "I knows it! An' I did purtect yo' property, sah! I sholy did! Dem ole cloes ain't wuth nothin' I'se feared to bresh 'em less'n I git a hole in 'em; but dis property," he said as he laid his hand on his chest, "dis property is wuth fifteen hundred dollars!"[109]

---

108 Yeary, II, pp. 470–471.
109 Yeary, II, pp. 470–471.

By late May 1862, General McClellan's strategy was obvious. He was within heavy artillery range of Richmond. Rather than take the city via costly infantry assaults, he intended to blast it into submission. The dirt roads of the Peninsula, however, were muddy, and it would take weeks for the Union siege trains to reach the front. Joe Johnston's army would have to push them back before then, if the capital was to be saved.

As the Rebel infantry marched to its assembly areas, its path was marked by discarded playing cards. Card playing was considered sinful by many people in those days. If a soldier was killed, his belongings were sent back home to his next of kin. Many Johnny Rebs (and Billy Yanks, for that matter) did not want their mothers and fathers to know they played cards, so they dropped them on the side of the road. They were replaced in the soldiers' pockets by New Testaments.

Johnston's attacks on McClellan were called the Battle of Seven Pines (May 31–June 1, 1862). During the fighting, the 5th Texas Infantry became separated from the rest of the brigade and became lost in the darkness. The night was so black the men could not see twenty yards in front of them, and they did not know was friend or foe. Their colonel, James J. Archer, ordered them to lie down where they were, despite the fact they were cold and wet. They carried nothing with them but their weapons. None of them had blankets.

Just as it got light enough to see, the Rebels discovered a Union camp about two hundred yards ahead. Some of them were cooking breakfast, but many had not yet gotten up. "…we raised the Rebel yell and charged them," Private William Henry Mathews recalled. "Surprised, they broke and ran, leaving behind everything they had, although a few took their guns with them. The Southerners captured breakfast, bedding, knapsacks full of clothes, and many other items. Every man liberated a blanket and wrapped up in it.[110]

The Battle of Seven Pines was fought within six miles of Richmond. Miss Constance Cary recalled: "It was so near that the first guns sent our hearts into our mouths, like a sudden loud knocking at one's door at night. The women left in Richmond had, with few exceptions, husbands, fathers, sons, and brothers in the fight. I have never seen a finer exhibition of calm courage than they showed in this baptism of fire. No one wept or moaned aloud. All went about their task of preparing for the wounded, making bandages, scraping lint, improvising beds. Night brought a lull in the frightful cannonading. We threw ourselves dressed upon our beds to get a little rest before the morrow.

"During the night began the ghastly procession of wounded brought in from the field. Every vehicle the city could produce supplemented the military ambulances. Many slightly wounded men, so black with gunpowder as to be unrecognizable, came limping in on foot. All next day, women with white faces flitted bareheaded through the street and hospitals, looking for their own. Churches and lecture-rooms were thrown open for volunteer ladies sewing and filling the rough beds called for by the surgeons. There was not enough of *anything* to meet the sudden appalling call of many strong men stricken unto death. Hearing that my cousin, Reginald Hyde, was reported wounded, two of us girls volunteered to help his mother to search for him through the lower hospitals. We tramped down Main Street through the hot sun over burning pavements, from one scene of horror to another, bringing up finally at the St. Charles Hotel, a large old building. What a sight met our eyes! Men in every stage of mutilation, lying waiting for the surgeons upon bare boards, with haversacks or army blankets, or nothing, beneath their heads. Some gave up the weary ghost as we passed them by. All were suffering keenly and needing ordinary attention. To be

---

[110] Yeary, II, pp. 470–471.

there empty-handed nearly broke our hearts. Bending down over bandaged faces stiff with blood and thick with flies, nothing did we see or hear of the object of our search, who, I am glad to say, arrived later at his mother's home, to be nursed by her to a speedy recovery.

"The impression of that day was ineffaceable. It left me permanently convinced that nothing is worth war!"[111]

A Prussian, Heros von Borcke was born into a Pomeranian noble family in 1835 and became an officer in the 2nd Brandenburg Dragoons. He experienced financial difficulties, resigned his commission, and ran the blockade to the Confederate States of America in the spring of 1862. He was commissioned captain on June 1 and was assigned to the staff of Jeb Stuart. Borcke was a large man and used an extremely large sword. He became known as "the Giant in Gray."

Borcke was assigned to Jeb Stuart's staff as a captain and was almost immediately in action at Seven Pines. He recalled: "Never shall I forget the impression made upon me by this first sight of death and devastation to which I afterwards became so well accustomed.

"The most horrible spectacle was that presented near the bastions and earthworks which the day before [May 31, 1862] had been stormed by our men. Friend and foe were lying here indiscriminately side by side, mown down in multitudes by musketry and by the guns which we had afterwards taken. The enemy's artillery had here lost all their horses, which lay by dozens, piled one upon another, and all around the ground was strewn with weapons, haversacks, cartridge-boxes, ammunition, &c. These articles, abandoned by the enemy, were used by us most profitably for the better equipment of our own troops."[112]

---

[111] Harrison, pp. 82–83.
[112] Borcke, p. 21.

Although Johnston's men scored some local successes, the Yankees rallied quickly and checked his attacks. In a vain attempt to get his offensive back on track, the general ventured too close to the front and was seriously wounded. He was replaced by Robert E. Lee.[113]

Lee launched his own offensive on June 25 and, in the Seven Days Campaign, successfully drove the enemy from the gates of Richmond. Bennett Wood of the 4th Texas Infantry Regiment (part of Hood's elite Texas brigade) recalled going into the Battle of Gaines Mill on June 27, 1862: "James Smiley was marching by my side. Solid shots were falling near us, and glancing up in the direction from which they came. I saw a ricochet shot coming toward me, I fell forward saving myself, but Smiley fell by my side, his entire head shot off. This was only a beginning..." They moved steadily down an open, gentle slope for about 750 yards to a creek, fixed bayonets, and attacked. "Oh, the slaughter as we charged! We [now] understood why Gen. Hood wanted us to go to the enemy without firing, for in piles all around us were other Confederates, who stopped to load their guns, lay dead and dying...on we went, yelling, shooting, seeing men fall and die, up, up to the top of that murderous hill." They captured a Union battery, pushed the enemy back, and cleared a road. Wood recorded later: "...as I knelt by a fence to take a shot at some artillery[men] in front a minie ball passed through a fence rail and I was blinded by a stunning blow below the eye." When he regained some of his vision, he staggered to the rear, where he saw Jack Smiley, who had borrowed General Hood's horse and was carrying his two brothers on it. Both of them were dead.

Wood learned that his brother, Lieutenant Peter S. Wood, had fallen. Bennett later found Peter in a hospital, where doctors had been forced

---

[113]   The Union Army of the Potomac lost five thousand men at Seven Pines. The South lost six thousand one hundred.

to amputate his leg. Bennett received permission to accompany him to Richmond and was with him when he died from blood poisoning on July 22. The regiment lost 212 of its 530 privates during this action.[114]

Bennett Wood was wounded in the face at Seven Days, was shot through the leg at Gettysburg, and was wounded in the foot in the Wilderness. He survived the war.

During the evening of June 27, Captain von Borcke returning from the front after carrying a dispatch for General Stuart. "…I felt a stunning blow across the spine," he recalled, "and at the same moment my horse rolled over with me. I was confident the animal had been struck by a cannon-ball; but, to my great surprise, I was not able to discover any wound. As I was myself unhurt, I remounted my brave animal, and continued on my way. A solid shot had passed close to my horse's back, and the current of air set in motion by its passage had knocked over both horse and rider. Afterwards, during the war, I witnessed many similar cases of 'windage.'"[115]

Later, in another battle, the major watched a young bullock (ox) suddenly turn a somersault when a shell exploded nearby. It was down for some time, and Borcke thought it was dead. But it found its legs again, and after reeling as if it was drunk, it took off again "with the speed of an arrow."[116]

During the Seven Days Battles, Jeb Stuart captured the main Union supply depot at White House, Virginia. The Yankees abandoned it but succeeded only partially in destroying it. Captain von Borcke was astonished at what he saw in the burning camp. "Never in my life had I seen such enormous quantities of commissary stores—never had I supposed

---

[114] Yeary, II, pp. 815–816.
[115] Borcke, p. 40.
[116] Borcke, pp. 239–240.

that an army of invasion would voluntarily encumber itself with such an incalculable amount of useless luxuries. Hundreds of boxes of oranges and lemons were piled up together…Great pyramids of barrels of white and brown sugar, and of salt fish, and eggs packed in salt, were blazing on all sides. One of the burning barrels of eggs we knocked open, and found its contents roasted à *merveille*, which gave us, with other edibles within easy reach, such a repast as we had not enjoyed for many months. Not far from us, as we thus feasted, were little mountains of hams, of bacon, and boxes of arms, uniforms, and equipments for more than 10,000 men. An equal number of the latter we discovered in the river, as well as two transports, laden with whisky and other liquors, which had been sunk by the enemy on our approach, but which we raised and secured with little difficulty. A large number of railway carriages and new locomotive engineers, and a pontoon train, also fell into our hands."[117]

The White House supply depot was burned by the time the 9th Virginia Cavalry arrived. "The evidence of the immense resources of the United States Government was displayed…" Colonel Beale wrote later. "The accumulation of commissary supplies seemed endless. We saw a lake of vinegar, which, bursting from the huge piles of barrels, had extinguished the fire, and covered the ground for some feet beyond the charred mass of staves and hoops. The houghs of hams and shoulders were still discernable over a surface of a thousand feet of charred back and smoldering ashes. Eggs packed in salt were here—some raw, some partly cooked, some cooked hard, and some burnt—in numbers larger than we had ever seen before. Many barrels of salted fish remained unscathed by the fire.

"…Cheeses, crackers, lard, butter, cakes, oranges, lemons, raisins, dry goods (embracing even hooped skirts), stationery, tobacco, and, in a few instances, trunks containing money, watches, and jewelry, fell into the hands of our troopers."

Riding in the twilight, the colonel also saw many chickens roosting in the Union's coups. He liberated two, which provided him his first meal of the day. "Immense piles of muskets we found burned, and many

---

[117] Borcke, p. 46.

wagons had been backed over the bank into the river." Many others were captured intact.[118]

The supply columns were unable to keep up with the Confederate pursuit, and the 9th Virginia Cavalry was just one of the regiments that suffered. They stopped near Malvern Hill just after the battle of July 1 and spent a night in the heavy rain without food. One officer took a detail out to purchase food locally and found seven fine bulls left behind by the enemy. The 9th immediately went into the butchering business and dined on steaks, cooked on sticks set into the ground in front of the fires.[119] Most units were not so lucky.

James P. Taylor was a school teacher in Pittsburg, North Carolina, when the war began. He enlisted as a private in the 5th North Carolina Infantry on April 15, 1861, two days after Fort Sumter surrendered. He was sent to Virginia and fought in the Siege of Yorktown (where he was slightly wounded in the ear), Dam No. 1, Seven Pines, and Seven Days Battles, including Malvern Hill, where Lee's Seven Days offensive was finally checked. Taylor's health failed that fall, and he returned to North Carolina, where Governor Zebulon Vance made him a brigade inspector. He served in this rear-area position until the end. "All the glory I want," he wrote later, "is the consciousness of having done my best on the side that I still know to be right."[120]

---

[118] Beale, p. 26. White House was owned by Colonel W. H. F. "Rooney" Lee, the commander of the 9th Virginia Cavalry.

[119] Beale, pp. 27–28.

[120] Yeary, II, p. 741.

Early in the war, there was a great deal of discussion on the subject of "dodging." Some said it was improper and unmilitary to dodge enemy fire. Others said there was no reason a good soldier should get his head blown off just to keep up appearances. Stonewall Jackson favored dodging, although he did not dodge himself. General Stuart did not commit himself on the issue.

The matter seemed to come to a head in Stuart's cavalry during the Seven Days campaign, Stuart sent one of his captains to deliver a message. On the return trip, he was exposed to plunging artillery fire from the enemy. The young staff officer rode "Comanche fashion" behind the neck of his horse, so that he was nearly in a prone position. He was greeted with howls of laughter from his general and his colleagues, who made fun of the young man.

They told the story to Robert E. Lee when he visited the cavalry headquarters shortly after. Lee listened gravely and came down solidly on the side of dodging. "That's right, captain," he told the young officer, "dodge all you can."[121]

---

[121]   King and Derby, p. 561.

The captain got even with Stuart later that year, during the Battle of Fredericksburg. The general was on a reconnaissance and took cover behind a cedar hedge, from which he observed enemy positions through his binoculars. A Union shell grazed the top of the hedge and Stuart made "a profound bow." When he raised up, he saw the young captain, who was laughing at him.[122]

---

[122]   King and Derby, p. 562.

CHAPTER VIII

SOCIETY CHANGES

Meanwhile, society changed on the home front.

Pattie Wright (later Pattie Hedges of El Dorado) was the daughter of Major Edward W. Wright. She lived in Lisbon, Arkansas, about sixteen miles from El Dorado. In 1861, nearly every man able to bear arms left for the war. The fall of New Orleans and the Federal blockade cut off most of their supplies. "The entire county presented a scene of remarkable activity, in which woman was the commanding figure. In the household, in the workshop, on the plantation, the hand of woman was displayed; and woman's mind directed nearly every undertaking, great or little"[123]

Women and children lived at the subsistence level. They survived on wild fruits, cornbread, sorghum molasses, and sassafras tea. Mrs. F. L. Sutton of Fayetteville, Arkansas, recalled: "Were there crops to be made, women made them; were fences to be built, women must build them. They raised houses, rolled logs, went to the mill, not with two fat sleek horses for a team, but more likely the family cow and a big calf yoked together. It was women that killed hogs and beeves [skinned and butchered them], and in the absence of these brutes, women shouldered guns and went hunting or fishing. In the absence of physicians (and there was a dearth of them for a long period), women practiced without leave or license..." They had to

---

[123] CWA, p. 63.

"offer final prayers, close sightless eyes, dig graves, make a pine coffin, and fill and mark the grave."[124]

First, in 1861, they made the uniforms the men wore when they marched away. Looms, spinning wheels and ad hoc tanneries were fully employed. All stations of wealth or rank were forgotten. Flowers, once appreciated only for their fragrance and beauty, were now prized for their medicinal qualities or food value, if any. Indigo was cultivated to dye uniforms. Beef tallow and candle molds were employed in making candles. Wicks were made from soft spun fabric, which was then doubled and twisted, waxed, and soaked in turpentine. Carpets were converted into blankets. Homemade shoes were created. The women fashioned different kinds of salves, manufactured corn cob pipes using bits of cane for stems, and manufactured red pepper for transport to the troops. Homegrown rice was popular and ground via mortar and pestle. Rolls of linen for bandages were produced from bed linen, tablecloths, and pillow cases.

An interesting story was told at the United Confederate Veterans' Reunion in Nashville in 1900. As General Grant pushed into northern Mississippi in one of his unsuccessful drives on Vicksburg, a young Southern soldier was seriously wounded and taken home on parole. Shortly after, Grant himself appeared and established his headquarters in this old Southern mansion. Alarmed for the boy's safety, the family hid him in the narrow space between the house and the ground. Unfortunately, his every groan (and there were many) was audible within the house. His elder sister solved this problem by playing the piano and singing all day. The little sister, however, was worried about her brother and decided to take matters into her own hands.

It was late afternoon when General Grant heard a soft tap on his door. He opened it to find a little girl, characterized by a mass of tangled curls. "I've got something to tell you," she declared.

---

[124] CWA, p. 73.

"You have? I shall be very glad to hear it," the future president answered.

"Well, before I tell you, you've got to promise that you'll never, never tell. Do you declare and cross your heart and wish you may die in a minute if you ever, ever tell?"

No doubt smiling, the general simply said, "Yes."

"Well, then do it."

He repeated the words after her and crossed his heart, as directed.

"My big brother is sick under the house; he's out there with the bugs and rats, and they're going to eat him up."

Shortly after, Grant crossed paths with the owner of the mansion. "I hear you have a wounded son under the house."

"What is that to you?" the startled old man replied.

"Simply this: if he is in need of medical attention, he should have it and be placed in comfortable quarters receiving it."

The young Confederate was immediately placed in a bedroom and eventually recovered. He was still alive at the turn of the century. It was many years before the little girl (then a woman) revealed what actually transpired.

General Grant apparently never told anybody about the incident. He crossed his heart, after all.

At first, wounds were considered a practical benefit. They often led to furloughs—often of indefinite length—and good food, positive attention from ladies, and sometimes a discharge.

This attitude changed fairly quickly. So did attitudes toward "rifle pits," which today are called "trenches." General Lee was perhaps the first to fully grasp their practical benefits. He ordered his men to dig in. Early in the war, they laughed at him and called him "the King of Spades," referring to a type of shovel. By 1864, however, it was easy to see where the Confederate army was halting for the night because dirt was flying everywhere.

Sara Pryor, the wife of Colonel Roger Pryor, the commander of the 3rd Virginia Infantry, heard the rumor that he was promoted to brigadier general. That day, Mrs. Pryor attended a reception at the Spotswood Hotel in Richmond, where she saw President Davis. "Is it true, Mr. President?" she asked. Had her husband been promoted?

Mr. Davis smiled benevolently and replied, "I have no reason, Madam, to doubt it, except that I saw it this morning in the papers."[125]

Robert E. Lee felt the same way as the president. He once sarcastically said to A. P. Hill: "We made a great mistake in the beginning of our struggle, and I fear, in spite of all we can do, it will prove to be a fatal mistake. We appointed all our worst generals to command our armies, and all our best generals to edit the newspapers."[126]

Colonel Daniel A. Wilson Jr. had a magnificent horse he called "Slasher," which was known for its "nimbleness and cat-like treads," according to Major R. H. Bigger. The boys in the 7th Louisiana said Slasher could jump over a church.[127] It easily carried "Big Dan," as the Louisiana colonel was called. At a time when the average Union soldier stood 5'8" and weighed 143 pounds, Wilson was 6'4" high and weighed three hundred pounds. One day, on a Virginia road, he ran into Stonewall Jackson, who was on his way to "preaching." After exchanging courtesies, Jackson said: "If it were not Sunday, colonel, and if you were disposed to sell 'Slasher,' what would be your price for him?"

---

[125] Pryor, p. 166.

[126] Clifford Dowdey, *Lee* (New York: 1955), p. 509 (hereafter cited as "Dowdey").

[127] As a captain, Wilson commanded Company I of the 7th Louisiana Infantry Regiment from June 7, 1861 until December 16, 1862, when he became judge advocate of the military court of Jackson's II Corps. He was promoted to colonel and held this post under Jackson and later Ewell until the end of the war.

"Well, General," Wilson replied, "if it were not Sunday, I might answer your question; but being Sunday, you will allow me to postpone the answer to some future day of the week."

"Certainly," Jackson answered, and rode on to worship.

General Lee was known to be a fine judge of horse flesh. One day, he asked Big Dan: "Colonel, in this world they say there is nothing perfect, but will you have the kindness to point out the defects of your horse?"

"Yes, General," he said, "they are very broad and distressing, and they are the cause of the dejected manner which you have observed in me of late. When I ride Slasher at the head of the regiment through villages and towns, everyone cries out, 'Oh, what a magnificent horse!' They never say, 'What a handsome, noble looking officer.'"[128]

In April and May 1862, General Beauregard brilliantly retreated to Corinth, Mississippi, which fell to Halleck's armies on May 30. Beauregard then retreated to Tupelo, Mississippi. Two weeks later, he took an unauthorized leave without informing President Davis. When he learned of it, he fired General Beauregard on June 17 and replaced him as commander of the Army of Mississippi (later dubbed the Army of Tennessee) with Braxton Bragg.[129]

Although undoubtedly a failure as an army commander, Bragg started out brilliantly enough. He moved thirty-five thousand men 776 miles via rail from Tupelo through Mobile to Chattanooga. Catching the Yankees flat-footed, he marched around Don Carlos Buell's left flank and invaded Kentucky. It appeared the Northerners would have to fight Bragg on his own terms, but the Rebel leader lost his nerve and retreated. The campaign ended in an indecisive meeting engagement at Perryville (October 8), and Bragg retreated to Murfreesboro, Tennessee.

---

[128] King and Derby, p. 445.

[129] The Army of Mississippi was officially redesignated the Army of Tennessee on November 20, 1862. A new Army of Mississippi was established under the command of John C. Pemberton.

During a skirmish in the Kentucky Campaign, Lieutenant Luther A. Williams of North Carolina became separated from his comrades. He came upon an abandoned cabin, from which he heard groans. He looked inside and found a severely wounded Union officer, who begged him not to kill him. Williams told the Yankee not to fear. He saw to the bluecoat's comfort and because it was a cold day, built him a fire, left wood handy, filled his canteen with water, lay his knapsack by his side, and left him to his fate.

Lieutenant Williams was later killed in action at Chickamauga in September 1863.

John E. Logsdon was a private in Company C, 9th Texas Infantry, and fought from Shiloh until April 10, 1865, when he was captured in the Battle of Spanish Fort, Mobile, Alabama.

During the Kentucky Campaign, he was at Cumberland Gap and for the first days received no rations except two ears of corn per day. He was always fond of coffee, so he would parch his corn until it was thoroughly brown, beat it until it was fine, and make a cup of "coffee." He did this three times a day. After finishing the coffee, he ate the grounds, thereby getting both stimulate and nourishment from the corn. "We endured hardships and privations with patience and fortitude," he said after the war, "for we knew that the Government was doing all it could for us."[130]

Elijah Perdue of the 37th Georgia was sent out on a foraging mission in the Cumberland Mountains. He crossed into a valley "where there was plenty to eat for man and beast." He found a house with the door wide open. No

---

[130] Yeary, II, pp.445–447.

one was home, but he found a cooked turkey and biscuits, so he filled his haversack and headed back to camp.

He traveled about one hundred yards when he met a couple of boys. They told him they lived in the house and their mother went to the neighbors to invite them to eat some turkey. "I expect that she gave me a blessing when she found the turkey gone," Perdue recalled.[131]

Frank B. Gurley enlisted in Forrest's Cavalry Corps (a battalion-sized unit) in 1861 and served with him in Kentucky. He was with "the Wizard of the Saddle" when he was surrounded at Fort Donelson but escaped with virtually his entire command. Shortly after, Gurley returned home and recruited his own company of 115 men. He was elected captain, and his command was designated Company C, 4th Alabama Cavalry. His regiment was attached to Forrest's cavalry division.

On August 5, 1862, U.S. Brigadier General Robert L. McCook led his brigade south from Decherd, Tennessee. He suffered from dysentery and was traveling in a wagon that was serving as an ambulance. It lagged behind the main body. Gurley spotted this outlier and attacked. McCook's teamster panicked and got the wagon stuck. McCook pushed him aside, took the reins himself, and began extricating the wagon. The general either did not hear the Rebels demanding he stop, or perhaps he ignored them. In any case, as he tried to escape, Captain Gurley shot him in the left side below the ribs.

Charles H. Word was with Gurley at the time and recalled: "Gen. McCook in an ambulance refused to surrender, surrounded by his body guard, and was shot in a fair fight, and wounded. (After his body guard had deserted him, those who were not killed or captured) we carried him to the home of the nearest citizen, Dr. Petty, a very aged man with a family of a noble wife and daughters, where in a few hours he died." (He actually died the next day.) McCook accepted his wound as an act of war and

<hr />

[131] Yeary, II, pp. 600–601.

never expressed any animosity toward Gurley. After McCook died and the 4th Alabama retreated, Word recalled, McCook's "'Dutch Hessions [sic]' burned the home and all of its buildings to the ground. Then they went through the neighborhood burning everything," Wood recalled. "Among them the home of my own dear mother, with her three daughters and one son eleven years old. They were not allowed to carry a single stitch of wearing apparel from the burning home, besides offering all the indignities and insults of which a brutal soldier is capable of offering to unprotected females."

Northern newspapers soon circulated the false story that Gurley murdered McCook as he lay helpless in the ambulance. Because the McCook family had considerable political influence, Gurley became a wanted man. Unaware of this, the captain continued to ride with Forrest and later Wheeler. During Forrest's famed West Tennessee Raid of December 1862, the captain personally captured Colonel Robert "Bob" Ingersoll, a Union brigade commander and the most famous agnostic of his day. Gurley briefly commanded the regiment as senior captain in 1863 but was captured on October 13, 1863, and was carried to Brownsboro, where the Yankees were split. Some wanted to hang him, others wanted to drown him, and others wanted to burn him at the stake. The town's commandant had to place a double guard around him to keep him alive.

Frank Gurley was taken to Nashville, locked in heavy chains, and confined to a four-by-seven-foot cell. He was put on trial. Because many of his men were in civilian clothes, the central issue became whether or not Gurley was a Confederate officer. The defense was unable to produce a commission, probably because the Yankees burned his house. Despite a letter from General Forrest that Gurley served with his command since July 1861, he was sentenced to death. Forrest's letter was threatening. Perhaps this is why the overall Union commander, General Thomas, suspended the execution and recommended that the sentence be commuted to five years' imprisonment. (Threats from Nathan Bedford Forrest were always taken seriously.) Union Judge Advocate Joseph Holt and Secretary of War Stanton, however, wanted their pound of flesh. Lincoln approved the verdict but because of Rebel threats of retaliation, delayed executing the sentence.

Gurley had been imprisoned over a year in January 1865 when the U.S. army's bureaucracy blundered and included Gurley in a prisoner exchange. He returned to Confederate lines on March 17. He surrendered in Huntsville, where he took the oath of allegiance and was paroled. Gurley returned to civilian life and was elected sheriff of Montgomery County in November.

Joseph Holt, meanwhile, still wanted to hang the former captain. He had him rearrested on November 28 and planned his execution for two days later. Seventy-four citizens petitioned President Andrew Johnson, asking the execution be suspended. Several of these people were pro-Union, which influenced the president to suspend the hanging. General Grant finally weighed in and called for Gurley's release. He was set free in April 1866.

Captain Frank Gurley never entertained malicious feelings toward the Federals. He resided in Gurley, Alabama, after the war. The town was named after his father. Frank died on March 29, 1920. He was eighty-five years old.

Private Word wrote later: "I am getting old enough now that I ought to forgive such inhumanity to my loved ones. But examine the passions and feelings of mankind (and especially Southern manhood), bring the doctrine of reconciliation to the touchstone of nature and then tell me whether you can hereafter love, honor, and faithfully serve the power that hath carried fire and sword, and dishonor (to our mothers and sisters) into our land... If you say that you can pass these things over, then I ask you, hath your home been burned, hath your property been destroyed before your face? Hath your wife and children been made destitute of a bed to lie on or food to live on? If you have not, you are not a judge of those who have."[132]

---

[132] *Confederate Veteran*, Vol. (1920), pp. 20, 236; Yeary, II, pp. 821–822.

Back at home, the women soldiered on and, in effect, fought their own war. Mrs. Mahaley Pollard of Gray, Arkansas, remarked: "Our soldiers acted bravely on the field of battle and we women tried to be worthy of them."[133] To do without for the boys in gray almost became a religion. Certainly, few of these women had any use for Yankees. One Southern woman wrote about the winter weather in her scrapbook: "The weather is as cold as a Yankee's heart, and as disagreeable as his company; as blustering as he is before a battle, and as dismal as he is after one."[134]

Granville County, North Carolina, was far from the front. The women wanted to help the Cause. They banned together and asked Richmond to send them one hundred or more sick and wounded soldiers. Richmond assented. The sick and wounded soon arrived by train. They were welcomed into each lady's private home, sometimes as many as four per household. They were nursed, fed good country food, and given fresh milk. With their health restored, they returned to the fighting.

"The Confederacy was very deficient in supplies of medicine—more necessary than ammunition at times," Marie Louise Benton Bankston recalled. "In the supreme moment of their country's need, the women rose to meet every emergency, from the making of bandages, knitting of socks to wearing of cloth. They dug up the floors of their smoke houses and tobacco barns to extract nitre [as niter was spelled in those days] from them; the corncobs were gathered up from the barns, that the soda and potash obtained from them might be used in making gunpowder. Women grew poppies, and from the gum they made an opiate for the sufferers in the hospitals. They learned to harvest and stew dogwood, which was used as a substitute for quinine. The black boys of the plantation were kept busy

---

133   CWA. P. 90.
134   CWA, p. 61.

in the woods gathering herbs and berries with which to make tonics and stimulants for the sick and injured soldiers.

"The carpets on their floors were cut up for blankets, and the draperies converted into underwear. When all else was exhausted, the women learned the art of weaving, and made the cloth from which the grey jackets and caps were contrived."

The town and church bells were melted and molded into bullets.[135]

In Fort Smith, Arkansas, the women organized a sewing society. They met at the Methodist church. They worked all day, making coats, pants, jackets, wagon sheets, tents, haversacks, and the like, and made hundreds of suits and bandages for the wounded. They knitted socks at night. Several women worked in their homes, making cartridges.

Later in the war, when there was fighting in the area (including Pea Ridge and Prairie Grove), the Methodist church became a hospital, as did the Presbyterian church, several stores, and vacant houses. Many of the ladies became nurses. Other women used the Episcopal and Catholic churches for sewing and preparing food for the sick and wounded.

Mrs. Anna Mitchell of Havana, Arkansas, recalled that war was a great equalizer. Women of wealth and station, who had never had to work before, "were glad to get their poor neighbors to show them how to spin thread and weave cloth to make their dresses, and when they were made those fine ladies were just as proud of them as if they had the finest silk."[136]

Southern women were noted for their generosity and self-sacrifice. Virginia Cleaver of Camden, Arkansas, was a little girl during the war. She recalled: "We suffered many hardships and privations, but it was all done very cheerfully. Provisions were very scarce, and it was hard to feed

---

135 Bankston, p. 29.
136 CWA, p. 96.

our families and our servants, but we always had enough to give to a Confederate soldier. No one who 'wore the gray' was ever sent away hungry from my mother's door."[137]

Soldiers' aid societies sprang up everywhere. Their members engaged in sewing, knitting socks, rolling bandages, feeding the troops, and other vital tasks. Some of them cared for wounded Rebels months after the end of the war.

"Few people living now have any idea what heroism it required to be a Confederate mother," Ms. Cleaver said later. "They lived in a state of constant apprehension, fear of death or wounds to their soldier boys at the front and fear of starvation and rags for the little ones at home."[138]

One beautiful Southern belle, age seventeen, visited a Confederate hospital in Richmond, bringing flowers to the patients. She heard a wounded officer use the Lord's name in vain. Displeased, she approached him. "I think I heard you call upon the name of the Lord," she declared. "I am one of His daughters. Is there anything I can ask Him for you?"

The man immediately brightened at the sight of the beauty. "Yes," he said. "Please ask Him to make me His son-in-law."

---

137   CWA, pp. 38–39.
138   CWA, p. 49.

CHAPTER IX

STILL MORE VICTORIES

Rumors are a part of every war—and indeed every organization, civil or military. During the Seven Days Battles, several Confederates became ill, and it was rumored that some died because the Northerners poisoned all the local wells and springs. Captain von Borcke investigated and wrote later: "...although I do not love Yankees, I am quite sure they were entirely innocent of this. The sufferers had been made ill by the too abundant use of bad apple-brandy, which will kill anybody."[139]

Unfortunately, like misinformation, rumor has a way of seeping into print and then into history.

⟳

As General McClellan evacuated the Peninsula, a new Union army was created around Washington under the bombastic General John Pope, who decreed that all male noncombatants who refused to take the oath of alliance be expelled from Union-held territory; anyone who returned could be shot. Under Pope's orders, a mother who wrote a letter to her son in the Confederate army could be shot as a spy. Local communities were financially liable for any damage a guerrilla did in their area, and Pope's subordinates took hostages. Lee was furious and declared that Pope must be

---

[139] Borcke, p. 44.

"suppressed."[140] This was the nastiest thing Robert E. Lee ever said about an opponent.

General George McClellan agreed that Pope was a scoundrel. On August 8, 1862, he wrote: "I will strike square in the teeth of all the infamous orders of Mr. John Pope, and forbid all pillaging and stealing, and take the highest Christian ground for the conduct of the war. I will not permit this army to degenerate into a mob of thieves, nor will be returned these men of mine to their families as a set of wicked and demoralized robbers."[141]

During the next campaign, the Rebels took Manassas and destroyed a huge Union supply depot. Seeing men in ragged gray uniforms eating lobster and drinking champagne while the depot was burning was amusing. Jeb Stuart saw a young officer whom he deemed to be too elated and reprimanded him. The young man did not recognize the general and curtly informed the cavalryman that he was in charge here. He ordered the general to mind his own business. General Stuart burst out laughing and rode away.[142]

Private Bennett Wilson of the 4th Texas Infantry observed the opening stages of the Second Battle of Manassas from a hidden position on Stonewall Jackson's right flank. "All day we watched," Wilson recalled, "and could see the enemy charge Jackson's position, see them fall back and others try till they got so persistent and so numerous that two or three batteries rushed out from our position and unlimbered for action. It was not a minute till bursting shells were tearing down their lines and not many minutes until the Yankees were hurrying to the rear. Still they tried again with

---

140   Douglas S. Freeman, *R. E. Lee*, (New York, 1933–1935), Vol. II, pp. 263–264.
141   Pryor, p. 193.
142   King and Derby, p. 557.

the same result, a retreat. I don't mean that Jackson's men were lookers on while the artillery did such effective work, for they held a constant line of fire while the enemy were in range."

"Up to this time the Texans were in line, waiting, ready and eager for orders. 'Forward.' Then James Drake Courier of Gen. Hood's staff, at full speed dashed down the line, and as he passed in front of his old company (C) yelled out, 'Boys, they are coming.' Every man was on his feet and in three minutes the order was given to go forward. We moved quickly through a thin skirt of timber where we met the enemy, Sickle's brigade of Pennsylvania and the New York Zouaves were chosen to meet the Texans (the enemy had learned our position in the reconnaissance the night before) as soon as we were in sight and range, our defiant 'Texas Yell' rolled out over the field, at the same time our rifles sent their death messengers among the foe, and they were soon on the move to the rear. Our pursuit was so hurried that their artillery could not 'time' their fuse to make the shells effective, for they passed over and beyond our line before they exploded. He drove the retreating enemy beyond the branch, where we had orders to halt that our support might relieve us and push the fight. Capt. W. P. Townsend of Company C (he was second in command of the regiment, and as brave a man as ever drew a sword) took observations, and then said, 'Men, the support is not in sight, the battery in front will be more difficult to take after its support rallies and returns, so I propose that we take it now.' (The battery consisted of five Napoleons—the finest I ever saw.) He gave orders to 'charge.' We did charge, thought it was only ninety or a hundred yards, and only took four or five minutes. I never saw more havoc in a few moments in so small a space. Those men worked their guns until we literally annihilated them. I never saw a man leave his gun, not even a driver, though some did attempt to take the caissons to the rear, but every horse and every man was shot down. Our colors were placed on the guns, we pushed the infantry back under the hill, halted to take breath, and looking forward to the left, the whole earth for a mile seemed a solid mass of Yankees. We then noticed a column passing to our rear, evidently to cut us off…so we moved back to the branch…Soon after taking position on the branch, I heard a mighty cheer in our rear, our support coming double quick, every foot seeming to move at once. And just in front, our artillery came at full speed for 300 yards, unlimbered and fired a dozen shots, limbered, and dashed forward, then repeated until they reached their position. The reinforcements passed us, and from then until after dark the battle raged …"

After nightfall, Wood went to General Hood and asked for permission to return to the part of the battlefield they had captured, to find his brother, Egbert, who had fallen. Permission was granted and Bennett found Egbert, who had a hole in his right breast from a grapeshot. It was an inch in diameter and had to be cut out of his backbone. Remarkably, he recovered.[143]

Famous author John Esten Cooke, a major on Jeb Stuart's staff during the war, wrote in 1867: "I never knew a braver or lovelier spirit than Hardeman Stuart's." He was the oldest son of Colonel Oscar James E. Stuart of the Mississippi State Guard. He went to war with the 18th Mississippi, was an aide-de-camp to his cousin, Jeb Stuart, during the Seven Days Battles, after which General Stuart secured an appointment for him as captain in the signal corps. He was an able, intelligent, and lighthearted young man who was liked by everyone who knew him. Known for his bright blue eyes and ready smile, he had a winning personality.

During the Second Manassas Campaign, Captain Stuart was in charge of the signal detachment, but he and his men were surprised by Union cavalry squadron. Only young Stuart and two of his men escaped the surprise attack by hiding in the woods. They lost all their equipment and horses but reached the main Rebel lines on foot. The captain and each of his men were given a captured Yankee musket and joined a Mississippi infantry regiment,[144] with which they fought in the Second Battle of Bull Run (August 29–30, 1862). Here Major John Esten Cooke of Stuart's staff saw him for

---

[143] Yeary, II, pp. 816–817

[144] Heros von Borcke reported that Stuart joined his parent regiment, the 18th Mississippi of Barksdale's brigade, but it was not present at the Second Manassas. He almost certainly joined a regiment in General Featherstone's Mississippi brigade.

the last time. "He had always been the neatest person imaginable in his dress and appearance," Cooke recalled. Now, however, "He was coatless, unwashed, his boots covered with dust; and his clothes had the dingy look of a real soldier, who is so often compelled to lie upon the ground, and to sleep in his apparel. His hair was unbrushed, and hung disordered around his face, and the gallant young captain of the Signal Corps had the appearance of a sapper and miner." But he kept his good humor and bright smile. He looked upon his disaster as part of the fortunes of war and opted to remain in the Mississippi infantry.

The next day, August 30, Stuart charged a Union battery in the Battle of Groveton Heights, as Lee and Jackson pursued the routed Yankees. Captain Stuart was shot through the heart and killed. Major Cooke lamented: "he died in the bloom of youth, before sorrow touched him, fighting for his native land."[145] He was twenty-three years old.

Hardeman's brother, First Lieutenant Oscar E. Stuart, was killed at Marye's Heights during the Battle of Chancellorsville on May 3, 1863. Their younger brother, Edward "Eddie" Stuart, joined the Confederate army in 1862 at age fifteen. Also in the "Bloody 18th," he was captured at Sayler's Creek on April 6, 1865.

Heros von Borcke recalled the climax of the Second Battle of Manassas (August 30, 1862). Colonel Stephen Dill Lee commanded the artillery, "and the accuracy with which the shells exploded in the very faces of the foe testified to the admirable service of the guns. It was as if an annihilating bolt out of the thundercloud had let loose its fury upon those doomed men, who until now had been pressing onward like moving walls, and they now wavered and swayed to and fro as if the very earth reeled beneath their feet. Again and again roared the thunder of our guns, again and again deadly volleys sent their hail of bullets into the dense ranks of the enemy, until all at once this splendidly-organized body of troops broke in disorder

---

[145] Borcke, pp. 110–111; John Esten Cooke, *Wearing of the Gray* (New York: 1867), p.152–157.

and became a confused mass of fugitives…With the utmost energy and courage they brought their men forward to three several assaults, and three times they were hurled back, leaving hundreds of their number dead and wounded on the plain. At last physical strength and moral endurance alike gave way before the terrible effect of our fire, and the whole force fled in disorderly rout to the rear, a flight which could no longer be checked. At this moment the wild yell of the Confederates drowned the noise of the guns. As far as the eye could reach, the long lines of our army, with their red battle-flags, lit up by the evening sun to a colour like blood, were breaking over the plain in pursuit."[146]

Losses at the Second Manassas were severe. Company C, 13th South Carolina Infantry regiment was part of Gregg's brigade, Jackson's command. It fought in fifteen major battles during the war. It had only twenty-two men going into the Second Battle of Manassas. It held its position all day. By nightfall, only three of its men were still standing.[147]

During the battle, Pope had seventy-seven thousand men as opposed to Lee's fifty thousand. General Lee tore Pope's Army of Virginia limb from limb, routed it, and inflicted 14,462 casualties on the Federals. Lee lost 7,298 men.[148]

From December 31, 1862 to January 2, 1863, Bragg's Army of Tennessee fought an indecisive battle near Murfreesboro, Tennessee, against William S. Rosecrans's Army of the Cumberland.[149] The fighting was extremely heavy. Rosecrans fielded forty-four thousand effectives against thirty-five

---

[146] Borcke, pp. 106–107.

[147] Bernard, p .423.

[148] O.R., Vol. XII, Part 2, pp. 262, 560–562, 738.

[149] This was the Second Battle of Murfreesboro. General Forrest had won a victory there in July 1862. The North called the Second Murfreesboro the Battle of Stone River.

thousand for Bragg. The Northerners suffered 13,249 casualties against 10,266 for the South.[150]

Some units naturally suffered heavier losses than others. Company C of the 11th Tennessee entered the action with fifty-two men. Only a dozen of them came out.[151] When Lieutenant William H. Ledbetter led Company K of the 9th Texas Infantry into action on December 31, 1862, he had fifty-eight men. At nightfall, he had seven left, and six of those were wounded. Meanwhile, Ledbetter captured two Union doctors and several wounded Yankees. He helped move them into a cedar brake and out of the range of fire.

Ledbetter was wounded three times in this battle and was captured. He was doctored by one of the physicians he took prisoner earlier. The doctor—Ledbetter's former prisoner—made arrangements with Ledbetter's guard, and the lieutenant was allowed to escape.[152]

◦◦◦

Charles T. Landrum of the 22nd Alabama managed to frighten himself during the Battle of Murfreesboro.

He carried a very large canteen, which featured several layers of thick, red flannel between the tin and the leather cover. During the fighting, a Yankee shot a hole clean through the canteen, pulling some of the red flannel through with it. "I could feel the trickling of water down my leg and thought it was blood," he recalled, "and saw the red string waving around and it looked like blood and I was sure that half of my hip had been shot away."

Later in the battle, Landrum was struck by a shell fragment, which knocked him down. He was carried back to a field hospital with his lieutenant, who was seriously wounded by the same shell.[153]

---

[150] National Park Service website, August 24, 2010.

[151] Yeary, Vol. II, p. 726.

[152] Bernard, pp. 426–427

[153] Yeary, II, p. 420. Landrum was again wounded at Chickamauga. He was captured at Missionary Ridge in November 1863 and in a POW camp until March 1865, when he was exchanged.

During the Battle of Triune (part of the Murfreesboro Campaign), Private Joe McBride and Captain Connor of the 45th Mississippi Infantry Regiment were engaged in a fight against Union cavalry. They were pushed against a fence they could not climb because it was wet from rain, and the Yankees demanded their surrender. McBride turned on them, threw himself on a Union major, and in hand-to-hand combat, practically bit the man's finger off. McBride was finally subdued and made a prisoner, although some of the Northerners wanted to shoot him. They took him to U.S. Brigadier General Peter J. Osterhaus and informed him that this was the man who bit the major's finger off.[154] What, they wanted to know, did the general want to do with him? The general looked McBride over from head to foot and said to the guard: "I want you to accord him every respect due a prisoner, and I want every one of you to fight just like he did."[155]

The Rebels joked a great deal. One, an old preacher with white hair and a long, gray beard, rode into camp. "Boys, here is old Father Abraham," one of them cried.

"Young men, you are mistaken," the preacher retorted. "I am Saul, the son of Kish, searching for my father's asses, and I have found them!" Everyone enjoyed the joke.[156]

Back in Richmond, things returned to normal. Constance Cary remembered: "Except for the numbers of people swathed in black met in its thoroughfares, Richmond showed little trace of its battle summer. As yet the

---

[154] Osterhaus was a Prussian. He retired from the U.S. Regular army as a brigadier general in 1905 and died in Germany in 1917, at the age of ninety-four.

[155] Yeary, II, p. 465.

[156] Johnston, n.p.

pinch of the times did not greatly affect the home commissariat, although we refugees had to be satisfied with simple living in other people's rooms, since a whole house to ourselves could not be thought of. When asked into private houses we found tables laid, as of old, with shining silver and porcelain and snowy damask, although the bill of fare was unpretending. The custom of giving the best of everything to the hospitals went on till the end of the war. Society was reinforced by a number of agreeable and high-bred women from all parts of the South, many of whom had previously graced a wider social sphere in Europe and America. Its peculiar attraction lay in the total absence of pretence [sic]. People thus bound by a common tie of interest and poignant sympathy tolerated no assumption of superior fashion in any of their number. In such an atmosphere flourishes best the old-fashioned grace of neighborliness. To the very last, each refugee family shared what it had with the other; while Richmond folk threw open their broad, delightful homes to receive their friends, with or without gastronomic entertainment; lent furniture to those in need, and sent dainty little dishes to the sick. All rejoiced in each other's joys, grieved with each other's griefs. Hardships in such company were lightened of their weight. Sorrows so shared were easier to bear."[157]

In 1861, the Confederacy had fourteen warships. The Union had ninety-four, along with the capacity to produce many more.[158] The South had only one naval shipyard, at Norfolk, and it fell early in the war, on May 9, 1862.[159] Except for the postmaster general, Confederate Secretary of War Stephen Mallory was the only member of Jefferson Davis's cabinet to hold his post throughout the war. A former U.S. senator who spent years on the

---

[157] Harrison, pp. 94–95.

[158] Most of the information on the CSS *Arkansas* was taken from Walter Trisler, "The Rebel Terror from Yazoo," *The Southern Defender* (November 2019), p. 4, and Walter Trisler, "The CSS *Arkansas*," lecture delivered to Camp 1714, Sons of Confederate Veterans, West Monroe, Louisiana, July 13, 2021. Mr. Trisler writes for *Southern Defender*.

[159] E. B. Long, p. 69.

naval affairs committee, he was under no illusions. He knew that the South could never even come close to matching the United States in ship production, so he did not try. Instead, he focused on harbor defense and innovations, such as ironclads and torpedoes (mines).

The Northern river offensive of 1862 consisted of two arms: Flag Officer Charles H. Davis's western gunboat flotilla (also called the Mississippi River squadron) and Flag Officer David Farragut's gulf-blockading squadron, which was supported by the mortar flotilla under David D. Porter, Farragut's foster brother. Farragut entered the Mississippi from the Gulf of Mexico and advanced northward up the river.

Because rivers were the South's highways and lifelines, Mallory authorized the construction of four large, shallow-draft river ironclads on the Mississippi. Two, the *Louisiana* and the *Mississippi*, were sunk in the Battle of New Orleans, and one, the *Tennessee*, was scuttled when Memphis fell on June 6, 1862. The *Arkansas* they towed south and then northeast, sixty miles up the Yazoo River. Here, Lieutenant Isaac Newton Brown assumed command on May 28, the day after his forty-sixth birthday. He joined the U.S. Navy as a midshipman in 1834 when he was seventeen years old. A veteran of the Mexican War, he made several trips around the world before resigning his commission when his native state, Tennessee, seceded. When he found the *Arkansas*, it was an abandoned derelict. Her engines were scattered around in various pieces, her guns had no carriages, her hulk was abandoned, and her armor was at the bottom of the river. Brown and his men fished out the armor and towed the boat to Yazoo City, where they set up an improvised naval yard. A local railroad provided Brown with iron, and local plantation owners furnished him with 214 laborers and fourteen blacksmith forges. They worked around the clock, and the lieutenant and his men had the *Arkansas* semi-battleworthy in five weeks. She was a formidable vessel, armed with two eight-inch Columbiads, two nine-inch Dahlgrens, four six-inch rifled cannons and two thirty-two-pounder smoothbores—ten heavy guns in all. The gunboat was big: 165 feet long and thirteen feet wide. She drew fourteen feet of water and had a maximum speed of six knots (about seven miles per hour).

Lieutenant Brown did a remarkable job. He created a functional iron-clad in the backwoods of Mississippi, behind enemy lines, with two enemy fleets only fifty miles away. On July 14, in spite of the *Arkansas's* question-able engine, Brown steamed down the Yazoo to attack the Union fleets. He had to. It was summer and the Yazoo River was falling. If he didn't leave his dock now, he ran the risk of having his ironclad stuck on dry land.

Coincidentally, the Yankees learned of the existence of the Rebel boat about the same time. The ironclad *Carondelet*, followed by the wooden gunboat *Tyler* and the *Queen of the West* (now a ram) entered the river in search of the *Arkansas*.

The *Carondelet's* captain was Henry Walke, a friend of Brown from the old navy. He and Brown had been messmates during Commodore Matthew Perry's famous voyage to Japan. When Walke saw the *Arkansas*, he prudently turned his ironclad around and fled. The *Arkansas* caught up with it quickly and opened fire. One of the shots from her bow guns damaged the *Carondelet's* steering. It made for shallow water, where the *Arkansas* hit it with a devastating close-range broadside, shattering its armor and almost causing it to "turn turtle" (i.e., roll over). Steam covered the badly damaged *Carondelet*, which was listing and helpless. Thirty-five of its crew were killed, wounded, or scalded. The Confederates could eas-ily have taken her as a prize, but their commander had other items on his agenda. Brown left it behind and headed for the *Tyler* and the *Queen of the West*, both of which fled. The running battle continued for ten miles, with the *Arkansas* pounding the two wooden Yankee vessels. Blood flowed freely on the *Tyler's* deck.

The Northern fleet watched with consternation as their two vessels entered the Mississippi, followed by the *Arkansas*. Because they were run-ning short on fuel and were conserving their coal, none of the Union ves-sels had their steam up and were ready for action, but all their gun crews scrambled to their weapons.

Inside the *Arkansas's* engine room, the temperature reached 130 degrees Fahrenheit, and fresh men had to be rotated in every fifteen min-utes. The *Arkansas* ran the gauntlet of the Union fleet. Brown faced what he called "a forest of masts and smokestacks, sloops, rams, ironclads and other gunboats on the left side, and ordinary river steamboats and bomb-vessels on the right." There were so many ships and boats that any Yankee gunfire that missed the *Arkansas* was likely to hit a friendly vessel. Several of them took the chance and fired nonetheless.

The ironclad was hit by dozens of shells. Sixteen men were killed or wounded when a shell smashed the forward gunroom. Another killed or wounded every man at the gunboat's huge Columbiad gun. Eight men were killed and seven were wounded at the starboard broadside station, and the *Arkansas*'s smokestack was riddled by sixty-eight shells. She could barely make one knot, but she was helped by the river current. Even so, the Rebel ironclad continued firing and hit several Union vessels, seriously damaging the warships *Hartford, Iroquois,* and *Benton.* The Union ram *Lancaster* came close to sinking her, but a Rebel cannon shot from one hundred yards out struck her boilers and covered her ram in steam. Much of her crew jumped into the river to avoid being scalded and the *Lancaster* drifted downriver, out of control.

After steaming all the way through two Union battle fleets, the *Arkansas* faced U.S. Commodore Porter's mortar boats, which posed no problem for it. The *Arkansas* ran one boat aground and forced the crew to burn it, to keep it from being captured. The Rebel ironclad then limped to the east bank, where it was covered by the heavy guns on the Vicksburg bluffs. It was in bad shape. Its ramming beak was broken, all of its lifeboats were shot away, and it was a mechanical mess. It had lost ten killed outright and fifteen badly wounded, and about thirty others were less seriously wounded, including Brown, who had a deep gash on the top of his head. Total casualties amounted to more than half the crew, and only forty-two crewmen were left to run the ship. The Union fleets lost forty-two killed and sixty-nine wounded, mostly aboard the *Carondelet.*

The *Arkansas* was now unfit for combat, but fortunately for the South, the enemy could not see inside it. Because they did not know how badly damaged it was, all the Union warships now had to keep up their steam in case the *Arkansas* sallied forth again. They were already short of coal. Soon they were dangerously low. They nevertheless continued their fruitless bombardment of the city.

It was summer in Mississippi, the river was falling rapidly, and Admiral Farragut was afraid his oceangoing vessels would soon be grounded. His ships weighed anchor and headed south on July 27, while Flag Officer Davis steamed north with his gunboats. Thus ended the first Siege of Vicksburg, after a sixty-seven-day bombardment during which twenty-five hundred shells fell on the city. They did little major damage. Only seven Confederate soldiers were killed and twenty-five wounded, excluding the *Arkansas*'s casualties. Only two civilians had died. One mother was decapitated by a shell as she rushed her young son to safety, and a seven-year-old girl was killed by another shell.

CHAPTER X

SHARPSBURG

In September 1862, General Lee invaded Maryland. His men were marching up to twenty miles a day. Straggling reached record levels because the state had many paved roads, many of Lee's men were barefooted, and the roads were rough on their feet. Private George S. Bernard recalled that they came across a large Confederate camp. "What brigade, boys?" one of them asked.

"General Straggler's brigade," one of them responded.[160]

"The morale of the army was superb," Sergeant Major Johnston recalled, with "officers and men alike inspired with confidence in the ability of the army to beat its old antagonist anywhere he chose to meet us. We were moving into the enemy's country in fine spirit…no desertion, no destruction of private property, no outrages committed upon non-combatants, the orders of the commanding general on this subject being strictly observed. Among the men were expressions of disapproval of the invasion of the North. We had uniformly insisted upon defensive warfare on our own soil; in other words, we steadfastly contended against the claim of the enemy to invade our own land, and logically we should

---

160   Bernard, p. 12.

be bound by the same reasoning. However, in the last analysis every man in the Army of Northern Virginia was loyal to his commander-in-chief, wherever he should lead. Here, indeed, was a spectacle: An army of more than sixty thousand freemen, every man a soldier in the true sense of the word, brave, resolute, fearless, the heroes and victors of many fields, marching unobstructed and thus far unopposed through an enemy's country, whose people had scarcely known that war was in progress; living in quiet and plenty."[161]

The level of Confederate sympathy in Maryland varied from town to town. "In Frederick our hearts were made glad by unmistakable signs of friendship and sympathy," one soldier recalled. "A bevy of pretty girls, singing 'Maryland, My Maryland,' on seeing our battle flag inscribed 'Seven Pines,' proposed 'three cheers for the battle flag of Seven Pines,' which were heartily and lustily given by us. In Middletown we met no smiles, but a decided Union sentiment was in evidence. In Hagerstown we observed indications and heard some expressions of Southern sentiment, but none that satisfied us that they were ready and willing to shed their blood for the Southern cause."[162]

Chalmers Glenn grew up in Rockingham County, North Carolina. He was raised with an African American servant named Mat. They shared all the boyish frolics and pranks of childhood and were as close as two boys could be.

Glenn joined the Confederate army and rose to the rank of captain. Mat followed him off to war. Near Boonsboro, Maryland, on the morning of September 14, 1862, Glenn turned to his friend and said: "Mat, I shall

---

[161] Johnston, n.p. Johnston's estimate of Lee's strength is high.
[162] Johnston, n.p.

be killed in this battle. See me buried, then go home and be to your mistress and my children all that you have ever been to me."

Mat did not fight in the battle but found his master late in the fighting. The prediction had come true, and Captain Glenn was already dead. With two of Glenn's comrades, Mat dug a grave with bayonets and sadly returned home with Glenn's letters and personal possessions. He visibly declined and died of a broken heart February 4, 1863.[163]

On Sunday, September 14, 1862, the Army of the Potomac attacked South Mountain positions in overwhelming force. Kemper's brigade was hurried to the Turner's Gap sector. It was a hot day and the road was hard and dusty, forcing many to drop out of the march. The brigade, Private Johnston recalled, "was now in a body of open timber, among stones— large boulders, with some fallen timber along the line, behind which, lying down, the men took shelter as best they could; the enemy occupying a skirt of woods with a strip of open land between their position and ours. For two or more hours the battle raged, or until darkness fell, the enemy making repeated but unsuccessful efforts to dislodge our men. The firing having ceased, there was heard in our front the tramp of the enemy's feet, evidently preparing to renew the assault. In a few minutes, a few yards to the right, in which lay a portion of the brigade in the edge of a field, where at the beginning of the battle was standing corn (now cut to the ground) came the sound of a voice, 'There they are, men! Fire on them!' Suddenly came a sheet of flame with a deafening crash from the guns of each of the combatants, plainly disclosing them to be within a few feet of each other. The flame from the respective muskets seemed to intermingle. The well-directed fire of the Confederates caused confusion in the enemy's ranks and compelled them to retire. Among the casualties on our side from this encounter was Adjutant John W. Daniel of the 11th Virginia, who received a severe wound in the hand. This same Daniel served with

---

[163] King and Derby, p. 350.

distinction in the United States Senate, dying a year or so ago.[164] Such was the character of many a noble man engaged in this horrid game of death."[165]

Before the war, Reverend George G. Smith was the pastor of "a charming little church in a beautiful valley in upper Georgia." He was recently married when the war broke out and recalled that he should have been content to stay at home, but he had Revolutionary War blood in his veins. When his parishioners went to the front, so did he. He joined Phillips's Legion, a fifteen-company Georgia regiment under the command of William Phillips, as a chaplain.[166]

"Somehow I got the name of the 'fighting chaplain,'" Smith recalled, "and candidly I did not like it...I did not go to the army to fight; I did not fight after I got there...I went to the army as a chaplain, and as a chaplain I did my work..."

On September 14, 1862, he got caught up in the Battle of South Mountain. The Union Army of the Potomac attacked Lee's screen, and the regiment was surrounded on the east, south, and west.

"Parson, we've been whipped," Gus Tomlinson told him through tears. "The regiment is retreating."

---

[164] John W. Daniel (1842–1910) was born in Lynchburg, Virginia. He enlisted in the cavalry but was commissioned second lieutenant in the 27th Virginia in May 1861. He was wounded in the First Battle of Manassas. He was transferred to the 11th Virginia Infantry Regiment as a first lieutenant and became its adjutant. He rose to the rank of major on the staff of Jubal Early. His leg was shattered by a minie ball during the Battle of the Wilderness. Unable to walk without a crutch, Daniels resigned his commission. He returned to Lynchburg and served in the Virginia House of Delegates (1869–72), the Virginia State Senate (1876–82), the U.S. House of Representatives (1885–87), and the U.S. Senate (1887 until his death). He defeated the incumbent U.S. senator and former Confederate general Wilhelm Mahone in the election of 1887.

[165] Johnston, n.p.

[166] William Phillips resigned his commission in February 1862 due to illness (recurrent typhoid), which cost him the sight in one of his eyes. The legion was led in Maryland by Major Richard T. Cook. It was part of Drayton's brigade in that campaign.

"And none too soon either," the chaplain replied, "for we are sur-rounded on all sides but one."

"Just then I felt a strange dizziness and fell, my arm dropping lifeless by my side. I knew that I was hit … But where was I hit? Was my arm torn off by a shell? No, here that is. Was I shot through the breast? Or—yes, here it was—blood was gurgling from my throat.

"The dear boys rushed to me, laid me on a blanket and bore me off the field," he remembered. The ball had struck his neck, done downward, and came out near his spine, paralyzing his arm. The reverend thought he was mortally wounded and so did the men. "It's all up with you," one of them said. "It's a good thing in such an hour to have faith in Christ and love toward all men," he remarked later. "… there was not one of the soldiers in the Federal ranks for whom I had any feeling other than love."

Reverend Smith was carried to the rear and survived the war.[167]

On September 14, 1862, Sergeant George S. Bernard was part of the 12th Virginia Infantry Regiment of Mahone's brigade, which was defend-ing Crampton's Gap, Maryland, during the Battle of South Mountain. The 12th and 6th Virginia took positions behind a rail fence at the foot of the mountain. The fighting was heavy. "I experienced a sudden pain in my right leg, just above the knee, as if some heavy substance had struck it with great force," Bernard recalled. "At first it did not occur to me that it was a bullet…" When he looked down, he discovered "an ugly orifice from which the blood was streaming." He bound the wound with his hand-kerchief and asked his friend, Private Branscomb, to strap up his leg with a leather strap, which he did. "I then lay as flat as was possible and won-dered how long the fight would last, thinking I would give the wealth of the Indies, if I had it, to be on the other side of the mountain, the constant whizzing of the bullets through and against the fence-rails, and against the timber and rocks on the side of the mountain reminding me unpleasantly

---

167 King and Derby, pp. 148–149.

that the enemy had not yet ceased to fire. Just at this point I heard a noise to my left where Branscomb was lying, and looking around to discover the cause, to my horror, saw that the fence and dry leaves were on fire..."[168]

Branscomb and the man to his left tried to extinguish it until Branscomb was severely wounded. Then the Yankees charged in overwhelming strength. The orders came quickly. "Fix bayonets!" and then "Fall back, men! Fall back!" The Rebels grabbed their knapsacks, canteens, and other supplies and retreated, but they were forced to leave Bernard behind. Someone yelled, "See yonder, boys!" Someone yelled, "Cavalry!" Bernard thought he would be either bayoneted by the enemy's infantry or trampled by his horses. Meanwhile, he faced a new danger. His own retreating comrades were firing down the side of the mountain and the Confederate artillery opened fire with canister. "If the enemy did not kill me, I thought our own men would," he recalled. He was grazed in the hip by a Southern bullet, but it was only a scratch. Bernard and another wounded Rebel, Lieutenant Mason, where taken prisoner. They proceeded to a Union field hospital with the assistance of two Union soldiers, whom Bernard called "kind and considerable." He was treated well by a Yankee chaplain and by the medical personnel.

Three days later, Bernard was transferred to Frederick, Maryland, where he was placed in the home of a Southern sympathizer. He was nursed back to health and was treated well as a prisoner of war, except by a captain, who thoroughly cursed him out for being a G****** Rebel. A Union soldier pulled Bernard aside and said: "Don't think anything of that man's talk. It was a mean thing to treat a prisoner so. We old soldiers who have seen service in the field don't approve to it. He is nothing but a recruit, a newcomer, and doesn't know how a true soldier should treat a prisoner."[169]

Shortly after, a Union officer learned that some of the Rebel prisoners were from Georgia. He asked them if they knew Colonel Pierce M. B. Young and said that they attended West Point together. The sergeant asked the bluecoat his name. It was George Armstrong Custer. They had

---

[168] Bernard, pp. 27–28.
[169] Bernard, pp. 34–35.

two other mutual friends. One was Major Richard K. Meade, C.S.A., who had died of typhoid fever in July. Bernard also knew Lieutenant Colonel John W. "Gimlet" Lea, who was Custer's best friend at West Point. Lea was wounded and captured in the Battle of Williamsburg, and it was erroneously reported that he died. Lea had fallen in love with his nurse and married her in a Union field hospital in Williamsburg. Captain Custer served as his best man. Custer was delighted that Lea was still alive.

Lea was exchanged in November 1862. He later led the 5th North Carolina Infantry and was wounded in the head at Chancellorsville. Promoted to colonel in 1864, he was again wounded in the Third Battle of Winchester. He was a brigade commander at the end of the war.[170]

Meanwhile, Bernard and his colleagues were sent to Baltimore, which was still very much a Southern town. They were easily identified as Confederate soldiers by their tanned faces and because Bernard was on crutches. They were free to roam the streets, where gentleman furnished them with the best and most fashionable clothes. The ladies met them with bows and smiles and were eager to engage them in conversation. Stores gave them whatever they wanted but refused to accept payment. Their meals were also free.

Sergeant Bernard was soon transferred to Fort Monroe, Virginia, and was exchanged for Federal POWs. Placed on a train, the prisoners reached Southern lines and were then slapped in quarantine for six or seven days—the government feared smallpox.

On September 16, 1862, the Confederate army concentrated at Sharpsburg, Maryland, which was filled with wagon trains. General Stuart set up his headquarters in a private home in the beautiful and formerly peaceful little village. About 11 a.m., the Union army began shelling the town, and by noon, the bombardment was "really appalling," according to Heros von Borcke, whom Stuart left in charge of the HQ. It knocked down

---

[170] Allardice, *Colonels*, p. 235; Bernard, pp. 35–37. Lea was called "Gimlet" because he was tall and lean. He became an Episcopal minister after the war.

the steeple of the principal church. Borcke was sitting on the sofa when a shell hit the house, exploded, covered the major with debris, and scattered the furniture in every direction. Almost simultaneously, another shell went directly through the house, exploded in the courtyard, killed the horse of one of the couriers, and threw the other animals into a panic. In the streets, dead and wounded soldiers lay everywhere. Borcke evacuated the HQ and expected a general battle to begin at any moment, but the Yankees did not attack until the following morning.[171]

Possibly the fiercest battle of the war was Sharpsburg (called "Antietam" in the North). It was the bloodiest single day in the war and in U.S. military history. Judge David Johnston, then a Confederate private, wrote that it "was fought on the part of the Confederates by a worn out, broken down, naked, barefooted, lame and starved soldiery, against a far superior force of brave, well rested, well clothed and well fed veterans. It was an all day, stand up, toe-to-toe and face-to-face fight, just as close as brave American soldiers could make it, and in none other did Southern individuality and self reliance—characteristics of the Confederate soldier—shine more brilliantly or perform a more important part. It was on this field that strategy and military science won the day for the Confederates. It was mind over matter. General Lee, the greatest military man of the age, was on the field, wielding the blade that was so admirably tempered, which brought blood and destruction at every stroke."

The battle was fought clockwise, from north to south. The Northern generals fought the battle piecemeal, launching one attack, then another, and still later another but all at different times. Lee was thus able to check one Union assault, shift his forces, and deal with another. Had the Yankees charged at once (i.e., launched all their attacks simultaneously), the Army of Northern Virginia would have been destroyed. It was a close-run thing as it was. At one point, James Longstreet, the commander of Lee's I Corps,

---

[171] Borcke, pp. 157–158.

held the horses of his staff, while they fired a cannon at the advancing foe. When a lieutenant general is a horse holder for his officers who are manning a single gun, things are bad all over.

"The failure of the Union soldiers to win this battle and utterly crush the Confederates," Johnston writes, "was no fault of theirs; they had the numbers and equipment, were courageous and brave. The truth is, their leader was timid, overcautious, and outgeneraled, fought his battle in detail, and was defeated in detail. General Burnside's, the largest single attacking corps [on the Confederate right], was beaten before he had his columns fairly deployed, and this because the Confederates outmaneuvered him on the field, had the flanks of his assaulting columns turned before he knew there was any Confederate force on the ground to turn them. Upon this occurring, he lost control of the battle…"

Judge Johnston later did a statistical study on the battle, especially on the right flank. He wrote: "The force engaged in this battle on the Confederate right, on the Union side, was that of General Burnside's 9th army corps [IX Corps], consisting of twenty-nine regiments of infantry, six batteries of artillery, and two companies of cavalry, making, according to the most reliable information obtainable, an aggregate of 13,083. His losses were: killed, 436; wounded, 1,796; missing, 115; total, 2,347.

On the Confederate side, the battle was fought by the brigades of Jenkins, Garnett, Toombs, Kemper, and Drayton (two regiments, 51st Georgia and 15th South Carolina); Gregg's, Archer's and Branch's (less the 18th North Carolina, on detached duty), of Hill's division. The 24th and the 7th Virginia, except their skirmishers, did not pull a trigger, but were under the fire of the artillery and partly that of infantry. Nor did the 18th North Carolina take part in the battle.

"From the best information I have been able to obtain, from the official reports and otherwise, I fix the number of Confederates in this battle against General Burnside's 13,083 men as follows:

Jenkins' brigade	500
Garnett's brigade	250
Drayton's brigade (51st Ga. & 15th S.C. Regmts.)	200

Kemper's brigade	300
Toombs' brigade (including Maj. Little's bat., 140)	600
Total Jones' division	1,850
A. P. Hill's three brigades, less 18th North Carolina, detached	1,900
Total, both divisions	3,750

He lists the casualties as follows:

Col. Walker, commanding brigade of Jenkins, reports	210
Taking 4 regiments of Garnett's and averaging the 5th	80
Drayton's two regiments, estimated	100
Kemper's regiments, estimated	160
Toombs, stated	346
Total	896

The disparity in numbers on this part of the field was thus 3.75 to 1.

"A careful examination of all the sources of information available to me," Johnston writes, "including official reports, and my own personal knowledge and observation on the march and on the field, inclines me strongly to the opinion and belief that the Confederate troops on the field of Sharpsburg on the firing line and actually engaged on the 17th of September numbered:

Jackson's division	1600
Ewell's division	3400
D. H. Hill's division	3000
D. R. Jones' division	1850
A. P. Hill's division	1900
Hood's division	2000
McLaws' division	2893
R. H. Anderson's division	3500
J. G. Walker's division	3200
Geo. T. Anderson's brigade	300
N. G. Evans' division	1500

Lee's cavalry brigade	1500
Artillerists	1800
Total	28,443"

His summary of the casualties are:

The Confederate casualties in the Maryland campaign as given in the war records	13,609
The Federal casualties, including the garrison at Harpers Ferry	27,767
Deducting the Harpers Ferry garrison, we have the Federal losses of the campaign	15,203
Deducting Federal losses at Boonsboro Gap of 1,813, Crampton's Gap 533, we have approximately as the Federal loss in battle of Sharpsburg	12,856
Deducting the estimated Confederate loss at Boonsboro Gap, Crampton's Gap and Harpers Ferry, 3,948, from the campaign loss, we have approximately as the Confederate loss at Sharpsburg	9,661

"The actual number of Union soldiers on the firing line in the battle of Sharpsburg could not have exceeded 68,000 men, but Porter's corps, some 19,000, was close up [and]…only a march away." For some reason, however, McClellan did not use Porter.

The next day, September 18, was generally quiet. That night, the Rebels retreated across the Potomac. They had crossed it earlier that month singing "Maryland, My Maryland." Now they sang "Carry Me Back to Old Virginia." Some of them sang: "Maryland, His Maryland."

On September 17, according to his own estimate, Lee had no more than thirty thousand men when the battle began, although he was joined that morning by McLaws's division of seven thousand men and a few smaller detachments. McClellan had at least ninety thousand men. Jackson commanded the left flank, Lee the center, and Longstreet the right.[172]

Heros von Borcke was conversing with Colonel Thornton, the commander of the 3rd Virginia Cavalry, when a piece of shell ripped off his (Thornton's) left arm. He died in agony a few hours later. The town of Sharpsburg caught on fire because of Union shells and "the sky was reddened by the glare of the conflagration." At the end of the day, however, von Borcke was able to report "we remained masters of the entire field of battle [which was] covered with the enemy's dead and wounded." It was astonishing, he recalled, 'to see men without shoes, whose lacerated feet often stained their path with blood, limping to the front to conquer or fall with the comrades"[173]

"The route of the extraordinary marches of our troops presented, for long and weary miles, the touching pictures of the trials of war," E. A. Pollard, the editor of the Richmond *Examiner*, wrote later. "Broken down soldiers (not all 'stragglers') lined the road. At night time they might be found asleep in every conceivable attitude of discomfort—on fence rails and in fence corners—some half bent, others almost erect, in ditches and on steep hill-sides, some without blanket or overcoat. Daybreak found them drenched with dew, but strong in purpose; with half rations of bread and meat, ragged and barefooted, they go cheerfully forward..."[174]

Dozens of men, however, fell out or could not keep up. When Mahone's brigade reached Sharpsburg, according to Joseph E. Spotswood,

---

172 Borcke, p. 158.
173 Borcke, p. 158–161.
174 Bernard, pp. 22–23 and 43, citing Edward Pollard, *The Southern History of the War.*

his company had only five men.[175] The 12th Virginia Infantry Regiment had twenty-three men, and there were only seventy in the entire brigade.[176]

Company G, 9th Virginia Infantry Regiment, marched from Harpers Ferry to Sharpsburg on September 16, 1862. It had six men and was commanded by a sergeant. It halted at midnight but only for an hour. They were supposed to continue their march at 1 a.m. on September 17 but were so exhausted, they could not be aroused. Two-thirds of the brigade (Armistead's) was in the same condition and could not be awakened.[177] They got an extra two hours' sleep.

After the Battle of Sharpsburg, wounded men who recovered and stragglers returned to duty. By November, the company had fifty-seven men, but seventeen were without shoes.

At Culpeper, they were given moccasins made from green hides of cattle killed for food, sewed up with thongs or strips cut from the hide, with the hair on the inside. Once the skin dried, the men could not get out of them unless they cut them.[178]

By nightfall on September 17, 1862, most of the men of the Army of Northern Virginia were living on ears of Indian corn (which they roasted on the side of the road) and green apples for days. After the battle, there were a great many pigs and chickens running around the streets of Sharpsburg. "Poor little things," one of the troops said, "they have nowhere to go, and we ought to take care of them." So they shot them and ate them.

---

[175] Spotswood was a member of Company E, 12th Virginia Infantry, which was previously known as the Petersburg Riflemen.

[176] General Mahone was wounded and Colonel William A. Parham (c.1830–1866) led the brigade at Sharpsburg. Here he was severely wounded and was eventually forced to leave the army. Allardice, *Colonels*, p. 298.

[177] Lewis, pp. 436–438.

[178] Lewis, p. 520–523.

Heros von Borcke had not eaten in forty-eight hours. He nevertheless 'felt obligated to rebuke a Texan, who, only a few steps from me, had just rolled over, by a capital shot, a porker galloping across the street at sixty yards distance, for his wanton disregard of the rights of property." The Texan gave him an incredulous look. "Major, did you have anything to eat yesterday?"

"No," von Borcke replied.

"Then you know what it is to be hungry. I haven't tasted a morsel for several days."

This shut the major up. He mounted his horse without a word and returned to the front.[179]

In September 1862, after the Battle of Sharpsburg, General Lee ordered the cavalry, along with a couple of infantry regiments, to cross the Potomac and demonstrate against the Army of the Potomac. A mile from Williamsport, Maryland, the infantry was attacked by a Union cavalry squadron. "I had here a very striking example of how little effect is often produced by volley-firing," Major von Borcke recalled. At close range, two Rebel infantry companies fired a volley into "the dense ranks of the horsemen," who fled "precipitately." Borcke galloped forward, expecting to find at least half the attackers on the ground. To his surprise and amazement, not a man or horse had been brought down. The volley had passed over their heads.[180]

---

[179] Borcke, pp. 162–163.
[180] Borcke, pp. 167–168.

CHAPTER XI

WINTER 1862-1863

O n November 1, 1862, a large force of Union infantry and cavalry advanced from Leesburg toward Union, Virginia. It was met by a much smaller force of Rebel cavalry under Jeb Stuart and Fitz Lee. The Yankees, however, did not press their advance until the next day.

Major von Borcke recalled it was a peaceful Sunday morning, "a rich, soft day, with all the splendor of the autumnal sunshine, and all the quietude of the Christian Sabbath, till, instead of the sweet church-bells from the neighbouring village calling us to the house of God, we caught the summons to the field in the rattle of musketry and the roar of cannon…"

"The enemy commenced his attack on us at an early hour with great vigour. A double line of tirailleurs [skirmishers] advanced in excellent order; four batteries opened upon our guns from different points; the air shook with the continuous roar of cannonade; on every side the bullets buzzed like infuriated insects; on the whole, the outward signs were rather those of a great battle than of a mere cavalry combat. This day the enemy's artillery was admirably well served, and its effect was very dreadful. Just as I rode up to a battery, which was answering as rapidly as possible the Yankee fire, a hostile shell blew up one of our caissons, killing and wounding several of our men, and stunning me completely for several minutes. For some time the fire was terrific at this spot. In less than half an hour one battery alone lost fifteen men killed and wounded, and I was obliged to force the frightened ambulance drivers to the assistance of their suffering and dying comrades, by putting my revolver to their heads and threatening to shoot them if they did not go."[181]

The Confederate cavalry continued to resist until the Yankees brought up their infantry; then General Stuart prudently retreated in the direction of Upperville, covered by Major Pelham's artillery. Unfortunately, young Captain Bullock of the 5th Virginia Cavalry had his horse shot out from under him. Before he could free his legs, the Yankee infantry was on top of him. Rather than surrender, Bullock pulled his revolver, killed two of his assailants, and made a run for friendly lines.

Jeb Stuart and von Borcke were only fifty paces from Bullock. They rushed to the rescue, carrying one of their spare horses with them. The young captain, however, was so exhausted by his ordeal that he could not mount his steed. They had to stop and lift him onto the back of the horse. All three, however, made good their escape.[182]

In 1862, Private Robert E. Lee Jr., of the Rockingham Artillery, appeared barefoot at his father's headquarters, carrying the remnants of a pair of shoes. He said to his father: "I only wanted to ask, sir, if I might draw a new pair, as I can't march in these."

"Have the men of your company received permission to draw shoes yet?" General Lee asked.

"No, sir. I believe not yet."

"Then go back to your battery, my boy, and wait until they have," his father replied.[183]

On December 11, 1862, the Battle of Fredericksburg began. Some Rebels met an old African American man, who was loaded down with haversacks,

---

[181] Borcke, pp. 233–234.
[182] Borcke, pp. 235–238.
[183] Harrison, pp. 90–91.

blankets, general baggage, canteens, and more He was puffing and nearly out of breath, and was sweating profusely, despite the cold.

"Hello, Uncle! Where are you going?" a soldier asked him.

"To de rear, Sah!" was the answer.

"To what command do you belong?"

"Barksdale's brigade, Sah."

"Is it running, too?" the Rebel asked.

"No boss, it never runs, but I always do."[184]

"In December, 1862, Fredericksburg was fought," Constance Cary remembered. "In that notable victory to Confederate arms our family met with an irreparable loss. My uncle's son, Randolph Fairfax, aged eighteen, a private in the ranks, fell beside his gun and was buried by his comrades after dark upon the spot. This youth, handsome and gifted, serious and purposeful beyond his years, the flower of his school and college, in all things worthy the traditions of his warlike ancestry, was killed by a piece of shell entering the brain, as he stood by his gun at sunset under a hot fire from the enemy's batteries. A day or two later his body, still wrapped in his soldier's blanket, was disinterred and brought through freezing weather to Richmond, where he was placed, uncoffined, on a bier before the altar in St. James's Church. An ever fresh memory is that of the sweet and noble face so unchanged, after two days' burial. Save for the cruel mark on the temple made by the piece of shell, and the golden curls matted with the clay of his rude sepulchre, he might have been asleep. He wore still the coarse flannel shirt, stained with battle smoke, in which he fell, and across him was thrown the blanket that had been his winding-sheet. When it was proposed to my uncle that the body be dressed again, he answered:

'No. Let my son sleep his long sleep as he fell at the post of duty.' And thus, his coffin draped with the flag he had died for, Randolph Fairfax was

---

[184] Johnston, n.p.

borne to his rest in Hollywood [Cemetery]. From camp at Fredericksburg, on December 28th, General Lee wrote to my uncle the words that follow:

> *'I have grieved most deeply at the death of your noble son. I have watched his conduct from the commencement of the war and have pointed with pride to the patriotism, self-denial and manliness of character he has exhibited. I had hoped that an opportunity would have occurred for the promotion he deserved; not that it would have elevated him, but have shown that his devotion to duty was appreciated by his country. Such an opportunity would undoubtedly have occurred; but he has been translated to a better world, for which his purity and piety have eminently fitted him. You do not require to be told how great his gain. It is the living for whom I sorrow. I beg you will offer to Mrs. Fairfax and your daughters, my heartfelt sympathy, for I know the depth of their grief. That God may give you and them strength to bear this great affliction, is the earnest prayer of your early friend.*[185]
>
> R. E. LEE"'

Heros von Borcke wrote of the Battle of Fredericksburg: "I could not rid myself of a feeling of depression and anxiety as I saw this innumerable host steadily moving upon our lines, which were hidden by the woods, where our artillery maintained as yet a perfect silence, General Lee having given orders that our guns should not open fire until the Yankees had come within easy canister range. Upon my mentioning this feeling to Jackson, the old chief answered me in his characteristic way: 'Major, my men have sometime failed *to take* a position, but *to defend* one, never! I am glad the Yankees are coming.'"[186]

Against Jackson's lines, the Federals launched attack after attack, with "fearful slaughter. Again and again, with the most obstinate courage and energy, did the Federals renew the attack, bringing more and more fresh

---

[185] Harrison, pp. 95–97.
[186] Borcke, p. 301.

troops into action; but their dense lines so much shattered by the appalling fire of our artillery that, upon coming within range of our infantry and being there received with a withering hail of bullets, they broke and fled time after time, leaving the ground strewn with hundreds of their dead and wounded."[187]

They also struck again and again at Marye's Heights, in Longstreet's zone of operations, along which ran a sunken road, fenced in with a stone wall on either side—the most formidable of all the Rebel defensive works. "...the folly of the Federal commander in sending his men here to certain death and destruction is utterly incomprehensible," von Borcke remembered. Rebel artillery fire—mainly from Colonel James B. Walton's Washington Artillery of New Orleans, Louisiana, and Lieutenant Colonel E. Porter Alexander's artillery battalion, "swept them away by the hundreds."[188]

After the Federals fled, General Robert Ransom, who commanded a division on Marye's Heights, took some of Jeb Stuart's staff officers on a tour of the battlefield. "The sight was indeed a fearful one," Major von Borcke recalled, "and the dead bodies lay thicker than I had ever seen before on any field of battle...The dead [in front of Marye's Heights] were here piled up in heaps six or eight deep. General Ransom told us that our men were ordered not to commence firing until the enemy had approached within a distance of eighty yards." At that point, the Rebels opened fire, and the Federals were "completely mowed down by our volleys...it became incomprehensible to me how even that small few of the most dashing assailants, who had run up within fifteen paces of our lines, could have survived this terrific fire long enough to do so."[189]

---

[187] Borcke, p. 305.

[188] Borcke, pp. 305–306. Walton was a descendant of George Walton, a governor of Georgia, U.S. senator, and signer of the Declaration of Independence. Colonel Walton survived the war.

[189] Borkce, p. 320.

There were not many cowards in the Confederate army, but like any army, it did have a few. Sergeant Major Johnston recalled: "In Company D was one, Dan East, who was never in a battle, and never intended to be; yet Dan knew more about it than anyone who had gone through it; always turning up after the battle with a full haversack, good blanket, overcoat and shoes. As usual, Dan walked into the camp after the battle of Fredericksburg, when the Colonel [Waller T. Patton] determined to punish him; he caused a placard with the word 'Coward' in large letters to be fastened across his back, and with rail on his shoulder he was marched to and fro in front of the regiment; but this had little effect on Dan, and the first opportunity he helped himself to a fellow soldier's clothing and other goods, which were found in his quarters."

Confederate enlisted men often did not bother their officers with cowards; instead, they handled these matters themselves. The men of the company decided to rid the service of Dan by whipping him out of it, which they did.[190]

⟋⟍

Stuart's staff had no meat to eat for days except tough (and almost inedible) beef and rancid bacon. They went hunting for small birds, using bullets cut into small pieces as a substitute for birdshot. They killed four or five blackbirds, robins, and sparrows, but a handful of small birds was not nearly enough for twelve fully grown men.

On the Lower Rappahannock (aka Tappahannock) River they captured a wagon load of oysters. They fed the staff for days, but without salt, pepper, butter, or any other condiment, they soon hated the very sight of an oyster.[191]

---

[190] Johnston, n.p. Waller Tazewell Patton was mortally wounded when his jaw was ripped off by artillery shrapnel during Pickett's charge. He was the great-uncle of George S. Patton, the famous World War II general, whose grandfather (who was a Confederate colonel) was killed in the Third Battle of Winchester in 1864. Waller T. Patton died on July 21, 1863.

[191] Borcke, pp. 338–339.

After Fredericksburg, the Army of Northern Virginia went into winter quarters. "The stroke of many axes rang through the surrounding forests and oak copses, and pine thickets dissolved," Borcke recalled, "…to give place to complete little towns of huts and log-houses, provided with comfortable fireplaces, from whose gigantic chimneys curled upwards gracefully and cheerily into the crisp winter air many a column of pale-blue smoke."[192]

The winter weather became worse and worse. There was rain, snow, ice storms, and severe frosts. The men were okay, but the horses and mules were not. They suffered from lack of fodder, exposure, vermin, and disease. They also lacked protection from the wind and cold. About one-fourth of them died. The mules withstood the suffering better than the horses.[193]

"Some of the most severe hardships we had to undergo was in standing guard, where we were exposed to the wind, sleet and snow, to say nothing of the danger from the rifles of the foe lurking behind rocks and bushes, ready to pick us off without warning," Sergeant J. W. Wynn of the 11th Tennessee Infantry recalled. He noted that camping in the snow and surviving on "one biscuit a day" was not much fun.[194]

A. Schappaul was born in Germany but immigrated to New York in 1858. Seven weeks later, he moved to Charleston, South Carolina. He enlisted in a South Carolina company, which contained 110 men. It was lightly engaged on the Confederate right flank at the First Manassas and suffered no casualties.

---

192 Borcke, P. 325.
193 Borcke, p. 326.
194 Yeary, II, p. 827

"It is a great mistake to think that our losses were all in battle," he recalled. "The fact is we lost more men outside the real battles than we did in them." He recalled one day during the winter of 1861–1862 when only nine men were available for duty. The rest had measles, which killed twenty-five of them. The following winter (1862–1863), mumps, "yellow janders" [jaundice] and typhoid fever struck, killing more Carolinians than did the Yankees.[195]

The Georgians had a similar experience. S. M. Wilkins of the 9th Georgia served at Yorktown in April 1862, where George Washington's old breastworks were clearly visible in places. "We suffered more there from measles than from the Yankees," he recalled. [196]

During the winter of 1862–1863, religious revivals swept the entire Confederate army. Sergeant Major David E. Johnston remembered: "When the call to arms was made in 1861, the sentiment of our people was a solemn appeal to God for the rectitude of our intentions and purposes, an appeal to the God of battles for His abiding presence and blessing upon our undertaking. Nearly every step taken was witnessed by religious services. Our whole Southland was permeated with the spirit and teachings of the Bible. The brave people of our land believed in God—indeed, the foundations of their state government were based upon their faith in the Author of their lives and liberty. This was no mere phantom. Most of our great leaders were Christian men, who feared and worshipped God.

"At the beginning of the war we had many wild, profane men who had joined the army, but from this it must not be inferred that our camps were scenes of vulgarity, and profanity. With but few exceptions, after the first year or so of the war, there was never an army freer from vice, immorality and anger. That which in the beginning would have been offensive and insulting, and probably brought the parties to blows, was now passed by. The men had come to understand each other's temperaments. They had lived, associated, marched, fought, slept and eaten together too long, had

---

195   Yeary, p. 666.
196   Yeary, II, p. 795.

suffered in common too many hardships, enduring the same privations, not to know each other's Christian convictions...

"Near the close of 1862, and throughout the greater part of the year of 1863, a religious spirit seemed to possess the army; at least this was true of our command. Christians had great reason to thank God and take courage when they thought on the remarkable progress the gospel was making in the camp. Thousands of young men embraced religion. While churches at home were languishing, the gospel was moving forward with marvelous strides among the soldiers in the field. Indeed, what could be more fitting, with real men accustomed daily to witnessing carnage and death. There was therefore much comfort to the men in having the gospel successfully preached and the standard of the Master borne aloft in the trenches, in sight of the enemy, even within musket and cannon's range. At the administration of the baptismal ordinance, the banks of the Rappahannock, Rapidan and the James and other streams resounded with the songs of praise. Our chaplains often proclaimed the glad tidings amid the noise of the booming cannon and rattle of musketry. This spirit was caught by our division at Taylorsville in the spring of 1863, when Dr. Pryor of Petersburg preached for us for several days in succession, hundreds professing faith in Christ. The whole camp was one religious gathering, and all men seemed greatly interested. There was a grand and glorious awakening. Many in the Spring of 1863 found the blessed Savior precious, to their souls and rejoiced in His love, I among the number." Johnston went on to note that, by the close of 1864, the Army of Northern Virginia "had in large measure become a band of Christian brothers."[197]

In Mississippi, several Union naval vessels were assigned to prepare the way for Sherman's Chickasaw Bluff offensive. One of them was the *Cairo*. It was huge by the standards of the day, displacing 521 tons, and was armed with three eight-inch smoothbores, three forty-two-pounder rifled cannons, six

---

[197] Johnston, n.p.

thirty-two-pounder rifled cannons, a thirty-pounder rifled cannon, and a twelve-pounder. It had a crew of 251. It was given the mission of conducting a reconnaissance and clearing the Yazoo River of Confederate mines.

Meanwhile, a Rebel naval lieutenant named Beverly Kennon arrived in Vicksburg. He was one of several innovative officers in Secretary Mallory's Naval Department, which was always looking for new and exciting ways to sink Yankee ships. Kennon approached Isaac Brown, the former commander of the *Arkansas*, and presented his latest idea: an electronically detonated mine. Brown liked what he heard and decided to detonate it himself. He, Kennon, and their men set up several five-gallon glass jugs in the Yazoo. (These mines were called torpedoes in those days.)

On December 12, 1862, the *Cairo* steamed up the river. When her bow crossed over one of the mines, Brown detonated it. The explosion was so powerful that it literally lifted the huge warship out of the water. As soon as she came down, Brown detonated a second mine directly beneath her. Although no Northerners were killed or even seriously wounded, the *Cairo* sank in twelve minutes in thirty-six feet of water. She was the first ship in history to be sunk by an electrical underwater mine.

Sherman tried to storm Chickasaw Bluffs on December 28 and 29, 1862. It was a complete debacle. The Rebels suffered two hundred casualties. The North lost nineteen hundred men.

Although there were occasional skirmishes, a relative lull descended on the major fronts from January to April 1863. Lieutenant Lewis recalled that "... Southern women sent cheerful messages to camp when in many cases their hearts were filled with sadness. It is no wonder that the women of the South of that day were looked on as very near angels by all of the Southern soldiers."[198]

---

[198] Lewis, p. 483.

Henry A. Morehead of the 11th Mississippi would have agreed with Lieutenant Lewis. In the 1910s, he said: "Just here let me digress a little and speak of the good women of Virginia. God bless them all, but the best women that the sun ever shone on were around Winchester, Va. They never tired nor failed to offer a helping hand to a sick or wounded Confederate soldier. I was there and sick and know whereof I speak, and I well know that my own mother and sister could not have done more for me. I have never forgotten them and never can."[199]

In early February 1863, Perry's Florida brigade arrived in Virginia. The troops were not properly provided with shelter and the food supply was irregular and insufficient. The temperature was zero degrees Fahrenheit, and the ground was covered with six inches of snow. Most of these men never saw snow before and their uniforms were inadequate. "…a more forlorn set of poor devils than they were in that, to them, Arctic experience it would be hard to imagine," Lieutenant William E. Cameron wrote later.[200]

This brigade became known as "the Florida Turkeys" because General Mahone kept a flock of turkeys. They got out one day and wandered into the Florida camp, where they were promptly killed and eaten.

Floridians were certainly not the only ones to suffer. In February 1863, Pickett's division of Virginians was transferred to North Carolina. En route, it spent the night at Chester, Virginia. When it went to bed the temperature was cool, but the sky was clear and the stars were shining. When the men awoke the next morning, they were under twelve inches of snow. The men were lying in rows which reminded one of them of a cemetery. When they got up, it resembled a mass resurrection.[201]

---

[199] Yeary, II, 538–539.
[200] Bernard, p. 46.
[201] Johnston, n.p.

CHAPTER XII

SPRING 1863

As spring approached, active skirmishing intensified. On March 17, 1863, the Army of Northern Virginia lost one of its most beloved officers.

John Pelham was born on his father's plantation near Alexandria, Alabama, the son of a prominent physician.[202] He and his brothers were known as "the wild Pelham boys," although one, John, was known for his modesty. He entered West Point in 1856 but was not a particularly good student. Because of Alabama's secession, he resigned from the Academy a few weeks before he would have graduated. Commissioned in the Confederate army, he fought in every major battle and many small ones, from the First Manassas to Kelly's Ford—more than sixty engagements. He had a particular talent for commanding horse artillery and became chief of Jeb Stuart's artillery by the time of the Battle of Sharpsburg (Antietam), where he set up his guns on Nicodemus Hill, inflicted heavy casualties on the advancing Northerners, and broke up several enemy formations.

Pelham particularly distinguished himself at Fredericksburg, where with a single section of artillery (two guns), he checked the entire Union left flank, inflicted severe losses on the Union army, and delayed the

---

[202] Pelham had six brothers, all of whom served in the Confederate army. Charles was a lieutenant in the 51st Alabama Infantry and became a congressman and a judge. Lieutenant Will Pelham served in the partisan rangers and was killed by a policeman during a drunken altercation in Anniston. The Pelhams also had a sister.

Federal advance for several hours. Watching through his field glasses, General Lee exclaimed: "It is glorious to see such courage in one so young."[203] Pelham lost one of his guns early in the contest but engaged in an artillery duel with thirty-two Union guns for hours. Three times, Jeb Stuart sent orders telling him to withdraw, but Pelham ignored them and fired until he ran out of ammunition. In the end, he helped load the cannon himself because most of the gunners were casualties. So rapid was his fire that one Federal commander thought he was facing an entire battery.[204]

After he fired his last shot, he took his gun off the field and rejoined the rest of his command, which helped repulse the disastrous Union attack of December 13, 1862. After this battle, he was known throughout the army as "the gallant Pelham."

John Pelham was not married but had at least three girlfriends in Virginia. One of them was Bessie Shackelford of Culpeper.

The Yankees advanced on this town in March 1863, and were met by Fitz Lee's brigade of Stuart's cavalry. On March 17, 1863, Pelham (who had been attending a court-martial) joined Fitz Lee in the Battle of Kelly's Ford, even though his artillery was en route to the ford and not yet engaged. The young Alabamian nevertheless took part in a cavalry charge. Minutes later, he was sitting on his horse next to Captain Harry Gilmor. The captain recalled, "The [Union] shells continued to explode all around us, but principally in our front; and so familiar had they become, that I had ceased to regard them, or watch the damage each had done, when...I was deafened by the explosion of one very near. Even then I did not look back till I heard Bailey exclaim, 'My God, they've killed poor Pelham.'"

"I had not heard the well-known *thud* of a bullet or piece of shell, which you never fail to hear when a man is struck as near as Pelham was to me. Turning quickly in my saddle, I saw Pelham's horse, without his rider, moving slowly off, and Pelham himself lying on his back upon the ground, his eyes wide open, and looking very natural, but fatally hurt." He had been struck by a shell fragment on the back of the head and was bleeding profusely.

---

[203] Burke Davis, *Jeb Stuart, The Last Cavalier* (New York: 1957), p. 255.
[204] *Confederate Veteran*, Vol. XXX (September 1922), p. 329.

Although skirmishers from the enemy's cavalry drew uncomfortably near, Gilmor, Bailey, and Lieutenant Minegerode of General Fitz Lee's staff put Pelham on the front of Gilmor's horse. After withdrawing some distance, Gilmor placed Pelham on the major's own horse and ordered two dismounted men to carry his body to the rear. Gilmor then galloped off to tell General Stuart of Pelham's death. Seeing the blood on Gilmor's shirt, Stuart thought he was wounded. "You're hurt," he exclaimed.

"No, General. It's not my blood. It's Pelham's."

"I shall never forget his look of distress and horror," Gilmor remembered. He bowed his head onto his horse's neck, wept, and cried: 'Our loss is irreparable!'"[205]

Toward evening, Gilmor overtook the two men who were carrying Pelham's body, which was draped over his horse with his arms and legs dangling. They carried him about eight miles. Gilmor ordered them to lay the body out. When they did, to his astonishment, he discovered that Pelham was still breathing. He soon got Pelham in an ambulance and rushed him to the nearby Shackelford house, where three surgeons worked feverishly on him, trying to save his life. They were assisted by Bessie Shackelford and other women. But the doctors soon announced that the case was hopeless. About 1 a.m. on March 18, Pelham opened his eyes, looked at the room as if he had never seen it before, breathed deeply, and expired.

John Pelham was only twenty-four years old when he died. His body was taken to Richmond, where it lay in state in the Confederate congress. Hundreds of mourners visited the fallen hero. His remains were then transported back to Alabama and buried in the Jacksonville City Cemetery. At every train stop along the way, women covered his coffin with flowers. Jeb Stuart wrote his wife: "He was noble in every sense of the word. I want Jimmie [Stuart's son] to be just like him."[206] When General Stuart's daughter was born the following October, she was named Virginia Pelham Stuart.

Robert E. Lee requested that Pelham be posthumously promoted to lieutenant colonel. Although this type of promotion was rare in the Confederacy, his request was granted.

---

[205] Gilmor, p. 60–67; Davis, *Stuart,* p. 273

[206] Davis, *Stuart,* p. 277.

Captain Gilmor, a recently exchanged prisoner, returned to the Army of Northern Virginia in mid-March 1863. He attended a jovial party at Culpeper on the 16th. Present were Colonel Thomas L. Rosser, severely wounded in the Battle of Kelly's Ford the next day;[207] Lieutenant Colonel Welby Carter;[208] Colonel Sol Williams, of the 12th North Carolina Cavalry, killed at Brandy Station on June 9; Major John Pelham and Major J. W. Puller, both killed the next day; Captain Rogers, 1st Virginia Cavalry; Colonel Jabez L. Drake, later commander of the 33rd Mississippi, killed near Shepherdstown on July 16, 1863; and Colonel Henry Clay Pate, killed at Yellow Tavern the same day Stuart fell.[209]

Meanwhile, the 4th Texas Cavalry was sent to Louisiana. When it passed through the streets of Opelousas, the women lined the streets, shouting: "God bless the Texans! We are safe when they stand between us and the Federals!" Private John T. Poe recalled, "They handed us trays filled with cake and lemonade and sandwiches and other good things to eat, and we were compelled to fill our pockets. We gave three cheers for the women of Opelousas and felt—every one of us—that we could fight for, and, if necessary, die for such heroic women…"[210]

Many Rebel soldiers found the Lord during the war. Private Poe was one of them. He survived the fighting, became a Baptist minister, preached the gospel for forty-three years, and baptized several thousand people.

---

[207] Rosser ended the war as a major general. He was a brigadier general of U.S. volunteers during the Spanish-American War.

[208] Later promoted to full colonel, Richard Welby Carter was a prisoner of war from December 1863 to August 1864. He was cashiered for cowardice at the Battle of Tom's Brook.

[209] Gilmor, p. 59. Pate and Rosser were bitter enemies. Pate led the 5th Virginia Cavalry from the autumn of 1863 and seems to have done a good job. Certainly, the men under his command thought more highly of him than did Rosser.

[210] Yeary, II, p. 613.

By now, the Rebel soldier looked much different than the volunteer of 1861. Certainly, he carried much less gear. "A musket, cartridge box with forty rounds of cartridges, cloth haversack, blanket and canteen made up the Confederate soldier's equipment," one sergeant recalled. "No man was allowed a change of clothing, nor could he have carried it. A gray cap, jacket, trousers and colored shirt—calico mostly—made up a private's wardrobe. When a clean shirt became necessary, we took off the soiled one, went to the water, usually without soap, gave it a little rubbing, and if the sun was shining, hung the shirt on a bush to dry, while the wearer sought the shade to give the shirt a chance. The method of carrying our few assets was to roll them in a blanket, tying each end of the roll, which was then swung over the shoulder. At night this blanket was unrolled and wrapped around its owner, who found a place on the ground with his cartridge box for a pillow. We cooked but little, having usually little to cook. The frying pan was in use, if we had one."[211]

Major John Esten Cooke recalled that the cavalry was a reserve of fun, "But the infantry of General Lee's army were, in camp, like a band of children turned loose for a holiday. The least trifle was sufficient to unloose the waters of the pent-up fun." If a rabbit appeared in camp, for example, the entire regiment would shout "hurrahs" and chase it. They also enjoyed huge snowball fights in which entire divisions took part.[212]

In the meantime, inflation devastated the Confederate currency. When the war began, the Rebel private was paid eleven dollars per month. This

---

211   Johnston, n.p.
212   King and Derby, p. 572.

figure was raised to eighteen dollars in June 1864. Before that, a corporal was paid thirteen dollars, a sergeant seventeen dollars, and a sergeant major twenty-one dollars. They were (theoretically) paid every two months. Officers naturally received more. A second lieutenant was paid eighty dollars, a first lieutenant ninety dollars, a captain $130, a major $150, a lieutenant colonel $170, a full colonel $195, and a general (whatever grade) $301. An army commander received an extra one hundred dollars a month. Generals also received allowances for rations and forage.

Prices soon made the pay of enlisted men almost irrelevant. According to a Mobile, Alabama, newspaper, apples cost sixty to seventy dollars a bushel in Confederate currency in 1863. Bacon cost four dollars per pound, butter cost six to eight dollars a pound, coal was $200 per ton, candles ten dollars a pound, coffee sixty dollars a pound, calico twenty dollars a yard, corn meal twelve dollars a bushel, cowpeas sixteen dollars a bushel, wheat thirty dollars a bushel, fresh beef $2.50 a pound, lard $3.50 a pound, and fresh pork two dollars per pound. Quinine cost $200 an ounce, while morphine cost $350 an ounce. Onions sold for seventy dollars a bushel, Irish potatoes ninety dollars a bushel, and salt was thirty-two dollars a pound. Whiskey ran sixty-five dollars to $150 a gallon, depending on the quality.[213]

Confederate money was, in fact, nearly useless by the summer of 1863. Private McDonald was with the 27th Louisiana when it surrendered at Vicksburg on July 4, 1863. He was approached by a Union officer, who was seeking souvenirs. He asked if McDonald had some Confederate money he could purchase. "I sold him a ream for seventy-five cents in greenback," McDonald recalled. It was the first "greenback money" he had ever seen.[214]

Lieutenant Colonel Richard T. Seckel was an engineer staff officer attached to Colonel M. Jeff Thompson's Missouri brigade. He was captured at Broomtown, Missouri, on March 1, 1863. He was imprisoned for

---

213 King and Derby, pp. 71–72.
214 Yeary, II, p. 488.

several months before he was slated to be sent by the steamer *Maple Leaf* to Fort Delaware. Off the coast of North Carolina, another prisoner told Seckel that he and his comrades were going to seize the vessel. Would the colonel like to join the coup? he asked. Seckel said he would be glad to. "At three taps you take that musket from that man," the leader said, pointing to a guard.

"I had that musket at the first tap," Secker recalled.

The coup was successful. The Rebels had the captain run close to the shore near Currytuck Sound, where they paroled the crew. They crossed part of the dismal swamps and, after they proved who they were, a young lady, Miss Adelaide Campbell, brought them a pound cake with a Confederate flag in the middle "...and you bet we gave her three cheers three times over." In 1909, Seckel recalled: "She was a daughter of the sunny South, lovely, pure and true. I hope she still lives, and I know if she does not that she is in Paradise."[215] Among the escaped prisoners was Raphael Semmes Jr., the son of the famous Confederate sea raider and admiral.

---

[215] Yeary, II, pp. 674–675.

CHAPTER XIII

THE MISSISSIPPI IS LOST

The Union forces began their tenth attempt to capture Vicksburg in April 1863.[216] This time they succeeded in establishing a bridgehead south of the city. They captured Grand Gulf, Port Gibson, Raymond, and Jackson, and won a decisive victory at Champion Hill on May 16.

Many historians don't seem to realize it, but General Joseph E. Johnston stripped the Army of Mississippi of most of its cavalry in late 1862. The army commander, Lieutenant General John C. Pemberton, was as blind in the final Vicksburg campaign as Robert E. Lee was at Gettysburg. This led to the Battle of Raymond, which was one of the most interesting fights of the Civil War. On May 12, a single Rebel brigade of four thousand men under Brigadier General John Gregg attacked a Union corps of about twenty thousand men. But the Rebels thought they outnumbered the enemy and fought the battle that way; on the other side, the Yankees thought they were outnumbered and fought the battle that way.

"As we moved down the wide road to the strains of 'The Girl I Left Behind Me,' I glanced back with a feeling of pride in the splendid army of gallant men, nearly all of whom I knew personally," Captain William E.

---

[216] For the story of the other nine attempts from the Confederate point of view, I humbly recommend *Vicksburg* by Samuel W. Mitcham Jr. (Washington, D.C.: 2018).

Cunningham, the commander of Company F, 41st Tennessee, recalled.[217] The streets of Raymond were crowded, mostly with women cheering them on.

Cunningham and his men were itching for a fight. "We were expecting nothing but cavalry," he recalled, "which we felt we could whip. Skirmishers were advanced in the thick black copse, and almost instantly the quiet was broken by the crack of the rifle, answered by the first big gun in our center."

"Suddenly the sound of the skirmisher's rifle was lost in the roar of musketry, while our three pieces belched defiance at the six gun battery of the enemy on the hill opposite. The force of the enemy was developed suddenly, for from right to left along our front of a mile, the battle opened at close range. At this junction, Colonel [Randal W.] McGavock advanced to charge the battery, supported by the 3rd [Tennessee]. We all saw him as with gallant bearing he led his men forward, capturing four guns. This was as gallant a charge as was ever made against terrible odds. In the moment of success, McGavock fell, shot through the heart.[218] Major Grace took command only to fall from a severe wound. The fighting around the battery was bloody in the extreme. The 3rd moved up in support, and in ten minutes 100 of the 500 men, comprising [sic] their number, were killed or wounded. By this time the battle along the whole line was raging with incredible fury." One of Captain Bledsoe's guns burst when it fired its 113th round.

General Gregg realized he was fighting more than cavalry. He examined the prisoners and found men from eighteen different regiments. He had attacked an entire corps. He faced a choice: retreat or eventually be overwhelmed. He retreated.[219]

---

[217] Gregg's brigade included the 3rd Tennessee, the 41st Tennessee, the 10th/30th Tennessee (an Irish regiment led by Colonel McGavock), the 50th Tennessee, and the 7th Texas. It also had Captain Hiram M. Bledsoe's Missouri artillery battery (three guns) and a few other attached units.

[218] McGavock was an attorney and former mayor of Nashville (1858–1859).

[219] King and Derby, pp. 170–172.

Outnumbered thirty-two thousand to less than twenty thousand, the Army of Mississippi was decisively defeated at Champion Hill on May 16 and retreated into the fortress of Vicksburg. One of the men trapped in the city was a musician named E. W. Krause.

He was born in Niederwaltersdorf (aka Nieder Waltersdorf, near Waldenburg), Germany, but immigrated to Texas. He was a music teacher at a female college in Waco, Texas, when the war began. Krause immediately enlisted in the Confederate army. After a tour of duty in Galveston, he became bandmaster of Waul's Legion and fought in the victory at Fort Pemberton and in the Siege of Vicksburg. He recalled: "From the day we entered the city of Vicksburg we were put on quarter rations, and it is a very peculiar sensation to be always hungry." The Yankees attempted to carry Waul's works by storm on May 19 and 22, and it was horrendous. "The terrific roar of cannon of all calibers, heavy siege guns, the unearthly roar of [Union] mortars from the river throwing 200-pound bombs high in the air and exploding over our heads, scattering their death-dealing fragments everywhere; the minie balls flying through the air like sleet; it was simply fearful. The loss on our side was great, but not as heavy as on the other side, but it was enough to make the heart sick to see the dead and hear the moans and shrieks of the wounded."[220]

The band played "Dixie" and other tunes to keep up the unit's morale. An "unharmonious" Union band was nearby and tried to outplay them. Simultaneously, dozens of Union muskets and cannons opened up on the bank which sheltered them. On the third night, however, they were not interrupted. An excellent Union band was stationed opposite them and a pattern emerged. Just after nightfall, the Confederate band would play "Dixie." Then it was the Union band's turn. They would generally start off with "America." Then the Rebel band would play, and so on (weather permitting) until bedtime. After the surrender, the U.S. players visited Krause's band, but as fellow musicians, not as enemies. When they saw

---

[220] Yeary, II, pp. 411–412.

how starved the Rebels were, they returned to their quarters and brought back a good store of provisions, including bacon, flour, sugar, crackers—and even real coffee.[221]

After the capitulation, Krause returned to Texas and served with the legion for the rest of the war. He settled in Waco and was still teaching music at age eighty-two.

"It would be impossible to tell of the sufferings from hunger and exposure at Vicksburg," Private W. F. Renshaw recalled. "We had to stay in the ditches [trenches] and take the rain as it came, as we had no shelter, and then the heat and cold with shot and shell, and hunger." The fighting was occasionally fierce. "When Gen. Grant made one of his desperate charges on our breastworks," Renshaw recalled, "a bayonet in the hands of one of his men tore the skin off the top of my head."[222]

The rations of the Vicksburg garrison were cut for the first time on May 30. The rations of the 3rd Louisiana for June 4 consisted of one-third of a pound of peas, five-ninths of a pound of meal, a half a pound of beef (including bones and shanks), and small amounts of sugar, lard, and salt. That day, the army seized all of the surplus provisions in the city and began issuing rations to soldiers and civilians alike. "It seemed wonderful that human endurance could withstand the accumulated horrors of the situation," a Louisiana soldier recalled. "Living on this slender allowance, fighting all day in the hot summer sun, and at night, with pick-axe and spade,

---

[221] Yeary, II, pp. 411–412.

[222] Yeary, II, pp. 636–637. Private Renshaw was captured when Vicksburg fell. He was exchanged, joined the 19th Texas Cavalry, and was part of Richard Taylor's Army of Western Louisiana during the Red River Campaign of 1864. He remained in the Trans-Mississippi Department until the end of the war.

repairing the destroyed portions of the line, it passed all comprehension how the men endured the trying ordeal."[223]

"Fair ladies, in all the vigor and loveliness of youth, hurried with light tread along the torn up pavements, fearless of the storm of iron and lead, penetrating every portion of the city, as they attended to the necessities of their brave, wounded and dying protectors. The annals of history can furnish no more brilliant record than did the heroic women of Vicksburg during this fearful siege. Regardless of personal danger, they flitted about the hospitals or threaded the streets on their missions of love, utterly forgetful of self… Many, very many heroic spirits, bade farewell to earth amid the thunder and din of the siege, feeling the soothing pressure of soft hands upon their clammy brows… as these ministering angels hovered about the lowly cots of the dying soldiers. No pen can describe in sufficiently glowing colors; no human language find words brilliant, forcible enough to do justice to the unwearying attentions, tender compassion, soul-felt sympathy, unvarying kindness, and unceasing labors of love, of the tender-hearted, heroic and fearless ladies of Vicksburg, toward their suffering countrymen."[224]

In Vicksburg, most of the civilians lived in caves. Due to the nature of the soil around the city, they were safe from all but a direct hit from Union heavy artillery. Small trenches, which the citizens called "rat holes," were dug along streets and in yards at irregular intervals. When the Federal guns opened up, the civilians would scurry to them, shouting "Every rat to his hole."

One day, a lady and her four-year-old daughter were caught in the open by a Union bombardment. They "hit the dirt" and were not harmed

---

[223]   W. H. Tunnard, *A Southern Record: The History of the Third Louisiana* (Baton Rouge: 1866), p. 245 (hereafter cited as "Tunnard").

[224]   Tunnard, 238.

by the flying shrapnel, but the little girl was nevertheless frightened and started to cry.

"Don't cry, my darling," her mother said. "God will protect us."

The young lady was not comforted. She replied that she was pretty sure God had already been killed.[225]

Near the end of the siege, rats in Vicksburg were selling at the public markets for $3.50 per rodent. The Confederate private at that time was being paid eleven dollars a month. If the reader can imagine paying more than a week's wages for a single rat, he or she can imagine how hungry people were. By the beginning of July, there was a shortage of rats in Vicksburg.

There were a great many close calls during the war. Few were luckier than Lieutenant Richard C. Walsh of Wade's Missouri battery. Described by Private Truman as "a talented, brave, competent officer," he had a habit of standing with both feet far apart. During the Battle of Grand Gulf (April 29), a Union heavy naval artillery shell passed between his legs below the knee. The shell was so large that it inflicted flesh wounds on both legs but no serious damage. It then buried itself behind Walsh but did not explode.

History does not record the lieutenant's reaction to his miraculous escape from death, but I doubt if he was of much use the rest of the day.

An African American named Abraham was even more fortunate. He and eight other men were engaged in countermining operations. They were about twenty-five feet deep but the Yankees struck first and detonated about two tons of high explosives directly beneath them. There is no record of the

---

[225] Mitcham, *Vicksburg*, p. 281, from a manuscript on file at the Old City Courthouse.

remains of the other eight men even being found. Abraham was thrown over Confederate lines, over the Union front line and supporting trenches, and into the Union rear. One would think that he would have been killed or at least suffered many broken bones and serious injuries, but he did not bust a pimple. He was, however, unable to speak for several hours.

One he got over the shock, the Federals asked him how high the explosion launched him. Abraham said he did not know, but he thought it must have been about three miles.

Some enterprising Yankees placed him in a tent and charged their comrades twenty-five cents each to meet Abraham and discuss his survival with him. When U.S. General Logan learned what they were doing, however, he shut the operation down. Abraham spent the rest of the siege as a servant in Logan's headquarters.

July 1, 1863, was a day of intense, suffocating heat in the Vicksburg trenches. At 2 p.m., the enemy exploded a mine beneath the 3rd Louisiana redan. "A huge mass of earth suddenly, and with tremendous force and a terrible explosion, flew upwards, and descended with mighty power upon the gallant defenders, burying numbers beneath its falling fragments, bruising and mangling them most horribly," a survivor recalled. "It seemed as if all hell had suddenly yawned upon the devoted band, and vomited forth its sulphurous fire and smoke upon them."[226]

Fortunately for the Rebels, Brigadier General Paul Hebert commanded that part of the trench line. He suspected what the Yankees were up to, had constructed a second line of defenses, and had three Missouri regiments ready to launch an immediate counterattack. The survivors were stunned, but only momentarily. They did not look for comrades but immediately rushed into the gap to check the Yankees.

The wounded were taken to the hospital, which was in the open under shade trees. "Surgeons, with sleeves rolled up to their elbows, hands, arms,

---

[226] Tunnard, p. 266

and shirts red with human gore, hastened hither and thither, or were using their keen-edged instruments in amputating some shattered limb, extracting balls and fragments of shells from lacerated bodies, or probing some ghastly wound…" Sergeant Tunnard recalled.[227]

The blast left a hole twelve feet deep. The Federals did not think to carry ladders and were trapped in the hole. Rebels slaughtered many of them by lighting artillery shells and simply rolling them into the gap. Grant threw in regiment after regiment, but without success.

Starvation did what Northern attacks could not do. Vicksburg surrendered on July 4, 1863. Almost every Yankee came into Rebel lines with a haversack full of provisions, which he would give to some famished Southerner, with the remark, "Here, reb, I know you are starved nearly to death."[228]

"When the Federal soldiers entered the city they mingled freely with the Confederates and expressed their sympathy with their deplorable situation by every possible means in their power," Sergeant Tunnard remembered. He remarked that they were "unusually kind."[229]

The Union expressed great astonishment that the place could have been held so long.

Major General Franklin Gardner surrendered the Confederate garrison at Port Hudson on July 9, 1863. The Mississippi River was now cleared of Rebel forces, and the states of Arkansas, Texas, and most of Louisiana, were lost to Richmond.

D. M. Shaw was the 23rd Arkansas was from Arkadelphia. He fought at Shiloh, the First and Second Corinth, Iuka, and in the Siege of Port Hudson. He was wounded three times and captured twice. After he was

---

[227] Tunnard, p. 267
[228] Tunnard, p. 267.
[229] Tunnard, p. 272.

exchanged, he served in Trans-Mississippi Department. "I want to say that no boy enjoyed the war more than I did," he wrote in 1909. "I was never sick, and loved my officers and comrades and my country, and I know that I gave it the best service I could. I am not ashamed of anything I did."[230]

The Rebels at Port Hudson held out for forty-eight days, mostly on small amounts of cowpeas and corn, ground into meal, with occasional helpings of mule and horse meat. Near the end, Captain Jube Turner received permission from General Gardner to break out with Company C, Louisiana Guards. They were stopped at Plains Store—almost within sight of Confederate breastworks—and were all but annihilated. It was considered by some to be the hardest-fought battle to take place on Louisiana soil.[231] About fifty Rebels were killed. A few succeeded in escaping.

When Lieutenant F. M. Bankston heard that General Gardner was about to surrender, he and three other officers of Company C, Louisiana Guards, broke their swords in front of Gardner's tent. Bankston's sword had been presented to him by Mrs. Jefferson Davis. They decided not to surrender, but hid themselves in a ravine and covered themselves with leaves and traveled by night.

With nothing to eat for days, they approached a plantation house looking for food. Nellie Gray, the daughter of the house, saw them coming and waved them back to cover—there were Yankees in the house. After darkness fell and the Northerners rode away, she went to them with a basket of food. Then she led them through the briars and brambles past the Union outposts. They eventually reached Rebel lines.[232] All four men survived the war.

As the Rebels retreated between Bisland and Franklin, Louisiana, before the Union Army of the Gulf, Private John T. Poe recalled, "I went into a fine residence to get some water. An aristocratic old lady sat on the front porch and watched the men go by. I noticed she had diamond earrings,

---

[230]   Yeary, II, p. 680.
[231]   Bankston, p. 114.
[232]   Bankston, pp. 114–116.

each one about three carats, and I said: 'Madam, go back into your back yard somewhere and bury those earrings and whatever such treasures you may have. Banks' Army is just behind us, and they will certainly rob you.' She thanked me, and went off to hide them. Many a Northern man got rich off such loot."[233]

[233] Yeary, II, p. 613.

CHAPTER XIV

CHANCELLORSVILLE

The Army of Northern Virginia broke from winter quarters in late April 1863, when U.S. General Joseph Hooker crossed the Rappahannock River with one hundred thirty-two thousand men. From May 1 to 6, Robert E. Lee won perhaps his most impressive victory at Chancellorsville, where he crushed Hooker's invaders with only fifty-eight thousand men. Unfortunately, Stonewall Jackson was mortally wounded on May 2 and died on May 10. One could argue that this was the turning point of the war.

On April 29, the Yankees crossed Ely's Ford, beginning the Chancellorsville Campaign. It rained heavily in Virginia during the night of April 29–30, 1863. The rain so moistened the leaves that they were able to gobble up twenty-three men from the Norfolk juniors "with not as much noise as a clever darkey would make in robbing a hen-roost," Lieutenant William E. Cameron recalled.[234] The pickets were unable to fire because their

---

[234] William E. Cameron (1842-1927) was a native of Petersburg, Virginia. He was educated at North Carolina Military Institute and Washington College in St. Louis. A member of the 12th Virginia Infantry Regiment, he ended the war as a captain in a Mississippi unit. Admitted to the bar in 1866. He was mayor of Petersburg and, in 1881, was elected governor of Virginia as a Re-adjustor candidate. He served from January 1, 1882 to January 1, 1886.

rifled muskets were made useless by the rain, and they were also captured. Mahone's brigade north of Chancellorsville and his artillery were caught napping and were entirely exposed; fortunately for Lee, the Federals did not take advantage of their opportunity. Mahone retreated and brought up the 12th Virginia Infantry, which stabilized the situation.

About noon on April 30, a Union sharpshooter climbed a tree a few hundred yards from the Confederate front (now about a mile east of Chancellorsville) and opened up on the men guarding the artillery. Two Rebels were wounded. One of General Posey's Mississippians asked permission to "hunt" the sniper, and it was immediately granted. It took him about fifteen minutes to find the sniper. He fired a single shot from a considerable distance and "brought the troublesome marksman down from his lofty perch, the body falling like that of a wounded squirrel from limb to limb until it struck the ground. Looking at the descent through my field-glasses I could almost hear the thud," Lieutenant Cameron recalled.[235]

On May 1, 1863, George W. Ivey of Company A, 12th Virginia, was captured along with several of his comrades. A few hundred yards to the Federal rear, he saw a large Union infantry column, led by a fine military band, which was playing music as they marched down the road. "In a few moments a shell from one of our batteries struck the head of this line of men and passed to about its centre and then exploded," Ivey recalled. "I never saw such destruction caused by one shell in all four years of the war." Although no band members were injured, it "scattered, leaving the bass drum on the side of the road with two or three horns to keep it company. Many of the infantrymen were killed by this shell, and after the line was reformed the musicians went for their dead comrades like so many birds of prey, rifling knapsacks and pockets, showing clearly by this act that they had not the instincts of soldiers."[236]

---

235 Bernard, pp. 50–51.
236 Bernard, p. 75.

As General McLaws's division moved forward at Chancellorsville on May 1, 1863, Union artillery opened up on the head of his column. Someone blundered and his ambulance and ordnance train were following immediately to the rear of Mahone's infantry and were now not only in the way but were exposed to enemy fire. Teamsters of both armies had a poor reputation. "A stampede followed," Lieutenant Cameron recalled, "each teamster whipping furiously into the woods with sublime disregard of getting out again. Wheels were locked against trunks of trees, teamsters swore, mules kicked, and the shells flew fast and furious. Presently a six-pound shell struck an ambulance 'midships, tore off all the rear parts of the vehicle, and left the driver perched on two wheels, himself and animals unhurt."[237]

On May 2, Stonewall Jackson executed a brilliant flanking maneuver, disappeared into the woods, emerged a dozen miles farther west, fell on the Federals exposed right flank with his entire corps, took it completely by surprise, and routed it.

Heros von Borcke followed Jackson's attack and reported: "It was a strange spectacle that now greeted us. The whole [U.S.] XI Corps had broken at the first shock of the attack; entire regiments had thrown down their arms, which were lying in regular lines on the ground, as if for inspection; suppers just prepared had been abandoned; tents, baggage, wagons, cannons, half-slaughtered oxen, covered the foreground in chaotic confusion, while in the background a host of many thousand Yankees were discerned scampering for their lives as fast as their limbs could carry them, closely followed by our men, who were taking prisoners by the hundreds, and scarcely firing a shot."[238]

---

[237]   Bernard, p. 52–53.
[238]   Borcke, p. 375.

Thomas Jefferson Smith joined the Confederate army the week after Fort Sumter as a private in the Mississippi battalion of Featherstone's brigade. Sent to Virginia, he was wounded in the Battle of Williamsburg. After he recovered, he fought in the Second Manassas, Harpers Ferry, Sharpsburg, Fredericksburg, and Chancellorsville, where, "…while lying down I was wounded, the ball striking my backbone just above the kidneys and ranged up about four inches then turned to the left and through the left shoulder." One of his messmates, a German, picked him up and carried him to a field hospital, three hundred yards to the rear. "I remained on that bed among the dead and wounded for twenty-six hours before I was removed; this was not very pleasant. I have the ball and hold it in remembrance of the great battle of Chancellorsville," he wrote in 1909.[239]

On April 15, 1861, Lincoln called for seventy-five thousand volunteers to suppress the "rebellion." Alfred H. H. Tolar of Elizabethtown, North Carolina, was the first man or boy from his hometown to enlist. Private Tolar was assigned to the 18th North Carolina and fought in most of the battles of the Army of Northern Virginia. He was promoted to second lieutenant after the Seven Days Battles. During the Battle of Chancellorsville, he and his comrades were waiting for orders to launch a night attack when Union cavalry approached their line. They were ordered to fire, which they did. But it wasn't Union cavalry. It was Generals Stonewall Jackson and A. P. Hill and members of their staffs. Jackson received his mortal wound here.

Tolar was slightly wounded in the leg at Malvern Hill and Cedar Mountain. He was struck in the chest by a bullet, but fortunately for him, it was spent. He was seriously wounded at Gettysburg, after which he was promoted to captain for meritorious conduct. Later, he commanded a "corps" of sharpshooters.[240]

---

239   Yeary, II, p. 706.
240   Yeary, II, pp. 752–753.

Despite Jackson's wound, Lee thoroughly whipped the Army of the Potomac, which barely managed to escape. It lost more than seventeen thousand men at Chancellorsville, as opposed to less than thirteen thousand for the South. Jackson's death, however, caused gloom to fall throughout the army. In 1862 and 1863, Jackson's men defeated or played a role in defeating armies under Milroy, Banks, Fremont, Shields, McClellan, Pope, Burnside, and Hooker. Private G. B. Scroggins of the 15th Alabama Infantry served with Trimble's brigade in all of these victories.

After Jackson's death, the army reorganized, and Trimble's brigade was dissolved. The 15th Alabama was transferred to Laws's brigade, Hood's division, Longstreet's I Corps. "The regiment regretted leaving the old brigade," Scroggins recalled, "because it severed us from Jackson['s Corps], for under Stonewall we had never known defeat."[241]

That was about to change.

Jeb Stuart's favorite scout was Captain Will Farley of South Carolina. He had a winning personality, although he seemed, according to Heros von Borcke, somewhat feminine. Indeed, the major, wrote, "it seemed difficult to believe that this boy, with the long, fair hair, the mild blue eyes, the soft voice and the modest mien, was the daring dragoon whose appearance in battle was always terrible to the foe. But Farley was a fierce warrior and a crack shot. He killed more than 30 Yankees by his own hand. He often went on the most dangerous missions and usually entirely alone. He was never wounded until June 9, 1863, during the Battle of Brandy Station.

---

[241] Yeary, II, pp. 671–672.

Matthew C. Butler

Colonel Matthew C. Butler's 2nd South Carolina Cavalry Regiment and little else held off an entire Union division for much of the day. Later, while Butler was laughing with Farley, whom he met just that morning, a Union shell from an unobserved battery bounded into them, tore off Butler's leg above the ankle, ripped through his horse, and cut off Farley's leg above the knee. Several officers came to Butler's aid but he said, "Go at once to Farley. He needs you more than I do."[242]

Dr. B. W. Taylor, a surgeon with the Hampton Legion, was summoned immediately. He saw at a glance that two amputations would be necessary. "Colonel," he said to Butler, "I have very little chloroform, but I will share it equally between you and the Major."

"No," Butler replied. "Keep it all for Farley, who is worse off than I am. I can bear the pain without it."[243]

The staff officers and medical orderlies immediately placed Farley on a litter. He asked them to hand him his leg, so it could be buried with him. "Now, gentlemen, you have done all for me possible. I shall be dead in an hour. God bless you for your kindness. I bid you all an affectionate farewell. Go at once to Butler."

---

[242] Borcke, pp. 228-229; *Confederate Veteran*, Vol. III (July 1895), p. 3.
[243] *Confederate Veteran*, Vol. III (July 1895), p. 3.

Farley died soon after. Butler's leg was amputated below the knee. He later returned to the field, was promoted to brigadier and then major general, and he became a United States senator after the war.[244]

Major Heros von Borcke was severely wounded by a Union sharpshooter during the Battle of Middleburg on June 19, 1863. The bullet entered his neck, traveled downward, cut through part of his windpipe, and lodged in his right lung. His surgeon did not expect him to live through the night. He was incapacitated until the spring of 1864, but was present at Yellow Tavern, where General Stuart was killed. He was promoted to lieutenant colonel in December 1864 and was sent to Great Britain on a diplomatic mission by President Davis.

Heros von Borcke of Jeb Stuart's staff,
shown here as a lieutenant colonel

---

[244] Borcke, pp. 228–229;

The Hart battery was formed in May 1861, shortly after the war began. The command was offered to Colonel Arthur Manigault (later brigadier general), Colonel William C. Heyward, Captain John B. Villepigue (later brigadier general), and Lieutenant John Pegram (later brigadier general), all of whom declined it. The appointment went to future lieutenant general Stephen Dill Lee, who was then a captain on Beauregard's staff. Lee was commander until November 8, when he was promoted to major and was succeeded by the senior first lieutenant, James F. Hart. He led it until the Battle of Burgess Mill (October 27, 1864), when he was badly wounded and lost a leg. He was later promoted to major.

In the Battle of Upperville (June 21, 1863), during the Gettysburg Campaign, the battery engaged in an artillery duel. The Federal batteries did well, repeatedly striking a stone wall protecting the South Carolinians. A Yankee shell struck Hart's Blakely rifled gun right in the muzzle, disabling it just as the Rebels retreated.

The Hart battery was under fire 143 times during the war. This was reportedly the only gun it lost during the conflict.[245]

---

[245] Brooks, *Stories,* ff. p. 246.

CHAPTER XV

THE GETTYSBURG CAMPAIGN

As part of John B. Gordon's brigade, George W. O'Neal of the 31st Georgia Infantry marched into Pennsylvania in 1863. As they approached the city of York, they were met by the mayor and several prominent businessmen. They asked the Rebels not to destroy their city. General Gordon replied that they did not intend to destroy private property or molest noncombatants. The brigade marched through the town without breaking ranks.

They pursued the retreating Yankees to the little town of Wrightsville, Pennsylvania. The Federals set the bridge over the Susquehanna River on fire, and Gordon's men, who had no buckets, where unable to put it out. The fire spread to a nearby lumberyard and threatened several upscale residences. When General Gordon announced that he and his men were willing to put out the fire if they were given buckets, the civilians produced plenty of them. Late that night, after the fire was extinguished, one of the grateful ladies visited General Gordon. She invited as many Rebels as could crowd into her dining room for breakfast, as a show of her appreciation for their saving her home. After a fine meal, the boys in gray marched away, toward Gettysburg.[246]

---

[246] Yeary, II, pp. 578–580. O'Neal was shot through the shoulder joint in the Battle of the Wilderness and was disabled from further service. He was later honorably discharged.

Dr. S. G. Welsh, a Confederate surgeon, recalled marching into Pennsylvania. He passed an iron factory owned by Thaddeus Stevens, a particularly hateful and sanctimonious abolitionist politician and anti-Southern bigot who took bribes from railroads but advocated confiscating all Southern estates larger than two hundred acres and giving them to "loyal" (Northern) men. His factory was burned by General Early. They stopped near a Pennsylvania farmhouse and asked for a meal. A smiling young lady agreed and fed several Rebel soldiers. The physician "was hungry as a wolf" and was served fried ham, stewed chicken, biscuits, light bread, butter, buckwheat cakes with molasses, several kinds of preserves, real coffee, cold milk, and several other dishes. Welch offered to pay for his meal. He was embarrassed because he had only Confederate money, but he offered it just the same since he had nothing else. The Pennsylvanian family readily accepted it, however. Welch offered a dollar, but they would only take fifty cents. A guard was posted around the house, so it would not be looted.[247]

When he returned to camp, Welch found that an order had arrived instructing them to cook one day's rations, place it in their haversacks, and be ready to march at 5 a.m. The soldiers immediately realized that a battle was imminent. About an hour after the march began, they heard cannon fire from the direction of Gettysburg.

Before long, the brigade came up on a hill and could see the infantry of Heth's division advancing in line of battle. Welch called the sight "magnificent." Shortly after, Welch's brigade was committed to the attack on Seminary Ridge. "Then such a rattle of musketry I never heard surpassed. It lasted for about two hours and a half without cessation…When the order was given to charge upon the enemy, who were lying behind some stone fences and other places of concealment, our men rushed forward with a perfect fury, yelling and driving them, though with great slaughter to themselves as well as to the Yankees."

---

[247] Letter from Dr. S. G. Welch, a Confederate surgeon, to his wife, August 2, 1863, published in Brooks, *Stories*, p. 33–.36 (hereafter cited as "Welch").

After his brigade charged, Dr. Welch spent most of the rest of the battle practicing his profession. He found the cannonading of July 3 "truly terrifying."[248]

The 14th South Carolina (Colonel Abner N. Perrin's brigade)[249] lost 209 men of 408 engaged at Gettysburg. Company K lost thirty-four of its thirty-nine men. Lieutenant Colonel Joseph N. Brown, the regimental commander, was wounded, as was Major Edward Croft. Commanded devolved onto Captain James Boatwright.

At Gettysburg, General Meade had about one hundred five thousand men; General Lee had about sixty-two thousand. These figures are given by Colonel Taylor, a member of General Lee's staff and adjutant general of the army, taken, as he states, from the official records. Many historians place Lee's strength at about seventy thousand. General Meade states his strength not less than ninety-five thousand men. The Federal loss was 23,190. David Johnston placed Confederate losses at 20,451.[250] Livermore put them at 28,063.[251] The actual total was probably about twenty-three thousand.

By anyone's accounting, the losses were staggering. Private L. N. Perkins of the 15th Virginia recalled, "There were places where one could have walked hundreds of yards on the bodies of the dead—blues and

---

[248] Welch, p. 39.

[249] Colonel Perrin previously commanded the 14th South Carolina but moved up to brigade commander when Samuel McGowan was wounded at Chancellorsville. Perrin was promoted to brigadier general on September 10, 1863. On May 12, 1864, during the battle of the Wilderness, he was shot seven times and died instantly. Being a Confederate brigade commander was dangerous business. McGowan had succeeded Maxey Gregg, who was killed at Fredericksburg.

[250] Johnston, n.p; O.R., Vol. XXVII, Part 1, p. 118. Meade later revised these figures to a total loss of 23,049 (p. 187).

[251] Livermore, p. 103.

grays—without ever touching the ground. At one place an old railroad cut was completely blocked with dead bodies."[252]

On July 1, the first day of the Battle of Gettysburg, Major Harry Gilmor's 1st Maryland Cavalry was supporting Major William T. Poague's artillery battalion of III Corps and Lieutenant Colonel Thomas H. Carter's artillery battalion of Ewell's II Corps. Just as he and his men rode up, four Union batteries opened up on them. The result was "a very pretty artillery fight," so Gilmor took his men back to a ravine. Then he and his aide returned to the guns, just as Northern shells exploded an ammunition chest and went through the lid of a limber-box. Minutes later, however, the Confederates silenced three of the Union batteries. He recalled General Early's division came up with "a heavy rattle of musketry, and then numbers of small squads of bluecoats could be seen straggling out of the woods, and hurrying toward Gettysburg. Soon we heard the yell of a line-of-battle charge; then, at intervals, heavy volleys; and at length the face of the earth seemed covered with blue-coats, all running toward the town of Gettysburg in the wildest confusion, with the grey-jackets after them, keeping up a constant fire." Then Rodes's and Johnson's divisions charged across the open field. Gilmor was too excited to remain with the guns, so he turned command of the battalion over to Captain Emack and took off after the Yankees with two men, slashing left and right with their sabers. Several of the Northerners surrendered, but "A small group of ten or more rallied round their colours. We dashed at them; two fired upon us, but so wildly that neither horse nor man was struck. They presented their bayonets, but, after knocking these aside and cutting down two or three of them, the rest surrendered." Gilmor personally captured the flag of the 149th New York.

---

[252] Yeary, II, p. 601.

Harry Gilmor when he was a captain

Major Gilmor and Captain Welch were the first two Confederates to enter Gettysburg. As they cautiously rode into town, they saw the street was lined with many capped and loaded muskets. A dismounted Union cavalryman fired at Gilmor, and the ball came within an inch of his ear. Gilmor picked up an abandoned Union musket, fired, "and had the satisfaction of seeing him fall." Gilmor took the Yankee's saber and pistols off his dead body and rode on.

"The enemy were crowding through the streets in the most inextricable confusion," Major Gilmor recalled, "and had we then pushed on, they must have been either captured or driven beyond the heights south of the town. But, unfortunately, this was not done, and they were allowed that night to throw up breastworks and fortifications, which, in the assaults of the next two days, cost us so many brave men."[253] This was one of the greatest tactical mistakes of the war.

---

[253] Gilmor, pp. 94–96.

Meanwhile, General Ewell ordered Gilmor to act as provost-marshal of Gettysburg, where he searched the town for prisoners, supplies, and guns. He policed up two thousand five hundred muskets.

The first day of Gettysburg was a Confederate victory. The second day was a Union victory but a marginal one. The third day was a decisive Union victory and, together with Vicksburg, was the turning point of the war.

As Lee's artillery blasted Union positions in preparation for Pickett's Charge, one fellow starting singing:

"Backward, roll backward, O Time in thy flight.

Make me a child again, just for this fight!"

Another man near him answered: "Yes, and a *gal* child at that!"[254]

As the infantry prepared to attack, one of the Rebels frightened a rabbit. "Run, old hare, run!" one of the soldiers shouted. "If I was an old hare, I'd run, too!"

John Lewis was a second lieutenant and file closer in Gen. Lewis Armistead's brigade during Pickett's Charge. He recalled that they left the woods and advanced about two hundred yards before about fifty Federal guns opened up on them. It made no impression on the men, who continued to advance, despite the fact that great gaps developed in their lines. They simply closed up and continued forward. They had crossed two fences when the roar of musketry joined the cannonade. "Men were falling in heaps." The division had not yet fired a shot.[255]

Three hundred yards from the Union works, Garnett's brigade roared its Rebel yell and charged at the double quick. At one hundred yards, they fired and dashed for the U.S. positions with their bayonets. Then Kemper's

---

254   McCarthy, p. 107.
255   Lewis, p. 805.

brigade charged, followed by Armistead's, which was on the left and a little to the rear. Armistead reached the stone wall when he went down.

Lieutenant Lewis was captured at the wall when the charge was broken and spent the rest of the war in POW camps. He recalled: "That we believed then that we were right and that we believe now that we were right then."[256]

Sergeant Major David Johnston of the 7th Virginia was wounded by Union artillery fire. As he lay there, he heard the order: "Fall in!" and Pickett's division assembled. General Pickett called out, "Up then, and to your posts! Don't forget today that you are from old Virginia!"

"The effect of this word upon the men was electrical," Johnston recalled. The regiments quickly formed up and closed to the left over the dead and wounded. A Union soldier from Massachusetts recalled:

"Then Pickett and his brave legions stood up and formed for the death struggle: three remnants of brigades, consisting of Garnett's—the 8th, 18th, 19th, 28th and 56th Virginia; Armistead's brigade—the 9th, 14th, 38th, 53d, and 57th Virginia; Kemper's brigade—1st, 3d, 7th, 11th, and 24th Virginia. Their tattered flags bore the scars of a score of battles, and from their ranks the merciless bullet had already taken two-thirds their number. In compact ranks: their front scarcely covering two of Hancock's brigades, with flags waiving as if for a gala day... It was nearly a mile to the Union lines, and as they advanced over the open plain the Federal artillery opened again, plowing great lanes through their solid ranks, but they closed up to guide center, as if upon dress parade. When half way over, Pickett halted his division amidst a terrible fire of shot and shell, and changed his direction by an oblique movement, coolly and beautifully made...To those who have ever faced artillery fire it is marvelous and unexplainable how human beings could have advanced under the terrific fire of a hundred cannon, every inch of air being laden with the missiles of

---

[256] Lewis, p. 888.

death; but in splendid formation they still came bravely on till within range of the musketry; then the blue line of Hancock's corps arose and poured into their ranks a murderous fire. With a wild yell the rebels pushed on, unfalteringly, crossed the Federal lines and laid hands upon eleven cannon.

"Men fired into each other's faces; there were bayonet thrusts, cutting with sabers, hand-to-hand contests, oaths, curses, yells and hurrahs. The Second [U.S.] Corps fell back behind the guns to allow the use of grape and double canister, and as it tore through the rebel ranks at only a few paces distant, the dead and wounded were piled in ghastly heaps; still on they came up to the very muzzles of their guns; they were blown away from the cannon's mouth, but yet they did not waiver. Pickett had taken the key to the position, and the glad shout of victory was heard, as, the very imper-sonation of a soldier, he still forced his troops to the crest of Cemetery Ridge. Kemper and Armistead broke through Hancock's line, scaled the hill and planted their flags on its crest. Just before Armistead was shot, he placed his flag upon a captured cannon and cried: 'Give them the cold steel, boys!' But valor could do no more, the handful of braves had won immortality, but could not conquer an army... Pickett, seeing his supports gone, his Generals Kemper, Armistead and Garnett killed or wounded, every field officer of three brigades gone, three-fourths of his men killed or captured, himself untouched, but broken-hearted, gave the order for retreat, but, band of heroes as they were, they fled not; but amidst that still continuous, terrible fire, they slowly, sullenly, recrossed the plain—all that was left of them, but few of five thousand."[257]

After Pickett's Charge, litter bearers carried Sergeant Major Johnston to a field hospital. About dark, he was removed by ambulance to a shed near a farmer's barn on Willoughby Run. Brigadier General James Kemper was with him, and the farmer placed the general in his home. Johnston visited the house twenty-two years later and saw Kemper's bloodstains on the

---

[257] Johnston, n.p.

floor. (Kemper was expected to die, but he did not, although he was incapacitated and no longer capable of service in the field. He was nevertheless promoted to major general in 1864 and was elected governor of Virginia after the war.) All that night, Johnston heard nothing but the groans and cries of the wounded and dying.

On Sunday night, the Confederate army withdrew. The brigade surgeon and General Early visited the field hospital and urged all who were able to ride in the wagons to go. A good many did, but Kemper and Johnston were too badly wounded. They were captured by the Federals on July 5. Johnston spent four months in Union hospitals.[258]

In mid-July 1863, the situation was not good for the Confederates. Their backs were to the Potomac River, which, swelled by recent rains, was past fording; most of the army's trains were parked on the northern bank, and were initially defended only by Imboden's calvary brigade and a few miscellaneous formations. Major Harry Gilmor was given command of 180 convalescent soldiers, as well as a variety of waggoneers, and commissary and quartermaster sergeants.

The Battle of Williamsport, Maryland, was fought from July 7 to 16.[259] "I could not say that I felt as much confidence in the 'crowd' I had now with me; however…To my surprise and satisfaction, the men behaved handsomely." Imboden was soon reinforced, most notably by Fitz Lee's cavalry and Heth's division, and the attacks were repulsed. Gilmor, however, lost consciousness and toppled to the ground. "I cannot say whether I was stunned by a shell, or fell from exhaustion," he wrote later. He woke up as a prisoner of war. Later that night, his two guards fell asleep, and he recovered his pistols and saber. He considered killing his erstwhile guards but could not bring himself to shoot sleeping men; instead, he made good his escape and reached Confederate lines three days later.[260]

---

[258] Johnston, n.p.
[259] Also known as the Battle of Hagerstown or Falling Waters.
[260] Gilmor, pp. 101–103

CHAPTER XVI

ON ALL FRONTS

After the failed Union amphibious attack on Fort Sumter (September 8–9, 1863),[261] several South Carolina Rangers were detached to escort them to a prison camp at Columbia. They arrived in the South Carolina capital about dark, turned in the prisoners, and were scheduled to return to Charleston via train the next day.

That night, some of the men wandered around town, looking for fun and entertainment. They strolled into a bar/restaurant, where the proprietor was about to raffle off a fifty-pound turkey. He offered sixty raffle tickets at fifty cents a ticket. It was agreed that the winner would buy drinks for everyone present.

While this was going on, Andrew Cunningham of the Rangers went to the back room and found himself alone with the gobbler, who was in a coop. He pulled his knife, decapitated the bird, and exited through the back door, leaving only the head. Meanwhile, the lottery was concluded and the winner stood drinks for all present. All the Rangers helped themselves liberally to the free whiskey. Then several men went to the rear of the building to see the turkey that was just raffled off. When only the head was found, some of them accused the bar owner of fraud, in spite of his pleas of innocence, and guns were drawn. The Rangers shot out the lights, and in the darkness, they confiscated (stole) all of the liquor, each Ranger helping

---

[261] Sometimes called the Second Battle of Fort Sumter.

himself to several bottles. The next morning, on the train to Charleston, they ate the turkey and consumed numerous bottles of adult beverages.[262]

The Confederate supply of tin was very short. Church bells contained tin and copper, of which there was an abundance. A twenty-four-hundred-pound bell contained enough tin for a six-gun battery. School house bells and plantation bells were also contributed.[263]

Meanwhile, the Yankees conquered east Tennessee and captured Chattanooga.

Confederate Brigadier General John W. Frazer surrendered Cumberland Gap to U.S. General Burnside on September 9, 1863—without firing a shot. William J. Wilson of the 2nd North Carolina was among the prisoners. The officers were sent to Johnson's Island, Ohio, and the enlisted men were condemned to Camp Douglas, Illinois. Here, Wilson remained until the end of the war. Conditions were deplorable. About 250 men from Wilson's regiment died. "The rigid Northern climate was severe on us," Wilson recalled, "and the prison treatment was not altogether humane, but on the whole I suppose we fared better than the thousands of other Confederates who were on the field struggling for independence." The prisoners passed the time in a variety of activities, depending on the man. They including writing poetry and studying medicine or the law or studying for the ministry.[264]

In the meantime, General Lee sent James Longstreet's reduced I Corps (two divisions) to Georgia. It traveled 923 miles over some very questionable

---

[262] Brooks, *Stories*, pp. 236–237.
[263] Bankston, pp. 103–104.
[264] Yeary, II, p. 811.

railroads and surprised Rosecrans's Army of the Cumberland at Chickamauga. For the first time on the western front, the Army of Tennessee outnumbered its opponents, if only slightly (sixty-two thousand to sixty thousand). The battle, which occurred on September 19 and 20, ended in a rout of half the Union army and a stinging defeat for the North.

J. C. Robinson of the 1st Texas Infantry Regiment (part of Hood's command) fought at Chickamauga. He fought on the eastern front from 1861 to 1863. He was alone and cut off at Gettysburg but managed to escape, just barely, as he was pursued by a squad of Union cavalry. At Chickamauga, a ball struck the left side of his chin, passed through his mouth, struck his right jaw bone, and broke it. Eventually, a physician extracted it from the right side of his neck.

Robinson never completely recovered from his wound and was finally discharged from the service in early 1865. "My wound has caused me suffering every day since I received it, and will continue until the end," he recalled in 1910. "Still if I were asked if I regretted having enlisted in the Confederate army, I would answer no, for I believe today, just as I did then, and would rather suffer as I do today than to have remorse of conscience for not having done my duty."[265]

In every army, there are officers and men who gravitate to the rear areas and are "invisible in war but invincible in peace." The Rebels referred to these men as "bombproof officers" because they were often found in bunkers, which were called "bombproofs." The Southern army seems to had have had fewer of this type than any other army on the planet. In its rear areas, one was more likely to find men like P. A. Smith or Zebulon York.

P. A. Smith joined the 39th Alabama. He fought in the Kentucky (Heartland) Campaign of 1862, including the Battles of Munfordville and Perryville. He also survived the hell of the Second Murfreesboro. His luck ran out at Chickamauga on September 20, 1863, when he was

265   Yeary, II, pp. 647–648.

shot through both arms. The muscles in his right arm were smashed. His three lower fingers drew crooked and could not be straightened, so he could only use the thumb and forefinger on his right hand. He was sent to Columbus, Georgia, on post (rear area) duty. He was paroled there on April 26, 1865.[266]

Zebulon York and his partner were the largest realty tax payers in Louisiana in 1861. They owned six plantations and fifteen hundred slaves—making them among the largest slaveholders in the United States. York, who was a native of Maine, raised the 14th Louisiana Infantry Regiment at his own expense but, because he had no military experience, initially refused to take a rank beyond that of captain. He nevertheless rose to brigadier general, despite being wounded at Williamsburg, Gaines' Mill, and the Second Manassas.

His luck ran out at the Third Battle of Winchester (September 19, 1864). His left arm was shattered by grapeshot as he charged a Union battery. Physicians in a field hospital amputated the arm. Meanwhile, the Confederate forces were defeated. A friend from Winchester tried to get him to come to his home where he could be taken care of. York replied that the enemy would never capture him—although they could have the arm. He then mounted a horse (!) and rode more than twenty miles to Fisher's Hill. There he got into an ambulance and rode to Staunton, where he got on a train for Richmond.

Frankly, it takes one heck of a fighter to ride a horse twenty miles after just having an arm amputated.

No longer fit for field duty, General York engaged in recruiting in North Carolina until the fall of Richmond. On April 12, 1865, he had the task of defending the Yadkin River Railroad Bridge against Stoneman's Union cavalry division of more than five thousand men. His troops consisted of about eleven hundred invalided soldiers, Home Guards, junior reserves, walking wounded, a few civilian employees, and about three hundred "galvanized Irish." Fortunately, Stoneman sent only a brigade of twelve hundred men and a battalion of artillery to attack York. General

---

[266] Yeary, II, p. 704.

York defeated the Federals in a battle that lasted five and a half hours. York's success kept Jefferson Davis's escape route to the south open. It was the last Confederate battlefield victory in North Carolina.

Zebulon's grandfather was Sylvester York, an aide-de-camp to General George Washington during the American Revolution.

As was usual for him, Braxton Bragg lost his nerve after the Battle of Chickamauga and instead of pursuing Rosecrans's beaten forces, lay siege of Chattanooga. The Yankees were allowed to rally, regain their balance, build up their forces, and break the siege in the Battles of Lookout Mountain (November 24) and Missionary Ridge (November 25). Much of Bragg's army was routed and retreated into northern Georgia, where Bragg submitted his resignation on December 2. He was initially replaced by Lieutenant General William J. Hardee (December 2–16) and then by Joseph E. Johnston.

In Virginia, the Army of the Potomac clashed with the Army of Northern Virginia in two indecisive operations: the Bristoe Station campaign (October 13–November 7) and the Mine Run campaign (November 26–December 2). Compared with previous operations, losses were not high.

In the second half of 1863, there was a considerable amount of patrolling and skirmishing in northern Virginia. Major Harry Gilmor's horses were nearly exhausted when they reached "White House," a plantation home near Summit Point, Virginia. Gilmor was talking with the ladies of the area when a bullet slammed between him and the women. "Here they are, boys! By G-d, we've got them now!" a Yankee roared. "I wheeled round and saw the head of a cavalry column on the rocky hill above," Gilmor wrote later, "and between me and Summit Point."

Seeing retreat was impossible, Gilmor decided to fight it out as best he could. Taken by surprise, the Rebel detachment (about fifty men) was completely disorganized. Fortunately for them, U.S. Captain Somers's company (about sixty men) would not charge, despite his urgings. "Captain Somers, who I must say was a brave man, spurred his horse down the hill, and engaged me with his pistol, firing wildly, for I saw he was much excited. I reserved my fire till he came within twenty paces, steadied my horse with the bit, took a long, sure aim, and Somers fell from his horse. The ball entered the side of his nose, and came out at the back of his head."

"Come, boys, it's a shame to leave the major there by himself," one of the troops shouted. The Confederates dashed forward, and a saber fight ensued. Gilmor noted a Union officer "fighting like a Turk." He shouted: "Come on, you damned rebel! I'll soon fix your flint."

"This promised good sport," Gilmor wrote later. He charged the officer and swung his saber. The Yankee parried the blow and cut at Gilmor's neck. The major brought his saber down in time, so his side caught the blow. Gilmor struck him in the cheek and created a large gash. The Federal fell to the ground and was quickly taken prisoner by one of Gilmor's men.

The Rebels lost one man killed, three wounded, and one captured in the skirmish. The Northerners lost four dead, three wounded, and twenty-three captured. Gilmor's men also took twenty-nine horses.[267]

Confederates not only fought Yankees; they also fought disease and Indians. Richard G. Walker of the 15th Texas fought at Corinth on the Western Front before being transferred to the Little Rock sector in the Trans-Mississippi Department, where he fought against U.S. General Samuel Curtis's Army of the Southwest. "Here the measles struck the army, and twelve hundred were buried before a drop of rain fell on their graves. I had measles and came so near dying that the doctors said I had consumption and gave me a discharge and I went home. After I had been at home about three months I joined a company to protect the frontier from Indian depredations, as the Indians were killing and carrying off women and

---

[267] Gilmor, pp. 108–110.

children and stealing horses. I was detailed as a special scout, and did some hard scouting and fighting. Four of us were attacked by eighteen Indians, and after some hard fighting we repulsed them and followed their trail and found where they had stolen children, recapturing them and brought them back."[268]

Walker joined a militia company and remained on the frontier until the war was practically over.

One cold winter night in 1863, Phoebe Pember, the Matron of Chimborazo Hospital in Richmond, was awakened by a nurse who said there was something wrong with Fisher. He was a favorite of hers—a nice, handsome young man, about twenty years old. He had been severely wounded high up on the leg ten months before and now was given a fair chance of recovering, although one leg would always be shorter than the other. Pember said he was "so gentle-mannered and uncomplaining that we all loved him."

She discovered that he had turned over in bed and part of a splintered bone had severed an artery. When he turned down his cover, a small jet of blood shot up. The artery could not be restored. "No earthly power could save him."

"The hardest trial of my duty was laid upon me," she recalled, "the necessity of telling a man in the prime of life, and fullness of strength that there was no hope for him."

Fisher took the news "patiently and courageously." He gave some directions for informing his mother about his death. "How long can I live?" he asked.

"Only as long as I keep my finger upon this artery," she replied.

There ensued a pause. "God alone knew what thoughts hurried through that heart and brain, called so unexpectedly from all earthly hopes and ties," she recalled. Finally, he said: "You can let go."

---

[268]   Yeary, II, p. 772.

But she could not. Tears poured down her checks. For the first and last time during the war, Phoebe Pember fainted.

"No words can do justice to the uncomplaining nature of the Southern soldier," she wrote later. "Whether it arose from resignation or merely passive submission, yet when shown in the aggregate in a hospital, it was sublime. Day after day, whether lying wasted by disease or burning up with fever, torn with wounds or sinking from debility, a groan was seldom heard. The wounded wards would be noisily gay with singing, laughing, fighting battles o'ver and o'ver [sic] again, and playfully chaffing each other..."[269]

Large-scale desertion was a problem for the Confederate army in the latter part of 1863. A typical example was the Rebel private who received a letter from home. It read: "Dear Will: The Yankees have raided our home and left nothing. I fear the children and me will starve. Our neighbors are not able to help us. Come home if you can honorably, but *don't desert.*"

The man asked for a furlough, but it was denied. He deserted that night but was caught, arrested, court-martialed, and shot.[270]

Others were treated with more leniency. Thomas J. Lokey of the 48th Georgia received a letter from his wife "that made it necessary for me to go home." He applied for furlough but it was denied, so he went anyway. "Of course, I knew that I had technically deserted, no matter for my intentions, and I realized the danger, but relied on my protector [God]." After he returned to his regiment, he was court-martialed and sentenced to thirty days on bread and water, but the sentence was never carried out. "My protector stayed by me on this occasion as he has on many others since."[271]

Most of the desertions from the Confederate army occurred late in the war. The men knew their families were suffering and even starving. One case in particular touched the heart of Colonel Cullen Battle (later major general) of the Army of Northern Virginia.

---

[269] Pember, pp. 74–77.
[270] Bowman, pp. 50–51.
[271] Yeary, II, p. 447.

Edward Cooper, a young artilleryman, was charged with desertion. He pled not guilty. He had no counsel and represented himself. The judge advocate had no difficulty sustaining every charge and specification. He called no witnesses on his own behalf.

"Astonished at the calmness with which he seemed to be submitting to what he regarded as inevitable fate," General Battle recalled, "I said to him, 'Have you no defense? Is it possible that you abandoned your comrades and deserted your colors in the presence of the enemy without any reason?'"

Cooper replied: "There was a reason, but it will not avail me before a military court."

Battle said that he might be mistaken. He reminded Cooper that he was charged with the highest crime known to military law, and he should make known what influenced his actions.

With tears in his eyes, young Cooper handed a letter to Battle, and soon the colonel's eyes also filled with tears. He passed it around the court, from one individual to another, until "those stern warriors who had passed with Stonewall Jackson through a hundred battles wept like little children." It was from Cooper's wife, and it read:

My Dear Edward:

I have always been proud of you, and since your connection with the Confederate army I have been prouder of you than ever before. I would not have you do anything wrong for the world; but before God, Edward, unless you come home we must die. Last night I was aroused by little Eddie's crying. I called and said, 'What's the matter, Eddie?" and he said, "Oh, mamma, I'm so hungry." And Lucy, Edward, your darling Lucy, she never complains, but she is growing thinner and thinner every day. And before God, Edward, unless you come home we must die.

Your Mary

Battle questioned Cooper and learned that he had twice applied for furlough after receiving the letter and had twice been rejected. Then, thinking in his mind's eye of his starving young daughter, he deserted.

Cooper reached his home, and Mary ran out to embrace him. "O, Edward, I am so happy. I am so glad you got your furlough."

Feeling her husband stiffen, she immediately realized what had happened and turned pale. "Have you come back without your furlough?" she asked. Without waiting for an answer, she told him he must go back. He did.

Every officer on the court-martial was moved, but they had no choice but to render a guilty verdict. The punishment for desertion was death. The case was sent to Robert E. Lee for confirmation. His answer was brief. "The finding of the court is approved. The prisoner is pardoned and will report to his company. R. E. Lee, General."

In a later battle, Cullen Battle was informed that one of his batteries had been silenced by the concentrated fire of the enemy. He rushed to the scene to discover every gun but one was dismounted. Only one soldier stood by the surviving gun. It was Edward Cooper, and he had blood streaming from his side. He recognized Battle immediately.

"General, I have one shell left. Tell me, have I saved the honor of Mary and Lucy?" he asked.

General Battle raised his hat. Cooper fired the last round. "Once more a Confederate shell went crashing through the ranks of the enemy, and the hero sank by his gun to rise no more."[272]

Other cases of desertion were more base. One fellow enlisted with the assurance from a wealthy planter that he would look after the man's wife and child while he was gone. After the soldier left, the planter made indecent propositions to the young wife and refused to give or sell her any food unless she yielded. The soldier twice asked for a furlough, but his application was rejected.

The young soldier deserted, kidnapped the planter, dragged him into the woods, tied him to a tree, and thoroughly flogged him. Assured his wife would receive better treatment, he returned to his regiment just as it was about to go into battle. He performed with such courage that his officers decided not to prosecute him, although he was technically a deserter for a short period.

---

[272] CWA, pp. 209–211.

Other desertions were treated more severely. In April 1864, General Forrest overran Fort Pillow, Tennessee. His attack was spearheaded by Tyree Bell's West Tennessee brigade. They faced the "homegrown Yankees" of the 13th Tennessee (U.S.) Cavalry Regiment. The Rebels knew many of the men in the Union ranks to be deserters from the Confederate army. After the order to attack was given, they overran the position in about five minutes and captured sixty-four deserters. All but seventeen of them were spared the ordeal of a long trial (i.e., they were forced to their knees and shot in the back of the head).

From November 1863 to May 1864, there was a lull on the western front. The Army of Tennessee was plagued by desertion. An unofficial agreement was reached between Joseph E. Johnston, the army commander, and the deserters. If they remained at home—where they were plowing the fields before planting season—until sent for, and then returned to the colors, nothing would be done to them when they rejoined the army. When Sherman began his drive on Atlanta in early May 1864, most of these men did come back. General Johnston kept his end of the unofficial bargain and these men were not prosecuted. Many of them, however, were killed or maimed during the struggle for Atlanta.

After Atlanta fell on September 2, 1864, many Southern soldiers decided—quite correctly—that the war was lost. Desertions picked up considerably after that.

General Lee had a problem with desertion as early as the Sharpsburg campaign. It was worse in February 1864, when he wrote that he feared "nothing but the death penalty, uniformly, inexorably administered, will stop it."[273]

---

[273] O.R., Vol. XXXIII, pp. 164, 168.

On February 2, 1864, Confederate forces under George Pickett captured fifty-three "buffaloes" or homegrown Yankees, i.e., North Carolinians serving in the Union army. (They belonged to Company F, 2nd North Carolina [Union] Volunteer Infantry.) Many of its men had deserted the Confederate army. Several were from the 66th North Carolina (Confederate) Infantry. Some of them stated that they were drafted into the Union army or intimidated into enlisting. Some were promised enlistment bonuses of one hundred to three hundred dollars.

When they were captured, the men of Company F were initially treated as prisoners of war. Many of Pickett's men, however, were from North Carolina. They identified the "buffaloes" as Confederate deserters. Pickett declared that "every G_____d man who didn't do his duty, or deserted, ought to be shot or hung." He told one of them: "I'll have you shot, and all other damned rascals who desert."

Pickett carried out his threat. He set up courts-martial, which were organized to convict. Twenty-two of the deserters were hanged in Kinston, North Carolina on February 22, 1864, in some cases in front of their wives and children. Most of the rest of the prisoners from Company F were sent to the newly opened prison at Andersonville, Georgia.

U.S. General Benjamin Butler and Abraham Lincoln called for retaliation. Grant, who become general-in-chief of the Union army in March 1864, disagreed. He wrote to Confederate General Joseph E. Johnston: "I would claim no right to retaliate for the punishment of deserters who had actually been mustered into the Confederate army and afterwards deserted and joined ours." He was also not inclined to punish Pickett after the surrender. They were friends since West Point, and their friendship survived the war. Secretary of War Stanton, however, ordered an investigation of General Pickett, who became alarmed and fled to Montreal with his family. A board of inquiry was called and recommended a trial, and Judge Advocate Holt wanted Pickett arrested, but Grant took the matter to President Andrew Johnson in March 1866. He called Pickett "an honorable man." He also pointed out that a trial would reopen old wounds and lead Southerners to question whether or not the government intended to honor the "contract entered into to secure the surrender of an armed enemy."

The matter was effectively ended when Grant was elected president of the United States. In 1868, he even offered Pickett an appointment as marshal of the Commonwealth of Virginia, but the general declined it. He died in obscurity in Norfolk in 1875.[274]

Meanwhile, a great many prominent people became refugees.

Judith Brockenbrough McGuire was born in 1813, the daughter of William Brockenbrough, a Virginia State Supreme Court justice. She married John P. McGuire (1800–1869), an Episcopal clergyman who became principal of the Episcopal high school in Alexandria, Virginia. Reverend McGuire introduced a new system of reporting grades—the report card. It was later adopted by virtually the entire public school education system in the United States.

The McGuires had two sons and several daughters. Reverend McGuire was elected to the Virginia Secession Convention and voted to leave the Union. He and his sons enlisted in the Confederate army when the war began; the women were forced to become refugees. Initially, they stayed in Richmond, but the rent was too high. Later, they settled in Lynchburg and then Charlotte. They resorted to making a living selling soap.

In November 1863, Mrs. McGuire obtained a clerk's job in the Confederate army's commissary department. She and thirty-five other women worked eight hours a day (7 a.m. to 3 p.m.) and were paid $125 a month. She also worked as a volunteer nurse.

---

[274] Donald E. Collins, "War Crime or Justice? General George Pickett and the Mass Execution of Deserters in Civil War Kinton, North Carolina," in Steven E. Woodworth, ed., *The Art of Command in the Civil War* (1998), pp. 50–83, accessed at http://homepages.rootsweb.com/~ncuv/kinston1.htm.

CHAPTER XVII

LULL AND THE HOME FRONT

"**N**ow," Constance Cary wrote, "came the winter's lull before the new fury of the storm should break forth with the spring. It was evident to all older and graver people that the iron belt surrounding the Southern country was being gradually drawn closer and her vitality in mortal peril of exhaustion. Our armies were dwindling, those of the North increasing with every draft and the payment of liberal bounties. Starved, nearly bankrupt, thousands of our best soldiers killed in battle, their places filled by boys and old men, the Federal Government refusing to exchange prisoners; our exports useless because of armed ships closing in our ports all along the coast, our prospects were of the gloomiest, even though Lee had won victory for our banners in the East. We young ones, who knew nothing and refused to believe in 'croakers,' kept on with our valiant boasting about our invincible army and the like; but the end was beginning to be in sight."[275]

There is a military adage that goes: "Amateurs discuss battles; professionals discuss logistics." Although this is not literally true, there is a great deal

---

[275]   Harrison, p. 166.

of truth in it. Most readers do not understand the huge amount of supplies, ammunition, and material an army consumes. King and Derby give us some indication of the huge supply demands of the Union army by listing the amount consumed by a single division—Henry Dwight's 2nd Division of Edward O. C. Ord's U.S. XVIII Corps, which was besieging Petersburg. A partial list of its supply requirements for August 1864 is as follows:

> Pork, 448 barrels
> Bacon, 13,109 barrels
> Ham 1,434 barrels
> Salt Beef, 76 barrels
> Fresh beef, 51,155 pounds
> Flour (soft bread) 528 barrels
> Dried applies, 4,611 pounds
> Coffee, 13,510 lbs
> Tea, 1,392 lbs
> Brown sugar, 42,469 lbs
> White sugar, 7,333 lbs
> Salt fish 15,205 lbs
> Candies, 3,075 lbs
> Potatoes, 69,066 lbs
> Hard bread (hardtack), 141,883 lbs
> Onions, 25,068 lbs
> Beets, 5,251 lbs
> Beans, 30,772 lbs
> Salt, 10,962 lbs
> Rice, 3,619 lbs
> Whiskey, 4,198 gallons.[276]

These figures include only foodstuffs for one month—not weapons, ammunition, medical supplies, or forage for horses and mules. The Army of the Potomac alone had fourteen divisions, as well as several independent

---

[276] King and Derby, p. 111.

brigades. These figures exclude several major commands. In the East alone, the Union had to supply the Middle Department (defending Maryland); the XXII Corps (defending Washington, D.C.); the Department of Virginia and North Carolina; the Department of the Susquehanna; the Department of West Virginia; and the Army of the Shenandoah, which alone had ten divisions. (Lee's entire army only totaled nine infantry and two cavalry divisions.) Several of these Union divisions were cavalry units and thus had higher supply requirements because horses also have to eat. Much of the supplies were taken from occupied areas within the South.

As they passed Petersburg on their way to North Carolina, several members of Pickett's division took a spot of unauthorized leave. One of them, Private Gardner, left wearing an old dingy hat. When he returned, he had a new, fine-looking hat. His comrades asked him about the change. "I swapped [hats] with a fellow," Gardner declared, "but he wasn't there."[277]

The 7th Virginia spent much of the winter at Taylorsville, Virginia, from November 1863 to January 1864. "Our rations were not abundant while at Taylorsville; one pint of unsieved meal and a quarter of a pound of bacon per day. Coffee was made of parched wheat, rye, and sometimes of rice when we had it." Occasionally, the men managed to get turnips or potatoes, of which they made fairly good soup. "There was so little of the bacon that we could not afford to fry it, so we generally ate it raw, with an ash or Johnny cake; we had but few cooking utensils, and had need of few."[278]

On January 20, they began a movement to Goldsboro, North Carolina, and on January 29, to Kinston, and to the New Bern sector. Here, they blew up a Union gunboat, captured a section of the 3rd New York Artillery (two guns), and several hundred prisoners. Some of them were from the

---

[277] Johnston, n. p.
[278] Johnston, n.p.

"2nd Loyal North Carolina Regiment," which included at least thirty-five deserters from the Southern army. They were recognized. Twenty-two of them were tried and executed.[279]

As 1864—the fourth year of the war—dawned, life was tough everywhere in the South. This was especially true in some of the rural areas which were overrun by the enemy. Often, law and order broke down completely.

Daniel Jeffers joined the Confederate army and left home for three years. He left his wife at home on the farm with two small children and no source of income. She had a young horse that a fifteen-year-old boy was unable to make work, so she broke it herself and plowed the field day after day. Her husband's brother came over occasionally to help her with the worst of the work.

After Confederate General Thomas Hindman retreated from Prairie Grove, small bands of marauders, rogue Yankees, bushwhackers, and outlaws raided the countryside and tortured old men and women for their valuables, usually by applying burning wood or hot coals to the soles of their feet. Often, these people had no valuables, which only made the outlaws madder.

Often, they appeared at Mrs. Jeffers's home and demanded she prepare them a meal, despite the fact she had little food. Her husband obtained a furlough and came home, but the 13th Kansas learned of it. He escaped into the woods. The Yankees entered her home and informed Mrs. Jeffers that they killed her husband. The ensuing hours were some of the worst of her life. The Federals, however, were lying. About 9 p.m., she heard her spouse's voice. He would not enter his home because enemy scouts were camped about a half a mile away, and he was afraid they were watching the house. She had little to offer. All the raiders left her was a small piece of meat and some corn they spilled and walked over.

Later, Mrs. Jeffers learned that her husband was captured and held at Van Buren, Arkansas, about forty miles away. She rode there with her baby, only to be cursed out by the commandant of the post, who turned his back

---

[279] Johnston, n.p.

on her. She made repeated appeals until the colonel realized she wasn't going to go away. He finally allowed her to spend the night with Mr. Jeffers in his cell, provided she promise to return home in the morning. When she left, she was sick in body and spirit, convinced that she would never see her husband alive again. Mr. Jeffers, however, was resourceful. He escaped the following night and reached home before his wife and child.[280]

M. C. Livingston of Hope, Arkansas, enlisted in the Confederate Army and left his wife at home with five children, ages ten years to six weeks. Mrs. Livingston hired the wheat sowed, raised her own meat, and bought corn. She taught two of her children how to card and spin, and they made yards of cloth, which they sold for corn. The quartermasters encouraged the women to weave jeans for sale to the Confederate government, so Mrs. Livingston had a little money all the time. She also traded jeans to a tanner, who made their shoes.

Federal raiders killed some of her cattle and stole all her honey, butter, and eggs, and all the chickens they could catch. They did not abuse any of them, however, and Mrs. Livingston felt she was treated better than many of her neighbors.

Isolated on the farm, she did not run the risk of going into town due to raiders and outlaws. She could not send her children to school, so she homeschooled them. She did not go to church for two years and felt guilty about that, but read her Bible daily.[281]

When Dorton Clark when off to war, he left his wife with four little girls to provide for. They had no shoes. She had to work hard every day just to keep a roof over their heads. Their staple food was roasted potatoes and boiled vegetables, and roasting ears (corn) was a welcomed treat. The only

---

[280] CWA, pp. 156–157.
[281] CWA, pp. 97–98.

seasoning was salt, and there was no meat. They drank Sassafras tea[282] and coffee made from potatoes. The children picked cotton, and their mother spun and wove the cloth to provide clothing.[283]

Women often had to think fast in order to save their homes, their loved ones, or their food supply. The Confederate army in Arkansas was in retreat. One lady, the "Ole Miss" of a plantation, stopped the commander of the rearguard. She asked where the Yankees were and if he planned to make a stand before they reached her plantation.

No, the Rebel cavalryman replied. The Yankees were about two miles behind him and should be here in thirty minutes. He resumed his retreat.

The Ole Miss knew that the Yankees would loot her smokehouse, which meant she, her family, and her servants would have no meat for the winter. Thinking quickly, she rushed into the smokehouse, grabbed a ham, stuck a knife in it, and twisted it, creating a hole. She did this with each ham as well as other pieces of meat and instructed her slaves to toss them out onto the lawn.

When the Northern cavalry arrived, they were astonished to see dozens of hams lying in the yard. Their officer asked the Ole Miss to tell him why hams were everywhere.

"The Confederate cavalry did that," she explained. She added that the Yankee could take the hams if he wished, but not to blame her if his men died of poisoning. In the mind of the Northern officer, that explained the holes in the hams.

When the bluecoats left, none of the hams had been touched.

Clothing became scarce. A calico dress was considered a luxury, and the ladies' hats were made of palmetto, which was grown in the swamps,

---

[282] A beverage made from boiling the root bark of the Sassafras tree. It tastes like root beer.
[283] Story by Mrs. L. A. Eason of De Queen, Arkansas, CWA p 53–54.

boiled, bleached in the sun until it was almost white, and was then split, braided, and sewn into a hat. The girls became experts at it, and the hats were said to be beautiful. The girls also made their own shoes, which were soled by a cobbler. They were proud of their homespun dresses. Real coffee was not obtainable, so they used sweet potatoes (dried and parched), burnt molasses, parched meal, and parched rye. Tea was made from willow bark fodder and was used as a medicine. The women—many of whom had never made a male garment—created whole suits of clothes, complete with undergarments. They also scoured the woods for roots and barks to dye the uniforms they made Confederate gray. "There was no sacrifice too great to make for our country and our boys in gray."[284] Some of the women formed societies and wrote cheerful letters to Rebel soldiers. Almost all of them knitted socks. When society women in Camden, Arkansas, and other places, made social calls, they walked to their appointments and knitted along the way. The conversation was accompanied by the click of knitting needles.

School children had a problem studying in winter and autumn. The days were shorter and there were no lights. There was no tallow, even for the little tallow lamps. Cows were all but extinct in most districts, so they were never killed, which eliminated them as a source of tallow, and hog fat was eaten. All that was left to use was pine torches for outside and a fireplace for inside

Sometimes, women might sell cotton to the Yankees, even though it was against Confederate law. To other women, this was an act of treason.

"...our breakfast, at 8 A.M., consisting of corn-bread with the drippings of fried bacon instead of butter, and coffee made of dried beans and peanuts,

---

[284] CMA, pp. 39–40.

without milk or sugar," Constance Cary recalled. "For luncheon we had, day in and day out, bacon, rice, and dried apples sweetened with sorghum. For our evening repast were served cakes made of corn-meal and water, eaten with sorghum molasses, and more of that unspeakable coffee. I cannot remember getting up from any meal that winter without wishing there were more of it. I went once to call upon a family antecedently wealthy, and found father, mother, and children making their dinner upon soup-plates filled with that cheerless compound known as 'Benjamin' hard-tack, soaked in hot water, sprinkled with salt or brown sugar. It is to be said, however, there was in our community no discussion of diets, fads, or cures, and the health chase of modern society was an unknown quantity. People in better physical condition than the besieged dwellers of Richmond..."[285]

Clothes were also in short supply. Worn-out garments could not be replaced. If two sisters were in a family, they went out singly, so the same dress could do double duty. "We borrowed, loaned, patched, lengthened, shortened, turned and twisted our garments until there was nothing left of them," Mrs. De Fontaine of Harrison, Arkansas, recalled.[286]

One Richmond belle at a starvation party was asked why she was not dancing. (They were called "starvation parties" because no food was served and water was the only beverage available.) She replied that she was in a borrowed dress which was too small, and she did not dare to laugh, much less dance, for fear she would burst the dress into pieces, and it was all her friend had.[287]

She wasn't the only one in ill-fitting clothes. John S. Wise of Virginia attended a similar party. He had no coat of his own, so he borrowed one from a larger friend, who was almost twice his size. The sleeves of the coat completely covered his hands, and the skirt of the coat hung several inches below his knees. His first dance partner was a Richmond belle who was

---

[285] Harrison, p. 191.

[286] CWA, p. 94.

[287] CWA, p. 94.

wearing a dress which originally belonged to her great-grandmother and was made when she was pregnant. He realized that they presented a ridiculous sight and burst out laughing. His partner gave him an angry glare, stormed off, and never spoke to him again.[288]

The "Feds" raided the Dickson farm in the Pine Bluff area. They destroyed all they could and robbed anything of value. They stole twenty bales of cotton from the storehouse and five horses. They searched the house and took every article that had any value. Mr. S. D. Dickson was in the Confederate army, and Mrs. Dickson had two small children to care for.

The Dicksons had three large barns full of corn. It was hauled off in twenty wagons. The Feds stole two thousand pounds of meat and threatened to kill Mrs. Dickson if she did not give them the key to a trunk. They killed or stole all the cattle. Sometimes, the family was without any food for a day and a half.

Her servants continued to work the farm with hoes because there were no animals to pull the plow. Mrs. Dickson worked right alongside them.

Judge James Green and his wife lived near Dalton in northern Georgia. They were wealthy. They sent six sons, who fought in battles from Virginia to Texas, in the Confederate army. Judge Green was too old to fight himself, but he offered his services to the Confederacy as a hospital worker. His offer was accepted, and he was named superintendent of the hospital at Tunnel Hill, Georgia. His wife was accustomed to a life of leisure, wealth, and comfort. She nevertheless pitched in and became matron of Judge Green's hospital. She worked day and night throughout the war, selflessly sacrificing herself for the sick and wounded soldiers. Mrs. Green was

---

[288]   CWA, p. 118.

fearless. She would go into the smallpox wards and nurse the men with her own hands.

In 1863, Green sold his plantation near Dalton and sent his slaves to a cotton plantation he owned in Hempstead County, Arkansas. Green remained with his hospital, which was moved to south Georgia as the Yankees advanced on Tunnel Hill. Later, it was relocated to Columbus, Mississippi, and Forsythe, Georgia, where it was when the war ended.

The stress of hospital work and the constant worry about her sons broke down Mrs. Green; she never fully recovered her health, although she did live to be seventy-six. Post-war, the Greens lived in Hope, Arkansas, where the judge served as county treasurer.[289]

Meanwhile, the armies went into winter quarters.

Confederate winter quarters were highly varied and depended on the material at hand. A favorite makeshift accommodation for two men was a large oak log, cut in half, with straw placed in between. The opening was covered with a rubber blanket in case of rain. Others built straw pens, several logs high, with a fly tent serving as a roof. Sometimes a chimney was added. Dry, clean straw was spread on the floor, followed by their blankets. Others slept in haystacks, barns, stables, porches, or for the very lucky, feather beds.

The infantry and cavalry tended to build "shelters" opened to the south, covered with brush or pine limbs. They built large fires in front of them.

While enjoying the makeshift accommodations, the Rebels built log cabins, usually one mess per cabin. Nails, door hinges, and the like were sent from home. Logs were cut from nearby forests and the gaps between the logs were sealed by clay. There were so many that they resembled villages. They also had makeshift chimneys. Several cords of firewood were stored in the cabins.

---

[289] CWA, p. 159.

Once the cabin was completed, the men usually received cloth parcels from home. Typically, they were wearing the same underwear and uniform for three months. They burned the old garments when clothes arrived from home. The boxes from home also often included bottles of whiskey, edibles, ink, pen, paper, and perhaps tobacco and a pipe. Most of it was shared by the mess.

For amusement, they played cards, had singings, revivals, church services, and games, which included huge snowball fights in which entire brigades participated. They played spin the top, marbles, hop-scotch, football, and other games. One of the happier activities was a visit to the unit's amateur barber, who might even give them a shave.[290]

On rare occasions, the family of a soldier would visit winter quarters. They were received with great hospitality. Additionally, many soldiers who not needed due to the lack of active campaigns were given furloughs.

Robert E. Lee

Most of the generals suffered with their men. In early 1864, the Mobile *Advertiser* wrote: "In General Lee's tent, meat is eaten but twice a week, the

---

[290] McCarthy, pp. 88–92.

General not allowing it oftener, because he believes indulgence in meat to be criminal in the present straitened condition of the country. His ordinary dinner consists of a head of cabbage boiled in salt water, and a pone of corn bread. Having invited a number of gentlemen to dine with him, General Lee, in a fit of extravagance, ordered a sumptuous repast of bacon and cabbage. The dinner was served and behold, a great pile of cabbage and a bit of bacon, or 'middling,' about four inches long and two inches across. The guests, with commendable politeness, unanimously declined the bacon, and it remained in the dish untouched. Next day General Lee, remembering the delicate titbit which had been so providentially preserved, ordered his servant to bring that 'middling.' The man hesitated, scratched his head, and finally owned up.

"'Marse Robert—de fac' is—dat ar middlin' was borrowed middlin'. We-all. didn' have no middlin'. I done paid it back to de place whar I got it fum.

"General Lee heaved a sigh of deepest disappointment, and pitched into the cabbage."[291]

Meanwhile, cavalry skirmishing continued. Near the Mount Airy, Virginia, estate of Dr. A. R. Meem, Major Harry Gilmor and his Maryland cavalry battalion launched a night attack on a Union camp and achieved a measure of surprise. "I must do them the justice to say that they fought desperately, firing from their blankets as they lay behind their shelters, and it was with difficulty that any could be secured." The Yankees were forced to retreat to a log house after setting fire to the shelters. The flames illuminated the Rebels, three of whom were shot. They attacked the house but could not force the door. Gilmor's cousin Willie was shot in the arm. Major Gilmor ordered him to mount his horse and go to Dr. Meem's home, where the ladies would dress his wound. Willie looked at him incomprehensively. "But, major, I've got two loads left!" he snapped. "Blaze away," Gilmor replied.

---

[291] Pryor, p. 268.

The major decided to burn the building. He gathered an armful of fodder and started for the house. He was within a step of it when a bullet struck the window sill and glanced off, throwing splinters into the major's face. Thinking he was shot, he dropped the wood. He ran behind the corner and discovered his wound was not serious. At that moment, two Yankees came out the back door. Unfortunately, Gilmor's revolver was empty. He ordered the Yankees to surrender. "I'll be damned if I do!" their leader shouted. He drew his pistol.

"Quick as thought, I seized the barrel and turned it aside. It went off, and the leakage between the cylinder and the barrel burned my wrist. I tried to wrench the pistol from him, but he managed to cock it again, determined to make the muzzle bear on me," Gilmor remembered

"Give him hell, captain," one of the Federals shouted.

"We were standing on a sheet of ice," Gilmor recalled, "my foe being the stouter man. After he had discharged two more loads, my hand still upon the barrel, my feet slipped, and I fell to the ground." Gilmor thought he was dead. "The captain took as good aim as he could in the night and under the excitement of the moment. I moved not a muscle, though I seemed to feel the ball crashing through my brain. I closed my eyes. He fired, and my face was covered with an avalanche of mud and ice. The ball had entered the ground two inches from my skull! The whole scene occupied but a few moments; it seemed an age to me."

The Union captain thought Gilmor was dead. He fled into the weeds and willows on the bank of the river. Gilmor quickly rejoined his men. Another attack on the house failed. The Rebels had to settle for taking their horses, of which they captured twenty-six. Five Union horses were killed by random shots.[292]

Colonel William F. Slemons of Monticello, the commander of the 2nd Arkansas Cavalry, served as a brigade commander under Forrest and

---

[292] Gilmor, pp. 125–129.

Chalmers in Tennessee and Mississippi, and Chalmers thought highly of him.[293] A brigade commander, he was the odd man out when Forrest reorganized his cavalry on January 25, 1864. He was transferred to the Trans-Mississippi Department, but before reporting, he decided to spend a few days at home, even though he was warned that there were Federals in the area. On his first morning back, he went into Monticello to conduct some business.

Someone must have tipped off the Yankees. About 11 a.m., a faithful slave girl, Beck, called out to the colonel's wife, Martha Slemons, that soldiers were coming. They were Yankees. Martha first ran to gather up her small children, who were playing in a nearby grove. She was halted by the Northerners but was eventually allowed to proceed. Meanwhile, Beck concealed everything the colonel brought with him just before the enemy cavalrymen entered the house. They searched it from top to bottom but found nothing.

The Yankees then interrogated Beck. With what Willie Slemons (one of the children) called "the native cunning of her race," she told the enemy that they were "not spectin' Marse Williams for two or three days." The Yankees went away after taking three valuable horses.

Colonel Slemons, meanwhile, hid in the loft of the Jones Hotel until the bluecoats passed through town. He was on foot when he ran into Mrs. Howard, Martha's grandmother-in-law, who was on horseback. She at once dismounted and gave Slemons her favorite horse. He immediately headed for Louisiana to join General Kirby Smith, who assigned him to command a cavalry brigade in Sterling Price's command.

The next day, some of the same Federals reappeared. They learned they were duped. In revenge, they thoroughly looted the house, taking off everything they could carry, including silver, dishes, food, and even the

---

[293] O.R., Vol. XXXII, Part 2, p. 614. Slemons (1830–1918) was a delegate to the Arkansas Secession Convention and voted to leave the Union. He entered the army as a first lieutenant in the 2nd Arkansas Cavalry and was elected colonel in May 1862. He often led a brigade and was recommended for promotion to brigadier general but was never selected. He was captured at Mine Creek and spent the rest of the war in the Rock Island prison camp. He was a lawyer and a judge postwar, and was a U.S. congressman from 1875 to 1881. Allardice, *Colonels*, p. 344.

dinner cooking on the stove. The stock of sugar and meat was too heavy for them to carry, so they scattered it along the road. They had a wagon with them loaded with former slaves and tried to induce Beck to join them by offering freedom and money, but she refused. As they were leaving, they poured a bottle of turpentine in the hall and set it on fire. Beck and Mrs. Slemons, however, managed to put it out before much damage was done.

Union Major McCauley, the commander of his squadron, did not approve this second "visit" and was not with the thugs. He soon turned up at the Slemonses' place and apologized for the vandalism. Thinking William Slemons must still be in the area, he asked Martha to tell the colonel to surrender. He assured her that he would see to it that he was treated right. She replied that, when their meeting did take place, perhaps he wouldn't be so glad of it.

Mrs. Slemons was right. They were both present at Marks' Mill, where Confederate General Marmaduke wiped out a Union column of fourteen hundred men. Major McCauley was captured by Slemons's brigade. After the battle, McCauley met Slemons and said, "Well, Colonel, I'm not half as glad to see you as I thought I'd be when I sent a message to you by your wife."[294]

Two Confederate soldiers were on leave and visiting their home area in Augusta, Arkansas, which was then behind Union lines. One was the brother of Miss Kitty of Augusta, the other was her lover, and they were visiting her home when suddenly, the house was surrounded by Yankees. An informant had alerted them to the presence of the Rebels. The lover climbed up the chimney, out of sight. Kitty stood and pointed to her voluminous hoopskirt. The brother understood and immediately ducked under the skirt. When the Yankees entered, Kitty affected a careless attitude and stood there, combing her hair. The Federals searched the premises, found nothing, and left.[295]

---

[294] CWA, pp. 146–147.
[295] CWA, p. 23.

Mr. Wilson was a wealthy old gentleman living in Baily Springs, Alabama, with his two small nephews. He was sick in bed when the Yankees arrived and demanded his money. When he failed to hand it over, they piled papers saturated with turpentine on him and set them on fire. Wilson burned to death, along with one of his nephews. The other was injured but escaped. From then on, the community lived in terror. People were afraid to light their homes at night or even go out and bury their dead. The Northerners picketed the roads and prevented people from passing, so there was no commerce. People had to make everything at home.[296]

Most fared better than Mrs. Lutetia Howell, who lived in Pittsburg, Arkansas, about nine miles from Clarksville.[297] On the night of February 20, 1864, six Union soldiers entered her house and demanded her money. When she refused to hand it over, they stripped her right foot and leg and thrust them into the large, open fireplace. They took them out and again demanded money. She again refused. They said they would burn her to death if she did not meet their demands. Again, she said no. They burned her until her flesh fell off the leg from knee to toe. Seeing that they could not break Mrs. Howell, they tortured her widowed sister, Mrs. John W. Willis, in the same manner but not quite as badly. She did not yield, either.

The Yankees locked the Negro servants in their quarters and told them that, if they came out before sunrise, they would blow their heads off. At dawn, three black women came to the sisters and nursed them as best they could. Later that day, the bluecoats burned the Howell home and shot most of the pigs and cattle. As flames engulfed the house, some Federal officers arrived in an ambulance to collect furnishings. Instead, they took the two burned women to Clarksdale, where they received medical attention. Yankee doctors were forced to amputate Mrs. Howell's leg. She never recovered but lingered in pain for two years before she died. Among her last words were: "I forgive them for the pain and poverty they have caused me."

---

[296] CWA, pp. 194–150.

[297] Her son, Captain John B. Howell, was an ordnance officer on General James F. Fagan's staff.

What happened to the Howells was not an isolated incident but a deliberate policy of terrorism on the part of higher headquarters. Fourteen other homes were burned that day. Among them was the home of Mrs. Adams, the widow of Governor Samuel Adams and mother of General Fagan.

One Union officer visited Mrs. Howell's daughter and told her: "If my wife or mother had been treated as yours, I would live only to kill Federals and when I came to die, I would regret that I could not live longer to kill more."[298]

Mrs. Sue James of Hot Springs, Arkansas, decided to take refuge in Texas. She was visiting her mother near Benton when the Yankees overtook them. They killed the milk cows, calves, and chickens, devastated the garden and orchard, and emptied the smokehouse. Six of them sexually assaulted her pregnant cook, Julia, an African American, beat her severely, and knocked out four of her teeth. Mrs. James recalled that they were drunk, raw recruits, and "low-down foreigners" (i.e., mercenaries).

Later, one of the soldiers passed Mrs. James's gate and exposed himself indecently. He did not know that her husband gave her a small pistol which she managed to save. She pulled it and fired at him two times. He ran away like a rabbit shot at twice and reported her to his commander. They planned to send Mrs. James to the prison at Alton, Illinois, which was a death sentence. Fortunately for her, a Rebel spy informed her husband, Lieutenant Henry James, a member of General Cabell's staff, of their plans. (They did not act immediately because of the military situation.) Cabell sent a detachment of Confederate cavalry to carry Mrs. James and her babies to Columbus (Hempstead County), where General Cabell was headquartered.

Mrs. James later returned to Benton, where she was captured, and the Yankees burned her home. She was taken to Little Rock. Fortunately, she

---

[298] CWA, pp. 31–33.

was a friend of Chief Justice English and his wife. He obtained a permit from U.S. General Steele, allowing her to remain at his home under house arrest. She was eventually released, even though she steadfastly refused to take the Oath of Allegiance.[299]

Mrs. Laura A. Wooten of Corsicana, Arkansas, recalled the Yankees plundering her house, taking all their meat and virtually everything she had. Her mother pled with them, saying she was a poor widow with two girls to take care of. They called her a liar. They then asked Mrs. Wooten where her husband was. In the Confederate army, she replied, exactly where she wanted him to be.

They also looted the home of Mr. Brazel Wooten, her father-in-law, who was blind. They took all his horses, stripped the beds, stole the dishes from the pantry, took all the meat from the smokehouse, dumped the flour on the floor, and poured a barrel of molasses on top of it. They ordered Wooten's black slave cook to prepare their dinner and tried to get her to run away with them. When she refused, they plundered her house as well. "Why the great army of the North should have made war upon women and children is hard to understand," Mrs. Wooten concluded.[300]

The ethnic diversity of the Confederate army is not appreciated by many historians. They included Irish dock workers in the Louisiana Tigers, the German Fusiliers who defended Charleston, men of Mexican descendent who rode with the victorious Texas cavalry in the Red River Campaign, Native Americans who rode with General Gano, Stand Watie, the only Indian to become a general officer during the Civil War, and African American Confederates who served everywhere. One example of the

---

[299] CWA, pp. 101–111.
[300] CWA, pp. 52–53.

ethnically diverse nature of the Rebel army is Ambrosio José Gonzales, who was born in Matanzas, Cuba, in 1818.

When he was nine, Gonzales's father sent him to New York to be educated. One of his classmates was G. T. Beauregard, who became a lifelong friend. After four or five years, Gonzales returned to Cuba and finished his education at the University of Havana, where he earned a law degree. Young Gonzales, however, decided to pursue a career in education. He was a professor of languages at the University of Havana in 1848 when he decided to join a group of Cuban revolutionaries. A. J. (as he was called) became the rebels' de facto ambassador to the United States, where he met with General Worth, President Polk, Secretary of the Navy Mason, and Secretary of the Treasury Walker. There was serious talk about annexing the island to the United States—especially in the South, which wanted more slave state senators in Congress.

The junta declared Cuba independent in 1849. They adopted a flag which is now the national flag of Cuba. When the Spanish government learned what was happening, they sentenced Gonzales to death in absentia. The rebels (i.e., the junta), however, promoted Gonzales to general and chief of staff and second-in-command to their leader, General Narciso Lopez. In New Orleans and Louisville, they raised a regiment of five hundred men, most of them people of means. They sailed for Cuba in 1849.

The junta forces (filibusterers) landed at Cardanas. Unloading took too long and the Spanish garrison was alerted. Cardanas fell to the junta in heavy fighting but not before General Gonzales was shot twice. Taken aboard the ship *Creole*, Gonzales still had not recovered when a Spanish counteroffensive forced the survivors to re-embark. The Creole escaped the Spanish navy and docked in Key West, Florida. Gonzales was taken to the home of Stephen R. Mallory, who also commanded the local militia.[301] When a Spanish warship approached and demanded that the rebels be turned over to them, a confrontation resulted. The Spanish, not

---

[301] Mallory (1812–1873) was a U.S. senator (1851–1861) and the only secretary of the navy the Confederacy ever had. After the war, he was charged with treason and imprisoned for a year but was never tried.

wishing to risk a war with the United States, withdrew, but Gonzales was still in danger.

After he recovered, General Gonzales was arrested for violation of the neutrality laws and ordered to report to Federal authorities in New Orleans, which he did. He was indicted, along with General Lopez, Mississippi Governor (and former general) John A. Quitman, and an impressive list of American dignitaries who supported the Cuban Revolution. After two mistrials, Gonzales was released. He remained in the United States, became an American citizen in 1849, and married Harriett Elliott, the youngest daughter of a rich South Carolina planter, in 1856. They had six children by the time she died in 1869.[302]

When the South seceded, Gonzales found a new cause. He threw himself into the Confederate war effort with the same enthusiasm he exhibited in the cause of Cuba libre. He joined the staff of General Beauregard as a captain and an assistant inspector general. He became a lieutenant colonel of South Carolina state troops in May 1861.

Colonel Ambrosio José Gonzales

---

[302] Brooks, *Stories*, pp. 286–291. Narciso Lopez led another filibuster expedition to Cuba in 1851.

Gonzales was associated with his old classmate and friend, General Beauregard, throughout his Confederate career, and was an aide during the bombardment of Fort Sumter. He also looked so much like Beauregard they were frequently mistaken for each other. After Beauregard left for Virginia, Gonzales was involved in the strengthening of South Carolina's coastal defenses as a special aide to Governor Pickens. He joined the Confederate army as a lieutenant colonel on June 4, 1862, and served under General Pemberton, who promoted him to chief of artillery for the Department of South Carolina, Georgia, and Florida on August 14. He was promoted to colonel that same day.

Colonel Gonzales served as chief of artillery from 1862 until 1865. He particularly distinguished himself at the Battle of Honey Hill, South Carolina, where part of Sherman's forces tried to cut the Charleston and Savannah Railroad. The battle, which was fought on November 30, 1864, is historically significant because most of the five thousand Yankees involved were African Americans, making it the first battle in U.S. history fought primarily by black soldiers. The famous 54th Massachusetts was part of the attacking force. The Rebels totaled fourteen hundred men and seven guns, but their position was well selected, and they were too well entrenched to be dislodged. The Federals were also badly cut up by Southern artillery. Major General Gustavus W. Smith, the commander of the Georgia Militia, reported: "I have never seen pieces more skillfully employed or more gallantry served upon a difficult field of battle." The Union army suffered eighty-nine killed, 629 wounded, and twenty-eight missing, as opposed to eight killed and thirty-nine wounded for the Southerners.

A. J. Gonzales was promoted to chief of artillery of the Army of Tennessee in 1865. Beauregard and Pemberton recommended him for promotion to brigadier general, but no action was taken by the end of the war. As part of the surrender of the Army of Tennessee, Gonzales was paroled on April 30, 1865.[303]

After the war, Gonzales tried to rebuild the family's fortunes and labored in Charleston as a merchant, mill owner, and planter. Like many

---

[303] Brooks, *Stories*, pp. 292–302; Allardice, *Colonels*, 146.

in the postwar South, he was not successful and basically went broke. He later worked as a teacher and translator, but eked out a bare living with inadequate means. He died in New York City on July 31, 1893, and is buried in Woodlawn Cemetery, the Bronx.

CHAPTER XVIII

ONSLAUGHT

O n May 4, 1864, the Union Army of the Potomac crossed the Rapidan with one hundred twenty thousand men. General Lee met them with sixty thousand men. The same day, Sherman ordered his army group (the Army of the Cumberland, the Army of the Ohio, and the Army of the Tennessee) to begin its drive on Atlanta. Sherman, who had one hundred twelve thousand men, was opposed by Joseph E. Johnston's Army of Tennessee, which had around fifty thousand men.[304] Johnston, however, would soon be reinforced by fourteen thousand men from Leonidas Polk's Army of Mississippi, which was defending the food producing regions of eastern Mississippi and Mobile. The Union was already engaged in secondary operations in Louisiana, Arkansas, Florida, South Carolina, and the Shenandoah Valley.

The fighting was fierce. In Virginia, it included the major battles of the Wilderness (May 5–7), Spotsylvania Court House (May 8–21), Cold Harbor (May 31–June 2), and Trevillan Station (June 11–12). In Georgia, it included battles at Rocky Face Ridge (May 7–13), Resaca (May 13–15), Adairsville (May 17), New Hope Church (May 25–26), Pickett's Mill (May 27), Kolb's Farm (June 22), and Kennesaw Mountain (June 27). On both major fronts, there were several battles of secondary importance and constant skirmishing, which produced many more casualties.

---

[304] David J. Eicher, *The Longest Night* (New York: 2002), p. 696. Also see O.R., Vol. XXXVIII, Part 1, pp. 89–117; Part 3, pp. 638–683.

Losses were appallingly high. Grant suffered sixty-five thousand casualties—i.e., he lost more men than Lee had. Sherman—who relied more on skillful maneuvering than trying to bludgeon the Rebel legions to death with ham-fisted frontal attacks—lost about a quarter of the men that Grant did. As a result, Grant reached the outskirts of Petersburg but was not able to take it. For the first time since Chancellorsville, the morale of the Army of the Potomac sagged; desertions increased alarmingly.

The battle for Richmond was fought outside Petersburg. Located twenty-eight miles south of Richmond, it was the key to the city. Five railroads radiated into Petersburg; without them, Lee could not feed his army, so Grant had no choice but to lay siege to the place. It would last from June 9, 1864 to April 2, 1865—almost ten months. Eventually, the trench line would extend to thirty miles in length.

"General Lee seemed to recognize that no part of the city [Petersburg] was safe, for he immediately ordered the removal of all the hospitals..." Sara Pryor, a Confederate nurse, recalled.

There were three thousand sick and wounded, many of whom could not be moved. "A long, never-ending line of wagons, carts, everything that could run on wheels, passed by the door," Mrs. Pryor, wrote later, "until there were no more to pass."[305]

Petersburg was frequently shelled. The citizens survived on peas, bread, and sorghum. Early in the siege, they mixed a little milk with roasted and ground corn. The children picked up grains wherever the army fed its horses. Not far from Mrs. Pryor and her family lived ran a sunken street with a hill, through which it was cut. Into this hill, some Negroes burrowed and remained there all day, selling small cakes made out of sorghum and flour, and little round meat pies made out of mule flesh.[306]

Mrs. Pryor's son, Theo, got sick from his diet, and his little brother developed a fever. Dr. Withers obtained a permit for Mrs. Pryor to get

---

[305] Pryor, p. 280.
[306] Pryor, p. 283.

a pint of soup from the hospital every day. One day, it even included a chicken drumstick!

"I cert'nly hope I'll not get well," the little boy said.

"Oh, is it as bad as that?" his shocked mother asked.

"Why, my soup will be stopped if I get better!" the child exclaimed.[307]

Sara Agnes Rice Pryor (1830–1912)

In 1864, a member of Company D, 5th South Carolina Cavalry (part of Butler's brigade) was scouting near Richmond, between Sheridan's U.S. cavalry and Wade Hampton's Confederates. Suddenly, he came upon five Yankee horsemen. Seeing he was in a tight place, he wheeled his mount and applied his spurs. Just as he fled, the sergeant who was commanding the Union patrol, shouted "Don't shoot him, boys." He wanted to take the Rebel alive. The Confederate, however, outran them all, but he attributed his escape from death to the sergeant.

Some weeks later, the Rebel was again alone, scouting between the lines. He heard the sound of a horse's feet coming down the road, so he hid behind a tree. Soon, a lone Yankee appeared, suspecting nothing. The

---

[307] Pryor, pp. 283–284.

Confederate dashed from behind the tree, gun drawn, and demanded he unbuckle his holster and surrender his weapons. The Northerner complied while simultaneously lamenting that he was captured. To the amazement of the Rebel, his prisoner was the same Yankee sergeant who ordered his men not to fire on him. He gave the Yankee back his weapons and released him, but instructed him to tell no man what had happened.

Before the Northerner left, he said: "Jonnie, you are a good fellow, and it is a pity we are obliged to fight one another. I hope the war will soon end. The trouble is, you fellows fight like hell, and when we get the advantage of you, you don't seem to know it, or don't care a damn, but keep on fighting, eventually getting us on the run. We can always tell when we strike Butler's South Carolina Cavalry."[308]

L. N. Perkins of the 15th Virginia (Ewell's Corps) recalled that "My experience at the Wilderness was short but exciting." General John M. Jones and his adjutant were killed within twenty feet of him. His nearest comrade was shot within a few feet of him and lost an arm. Perkins himself was shot in the head. The ball went through the front of his ear and bounced to the back of his neck. He was in action only five minutes.[309]

Fortunately for him, Emory Perkins, a cousin, saw him fall. Emory carried him to a creek and bathed his wound until he regained consciousness. The regimental surgeon rode up at that moment, cut out the bullet with his pocket knife, and sent him to the field hospital. He was eventually sent to a hospital in Richmond and did not return to the army until early August.[310]

Casualties were high in all units. During the spring campaign, the 24th Georgia of Lee's army lost eight color guards. All were killed or wounded.

---

[308] Brooks, Stories, pp. 239–240.
[309] Yeary, II, pp. 601–602.
[310] Yeary, II, p. 602.

At Spotsylvania Court House, a gun was too far forward, was in advance of the Rebel line, and was so exposed to heavy enemy fire that it was abandoned. Later in the day, the captain ordered a sergeant to take a detachment and bring the gun in by hand. Two men lifted the gun trial and began moving, but *in a circle*. The fire was so hot that every man was on the same side—the one farthest from the Yankees. The sergeant and a corporal were able to get a man or two to the other side and were moving the gun when shrapnel broke the sergeant's ribs and tore into his arm. The men (who knew their only chance to escape was to complete their task) continued to slowly roll the gun to safety.[311]

First Sergeant W. L. Young of the 17th Mississippi was also present at Spotsylvania Court House. He "saw a pine tree, 12 inches in diameter, cut down by minie balls," he reported later. "My gun barrel got so hot that I could not hold it in my hands. It is hard to understand how I escaped or why I am still here," he wrote in 1909.[312]

Despite incredibly high losses, Grant continued to butt his head against General Lee's defenses. Colonel Pinckney D. Bowles commanded a brigade of five Alabama regiments at Cold Harbor on June 3, 1864. Well-fortified, he ordered three of every four men to stay undercover and load rifles for the fourth man, who stood on the works, fired, and handed empty weapons back to the other three. He thus always had a freshly loaded weapon.

When the Yankees advanced out of the woods, Bowles ordered his men not to fire until they were within seventy yards. The Federals charged

---

[311] McCarthy, pp. 109–110.
[312] Yeary, II, p. 834.

without any caps on their guns (!) so they could not fire. They were supported by only one battery of six guns. When they were within one hundred yards, the Rebel artillery opened up, firing double-shotted canister, "cutting wide swaths through their lines at every fire, literally mowing them down by the dozen, while heads, arms, legs, and muskets were seen flying high in [the] air at every discharge," Colonel Bowles recalled.

Bowles noted that: "We were opposed to a brave, determined, and gallant foe" and fighting them "was no child's play." They quickly closed up their ranks, but the carnage was too much, even for them. They sought cover in a ravine to Bowles' right, in the zone of Anderson's brigade. "The blood ran down the gully past our lines…Such invincible resolution I never saw before or since. They advanced again and again only to be shot down until the ground was blue with the dead and wounded…" In places, Union dead were piled five and six deep, one on top of the other. Colonel Bowles said he saw no more heroic act in the whole war than the Yankee charges that day.[313]

In the summer of 1864, a Union private in Grant's army told his captain that they had killed enough men and lost enough men that the war should be over. How, the officer wanted to know, could the war be ended?

"Take Richmond," was the answer.

That is what Grant was trying to do, the captain replied.

I know how to do it, the private answered.

"How?"

"Swap generals," he replied.[314]

---

[313] King and Derby, p. 311. Pinckney Downie Bowles (1835–1910) normally led the 4th Alabama Infantry but commanded Evander Law's brigade from early June to September 1864, when that officer was recovering from wounds. Bowles was noted for his bravery and his pleasant nature. He was a judge and a general in the United Confederate Veterans after the war. Allardice, *Colonels*, p. 69.

[314] Johnston, n.p.

The summer of 1864, Phoebe Pember recalled, "began what is really meant by 'war.'" The problems the Chimborazo Hospital faced included worthless money, which increasingly limited the hospital fund, which limited what they could buy; the constant cutting of the railroads, which made chickens and vegetables useless by the time they reached Richmond; and a "growing want of confidence" in the ultimate success of the Cause.

"The rations became so small about this time that every ounce of flour was valuable, and there were days when it was necessary to refuse with aching heart and brimming eyes the request of decent, manly-looking fellows for a piece of dry corn-bread." They had to constantly fall back on dried apples and rice for convalescing patients. Herb tea and arrowroot were given only to the very ill or badly wounded. Arrowroot could only be made palatable, according to Mrs. Pember, by drenching it in whiskey.[315]

Old stoves could not be replaced because of the blockade. The quality of the wood furnished to the hospitals was also poor due to the expense and trouble involved in land transportation. The wood at Chimborazo was light, soggy, and decayed, and was condemned as unfit for use as lumber.

The quality of bacon was also poor. It required salt to be cured, and salt was expensive and became exorbitant. Hence the bacon often spoiled before it arrived.

"...there was absolutely nothing to be bought that did not rank as a luxury."

Of rats, she wrote: "Hunger had educated their minds and sharpened their reasoning faculties." Pember fought a long battle with an old, gray rat. He would eat nothing but butter, which cost twenty dollars a pound. She caught him by hiding a fishhook in a lump of his favorite butter.[316]

---

[315] Pember, pp. 98–99.
[316] Pember, pp. 100–105

A lieutenant in the 3rd Georgia had just received a new hat from home when the Battle of Cold Harbor began. A bullet struck him in the side of the head, cutting a large hole in the hat and giving him a severe flesh wound. "At first we thought he was killed," T. H. Stewart recalled, but he soon got up. "They ruined my hat, didn't they?" he asked. He was bleeding so profusely they had to take him to the rear.

Later, the lieutenant returned to action, although he was still very bloody. Stewart asked him how was his hat. "You fool," the officer snapped, "it is my head, not my hat, that I am interested in."[317]

John West (aka Kildee) of the Twiggs County, Georgia, volunteers was considered by some to be the best Confederate sharpshooter. After three months of special training in Georgia, he and a dozen other trained marksmen were sent to Virginia in 1861, where General Lee received thirteen English Whitworth rifles, which could kill at eighteen hundred yards. They were considered by many to be the best rifle on either side.

"Artillerymen could stand anything else better than they could sharpshooting, and they would turn their guns upon a sharpshooter as quick as they would upon a battery," West recalled. "Myself and a comrade completely silenced a battery of six guns in less than two hours."

"We frequently resorted to various artifices in our warfare. Sometimes we would climb a tree and pin leaves all over our clothes to keep their color from betraying us. When two of us would be together and a Yankee sharpshooter would be trying to get a shot at us, one of us would put his hat on a ramrod and poke it up from behind the object that concealed and protected us, and when the Yankee showed his head to shoot at the hat the other one would put a bullet through his head. I have shot 'em out of trees and seen 'em fall like coons. When we were in grass or grain we would fire

---

317   Yeary, II, P. 721.

and fall over and roll several yards from the spot whence we fired, and the Yankee sharpshooter would fire away at the smoke."

At Cold Harbor in June 1864, West and Colonel Brown[318] were cut off behind enemy lines with Sheridan's wagon train between them and liberty. Both Rebels were wearing blue coats, and they rode along up the wagon train trying to find its head, but they could not do it. Finally, the colonel rode up to a driver and ordered him to turn to one side so they could pass.

"By whose authority?" the driver demanded.

"By my own," Brown snapped.

"Who are you?"

"Colonel Coleman," Brown replied. He had learned that Coleman commanded the wagon train.

The driver began to question Brown closely—too closely. The colonel drew his revolver and put a bullet into the driver's brain. Brown and West took off at maximum speed and ran into a company of Union cavalry. Under a hail of bullets, they turned right and jumped a stone wall, just as a bullet brought down West's horse. Colonel Brown's horse went down about twenty paces ahead of West's.

Thinking fast, Kildee threw his rifle into some tall grass. Then they were captured. The Confederates, who were in Yankee uniforms, thought it likely they would be shot as spies. That night, West told Brown he intended to escape. The colonel wanted to know how. West replied that he would rather risk four bullets in the dark than twenty in daylight at Fort Delaware. They low-crawled "like snakes" past the sentinels and, remarkably, were not detected. They straightened up about fifty yards from the sentries and spent three weeks behind enemy lines. They came "near perishing for want of food" before reaching friendly lines. On the way back, West retrieved his Whitworth.

Later West was severely wounded and sent to the hospital. While he was away, Charley Grace of LaGrange, Georgia, used his gun.[319]

---

[318] Probably William A. J. "Jack" Brown (1830–1891), the commander of the 59th Georgia.

[319] King and Derby, p. 268–273.

General Lee had to use every man at his disposal to hold the Yankees at bay. In the Shenandoah Valley, he assigned cadets from the Virginia Military Institute to General Breckinridge. They were only boys, aged twelve to seventeen, but they played a decisive role in the victory at New Market. He took similar drastic measures at Petersburg.

Colonel Fletcher H. Archer was born in Petersburg on February 6, 1817, the youngest of nine children. His father was a prosperous miller and sent him to the University of Virginia, where he studied law. Archer graduated in 1841, returned to Petersburg and served as a company commander in the 1st Virginia Volunteer Regiment during the Mexican War. He returned home and resumed his law practice but became commander of a battalion and then a militia brigade during the first year of the war. He was no longer up to the rigors of active campaigning, however, so he resigned in May 1862.

Two years later, as Grant pushed on Richmond, Archer was commissioned major, C.S.A. and in early May, assumed command of "Archer's battalion," Virginia reserves. His men were ages sixteen to eighteen and forty-five to fifty-five, from Petersburg and the surrounding area. They underwent a brief training period in April. In May, they were charged with defending the Jerusalem Plank Road, which led directly to Petersburg.

Meanwhile, U.S. General Butler moved against Petersburg from the south with thirty thousand men. On June 9, he was opposed by an ad hoc force under General Beauregard, totaling about eighteen thousand men, of which Archer's battalion was a part. It formed part of Henry Wise's division and Raleigh E. Colston's brigade.

Sara Pryor was in Petersburg that day. "The morning was so sweet and bright that the women and little children were abroad in the streets, on their way to market, or on errands to the shops…Lossie Hill, the daintiest of dainty maidens, was picking her leisurely way in the dusty streets, going to spend the morning with old Mrs. Mertens, when she heard the frantic shout: 'Get out of the way! Damn the women! Run over them if they won't get out of the way!' This was the morning greeting of the politest of gentlemen,—Captain Graham,—whose guns were thundering down the street to the rescue of the slender line at the front…"

When the alarm was given, "every one dropped his business and rushed to the firing line," Mrs. Pryor recalled. "the oldest men were as ardent as the youngest...'I am going to the front!'" an old druggist snapped to his clerk. "I'm just like General Lee. I should be glad if these fellows would go back to their homes and let us alone, but they won't they must be made to, that's all." The wife and two daughters of Mr. William C. Banister, the president of the Exchange Bank, implored him not to go. "The duty of every man lies yonder," he said, pointing to the front. He shouldered his musket and marched away.[320] Banister was old, partially deaf, and feeble. His family begged him to stay behind because he could not hear the orders.

"If I can't hear, I can fight—I can fire a gun," Banister declared. "This is no time for anyone to stand back. Every man that can shoulder a musket must fight. The enemy are now right upon us."[321]

The enemy that day, more than twenty-three hundred Union cavalry under General Kautz, attempted to take Petersburg from the east. All that stood between him and Petersburg was Archer's battalion, and much of it was detached on special duties and on guard duty. Archer met Kautz with 125 men and two guns. They had to cover six hundred yards of frontage, which no doubt represented one of several weak spots in the Rebel line. "And what a line!" Archer recalled. "In number scarcely more than sufficient to constitute a single company, in dress nothing to distinguish them from citizens pursuing the ordinary avocations of life, in age many of them silvered over with the frosts of advancing years, while others could scarcely boast of the down upon the cheek of youth; in arms and accoutrements such as an impoverished government could afford them. But there was that in their situation which lifted them above the ordinary rules of criticism. They stood there, not as mercenaries who, having enlisted on account of profit, required the strong arm of military law to keep them to their post...but they stood as a band of patriots whose homes were imperiled and whose loved ones were in danger of falling into the hands of an untried foe." His troops were inadequately armed with old-fashioned muskets, and many of the men were in civilian clothes, but a good number of them could glance over their

---

[320] Pryor, pp. 274–275.
[321] Pryor, pp. 275–276.

shoulders and see the roofs of their own homes. That made all the difference. "When I addressed them in a few words of encouragement, they listened with gravity and a full appreciation of their situation," Archer recalled. "There was no excitement, no shout, only calm resolution."[322]

In what was called "The Battle of Old Men and Young Boys," Archer's men repulsed the first attack, but it was obvious they needed reinforcements from General Wise's nearby brigade. Meanwhile, Brigadier General Raleigh E. Colston arrived and offered his horse to the dispatch rider, eighteen-year-old Lieutenant Wales Hurt of the junior reserves. He quickly rode off—and nobody ever saw him alive again. Colston's horse returned with the saddle empty, and the general returned to his own headquarters. Meanwhile, a second Northern assault was crushed. "The position occupied by the enemy was well chosen and defended with obstinacy," Colonel Samuel P. Spears, commanding one of the Union brigades, reported.

The old men and young boys delayed the third Union attack but were unable to defeat it. "I wish to bear full and explicit testimony to the steadiness and gallantry of the citizen soldiers who composed Major Archer's command," General Colston wrote later. "They stood to the breast-works like veterans, and did not fall back until ordered to do so, when they were surrounded on three sides, and almost entirely cut off. Knowing how important it was to hold the position, and expecting reinforcements every moment, I delayed giving the order to retreat until it was evident that a minute or two longer would have rendered inevitable the capture or death of every man in the breast-works."[323]

It was too late for about thirty of the Confederates. They were captured, along with both of Archer's company commanders. The survivors fell back into the last Petersburg trench line, about half a mile from the city, in good order. Before the Yankees could seize the vital railroad hub, regular Confederate cavalry and artillery under Brigadier General James Dearing arrived, and the opportunity to take Petersburg was lost to the Union. Only three Yankee horses managed to enter the city, and they were riderless. Archer's battalion lost seventy-six casualties—more than half of those

---

[322]   Pryor, p. 272.
[323]   O.R., Vol. XXVI, Part 2.

engaged. Union General Butler later lamented that "forty-five hundred of my best troops have been kept at bay by some fifteen hundred men, six hundred only of which were Confederate troops and the rest old men and boys..."[324]

Unfortunately, William Banister, the bank president, was among the dead. There was wailing in Petersburg that night, and Banister's daughters "wept for the good, gray head gone forward to the 'eternal camping ground' after a long life of peace."[325]

Not all the Confederate emergency units fought as heroically as Archer's men or the V.M.I. cadets. During the Battle of Fort Harrison on September 29, part of the line was held by the "department battalion," which consisted mainly of bureaucrats and clerks from various government offices in Richmond. They presented a very soldierly appearance. Just before sundown, the Union artillery fired on them. It was a heavy but brief bombardment. The terrorized bureaucrats ran for shelter, leaving a gap in Confederate lines. General Custis Lee witnessed the panic. He stepped up to the parapet of the forward works, folded his arms, and walked back and forth, without speaking or looking to the right or left. "His cool behavior... soon reassured the trembling clerks, and one by one they dropped into line again."[326] Fortunately for the South, the Yankees did not launch an infantry attack on that particular sector in the interim.

Back at the home front, the women performed as courageously as they had since the war began. Great, cumbrous looms with beams supported against the ceiling were brought out of attics. Pins became scarce. "People

---

[324] Pryor, p. 277.

[325] Christopher M. Calkins, "Archer, Fletcher H. (1817–1902)," Encyclopedia of Virginia https://encyclopediavirginia.org/entries/archer-fletcher-h-1817-1902/, accessed 2021 (hereafter cited as "Calkins, 2021"); Bernard, pp. 123–172; Pryor, p. 277.

[326] McCarthy, pp. 111–112.

walked about with downcast eyes," Sara Pryor recalled, "they were looking for pins. Thorns were gathered and dried to use as pins. Dentists' gold
soon disappeared." Morphine, chloroform, and opium (anesthetics) disappeared. The United States gave its maimed soldiers artificial limbs. The
Confederacy could give its disabled soldiers only rude, home-manufac-
tured crutches."[327]

Never was Petersburg so healthy: there was no garbage in the streets.
"Every particle of animal or vegetable food was consumed, and the streets
were clean...Rats and mice disappeared. The poor cats staggered about
the streets, and began to die of hunger. At times meal was the only article
attainable...An ounce of meat daily was considered an abundant ration."

Meanwhile, nearly every regiment in Lee's army reenlisted for the war.[328]

In the Shenandoah Valley, Major General John C. Breckinridge defeated
a Union army under General Sigel at New Market. He was ultimately
replaced by Lieutenant General Jubal Early as commander of the
Confederate forces in the area. Although outnumbered, Early defeated
another U.S. army under General Hunter in the Battle of Lynchburg (June
17–18), pursued it sixty miles in three days, reconquered the Shenandoah
for the South, invaded Maryland, and launched a raid on Washington.
He actually penetrated into the District of Columbia before he was
turned back.

Eventually, General Early's Army of the Valley (fifteen thousand five
hundred men) was defeated in the Third Battle of Winchester (September
19) by Sheridan's Valley of the Shenandoah, which had forty thousand men. It was defeated again at Fisher's Hill (September 21–22) and
Cedar Creek (October 19). Early was ultimately crushed in the Battle of
Waynesboro (March 2, 1865), after which the Shenandoah was finally lost
to the Confederacy and the Army of the Valley virtually ceased to exist.

---

[327] Pryor, p. 266.
[328] Pryor, p. 267

In May 1864, Lieutenant Colonel Harry Gilmor, who commanded "Gilmor's raiders" (the 1st and 2nd Maryland Cavalry battalions), opposed Sigel's advance up the Shenandoah Valley. He was forming his command for another attack when he saw a Union officer dismount, seize a carbine from one of his men, and aim at Gilmor. The major wheeled and applied his spurs to his mount, and took off at full speed. "All this occurred in a few seconds," he recalled, "but it seemed an age to me until the carbine cracked. I was not surprised when the ball struck me in the back, within two inches of the spine, on the upper part of the right hip-bone. The force...nearly knocked me over the front of my saddle, and made me deathly sick; besides, I felt a sort of paralysis of the spine, and right hip and leg. I expected to fall every minute; nor had I strength to manage the horse..."[329]

Gilmor was lucky. He managed to reach Confederate lines, the bullet had not struck a vital organ, and no bones were broken. Despite being in severe pain, he rode without assistance to Dr. Meems's home, where Mrs. Meems and the ladies took care of him. [330]

Colonel Gilmor recovered sufficiently to command his raiders during Union General Hunter's advance up the Shenandoah. Hunter was very effective when operating against unarmed women and children, but against armed Rebels? Not so much.

During a raid on a wagon train, Harry Gilmor shot a Union sergeant in the neck. He thought his face looked familiar. He later turned out to be a sergeant from the 18th Connecticut. Earlier in the war, when Gilmor was a prisoner of war at Fort McHenry, near Baltimore, Maryland, this man was often his guard, and always treated him with kindness and consideration. Gilmor was delighted to learn that the wound—though ugly—was not dangerous. He saw to it that the sergeant's wound was dressed, gave him a crippled horse (so he would travel slowly), and sent

---

[329] Gilmor, p. 150.
[330] Gilmor, p. 125.

him back to Union lines. "He could not sufficiently express his gratitude," the colonel recalled.[331]

Meanwhile, Gilmor's men captured the wagon train. Its cavalry escort took to its heels and escaped. Three Yankees were killed, seven were wounded, and forty-one captured, along with seventy horses. No Rebels were killed, but Gilmor was in for a shock when he entered Newtown. He recalled:

"General Hunter had issued a circular to the citizens, telling them that if any more trains were attacked or pickets captured, he would burn every house within reach of his cavalry. This seems almost incredible for the nineteenth century, but it is nevertheless true...He had already burned the parsonage and Mr. White's, and two other houses in Newtown. When I rode into town, the people, although overjoyed at my success, were alarmed at the consequences to themselves, and with pallid countenances said, 'We shall be houseless before to-morrow night.' This was more than I could bear; so seizing a pen, I wrote a communication to General Hunter, telling him that I held thirty-five men and six officers as prisoners; that I would take them to a secure place in the Blue Ridge, and upon receiving intelligence that he had carried out this threat, I would hang every one of them, and send their bodies to him in the Valley. And *Hunter knew that I would do it.*"

The next day, Hunter sent three hundred cavalry to burn Newtown. The Union commander proclaimed to the citizens that he was about to burn their homes and, to his credit, actually cried when he made the announcement. But after someone handed him a copy of Gilmor's message to Hunter, he decided not to burn the town.

Lexington and some other towns in the Valley were not so fortunate. Meanwhile, the Yankees adopted the policy of sending large escorts of a thousand men or more with the wagon trains.

---

[331] Gilmor, pp. 169–170.

Lieutenant Colonel Harry Gilmor

Following Hunter's defeat, Gilmor took part in Early's Raid on Washington and his "invasion" of Maryland and Pennsylvania. He was ordered to burn a Susquehanna River bridge near Havre de Grace, Maryland. He found it guarded by two hundred infantrymen and the gunboat *Juniata*. He did not attack immediately but captured a twelve-car passenger train. After making sure the civilian baggage was unloaded, he sent his sharpshooters to deal with the infantry, most of whom soon left the bridge and sought the protection of the gunboat. Gilmor then set the train on fire and backed "the whole flaming mass" onto the bridge. The few Union infantry still on the bridge jumped into the water. Gilmor stopped the train on the bridge, where it burned through, caught the bridge on fire, and soon, the most important part of the bridge fell into the water, train and all.[332]

During his foray, Gilmor captured U.S. Major General William B. Franklin, who was on medical leave. (He was wounded commanding the XIX Corps in the Red River Campaign in Louisiana.) The Rebels

---

[332] Gilmor, pp. 205–206.

had gone days with little or no rest, however, and the guards fell asleep. Franklin seized the opportunity and slipped away. "Right glad am I that my pious friends were not there to hear me when I found that Franklin had escaped," the colonel wrote later.[333]

Gilmor pushed on to within a mile of Baltimore.

After the Washington incursion was repulsed at Fort Stevens, Early slowly retreated back toward the Shenandoah. He sent Brigadier General John McCausland with twenty-eight hundred men to Chambersburg, Pennsylvania. In retaliation for Hunter's deprivations in the Shenandoah, the city leaders were ordered to pay a levy of $200,000 in gold or the equivalent in greenbacks; if they failed, the town was to be "laid in ashes." Just then, scouts returned with a prisoner from U.S. Brigadier General William W. Averell's command. The POW said Averell was only two or three miles from town with a heavy force of cavalry. "The citizen knew it too, and positively refused to pay the money, laughing at us when we threatened to burn the town."[334]

General McCausland ate breakfast at the hotel and ordered Colonel Gilmor to arrest fifty or more of the most prominent citizens of the town. Gilmor had arrested about forty when McCausland sent for him and said the town must be burned. "... he was sorry for it, on account of the women and children, but it must be done, to check the burning of private property in Virginia, and they had none to blame for it but General Hunter, and their own press for extolling such fiendish acts of Vandalism."

"Deeply regretting that such a task should fall upon me, I had only to obey," the major recalled.[335]

"I took two men with me to fire a fine brick dwelling..." Gilmor recalled. "Dismounting, I went in, and told the lady who came to the door that I was there to perform the extremely unpleasant duty of burning her

---

[333] Gilmor, pp. 210–211.
[334] Gilmor, p. 219.
[335] Gilmor, pp. 219–220.

house, which I much regretted: that we were obliged to resort to such extreme measures in order to prevent or check the terrible devastation committed by such men as General Hunter. I told her that the people of that town had seen us twice before, and that all had spoken in the highest terms of our behavior, saying that our soldiers had behaved better than their own. She was weeping, evidently much distressed, but she acknowledged the justice of my remarks, and declared that she blamed none but the [Lincoln] administration for allowing such horrible acts of cruelty to go unpunished. She was in deep distress, and shed many bitter tears; did not beg me to spare her house; only asked time to remove some articles of value and clothing. This was readily granted."

The lady already had breakfast on the table. She invited the Rebel officer to eat while she was gathering her things. Gilmor readily accepted and even drank some wine. He was already thinking about disobeying his orders and not burning this particular house when she engaged him in conversation. He asked her husband's name.

"Colonel Boyd, of the Union army," she responded.

"What?" the Confederate snapped. "Colonel Boyd of the 1st New York Cavalry?"

"The same, sir."

Gilmor had operated against Boyd in the Valley for two years. He was a gentleman of the first order with a reputation for kindness to women, children, and old men. He only waged war against armed soldiers who were capable of defending themselves. "Then, madam, your house shall not be destroyed," Gilmor said. The purpose of burning Chambersburg was to punish vandalism. This did not apply to Colonel Boyd. Gilmor assured her that nothing that belonged to her would be disturbed. He even posted a guard at this house to make sure it was not set on fire. It was a good thing he did, too, because a drunken officer showed up later and ordered the guards to fire the house. They refused.

Mrs. Boyd was at first completely overwhelmed by Gilmor's generosity. The guards later told him that, after he left, she brought them baskets of food, hot coffee, and as much wine as they cared to drink.

"The burning of Chambersburg was an awful sight," Colonel Gilmor recalled, "…although I had been hardened by such scenes in Virginia. One hundred eighteen houses were torched. When he saw the houses of some of his friends go up in flames, feelings of vengeance stirred the colonel; but when he saw this Pennsylvania town going up in smoke, he felt more like weeping. But, he added, taking a dispassionate view, who could condemn the Confederate government for "this act of righteous retribution?"[336]

Gilmor also captured McConnellsburg, Pennsylvania, but did not allow his men to enter a single private home. His men captured a number of horses and cattle, but Gilmor ordered his men to leave two plow-horses to each family and not to take any milk cows at all. "…the people were much surprised and pleased at the good behavior of the troops," he wrote later. "A large proportion of my men were of the best families in Maryland, and there was no difficulty in controlling them."[337]

After he was forced to retreat back to Virginia, Early met the invaders in the Third Battle of Winchester. L. N. Perkins of the 15th Virginia watched a Union artillery piece about eight hundred to one thousand yards in front of the 45th Virginia, to which he attached himself. He suggested he and his comrades move because they were in an exposed position. At that moment, the cannon fired "and that was the last I saw of the battle of Winchester." The shell took off much of his right leg, including four inches of bone, "leaving a hole that I could easily run my hand through." Two of his buddies put him in a blanket, carried him to a big brick house, shook hands with him, and bid him goodbye. It was clear they thought his wound was mortal.

The Federals captured the house when the Confederate army retreated, and the Rebel surgeons went with them. Perkins lay on the bare floor for four days. The only medical attention he received was an orderly

---

[336] Gilmor, pp. 220–222.
[337] Gilmor, pp. 92–93.

pouring water on his wound a few times. Finally, a surgeon amputated his leg and sent him to a hospital, where he lay on a blanket on the floor.

On the fourth day after the amputation, he felt something was wrong and summoned a nurse. He raised the blanket and a stream of blood shot up and almost hit the ceiling. An artery had burst. Perkins and the male nurse both started screaming for help. A surgeon rushed in and stopped the bleeding before Perkins died, but it was a close thing. He was better cared for after this, especially by the ladies of Winchester, who volunteered to nurse the wounded without pay.

Perkins improved rapidly and was sent to the prison at Point Lookout, Maryland. He survived, was released on June 4, 1865, and was transported to Richmond. From there, he walked one hundred miles on crutches and reached his home in Grayson County on June 18.

CHAPTER XIX

PRISONS

When it comes to discussing prisons, Civil War historians have generally shown absolutely no objectivity. According to the U.S. Record and Pension Office, 30,218 Union prisoners died in Southern prisons, a 15.5 percent morality rate. This has led to what Dr. Long called the "Andersonville complex," which establishment historians discuss the miserable conditions in Southern prisons ad nauseam.[338] Usually, Andersonville is the only Civil War prison mentioned. The implication is that the Rebels deliberately starved their Yankee prisoners. Union prisoners, however, received the same rations as Confederate soldiers—even when the Army of Northern Virginia had nothing but cornmeal to eat. At a cabinet meeting, Commissary General Lucius B. Northrop advocated putting prisoners on half rations. General Lee opposed the proposal. President Davis sided with Lee.[339] Some Northern prisons, in fact, were just about as bad as Andersonville. Some 25,976 Southern prisoners died in Northern prisons—or a little more than 12 percent.[340] And yet the entire South was starving. The North had plenty of food and an abundance of resources of every kind.

According to Eliza Andrews, Mr. James Tanner, the former commander of the Grand Army of the Republic, said, "It is true that more

---

[338] Long, p. 715.

[339] Pember, pp. 110–111.

[340] Long, p. 715. These figures exclude captives paroled in the field, who had a death rate of zero.

prisoners died in Northern prisons than Union prisoners died in Southern prisons." He blamed the South for this phenomenon, saying: "The explanation of this is extremely simple. The Southern prisoners came North worn and emaciated—half starved. They had reached this condition because of their scant rations. They came from a mild climate to a rigorous Northern climate, and, although we gave them shelter and plenty to eat, they could not stand the change."[341]

Few Confederate veterans who survived the Northern prison system would have agreed with Mr. Tanner (see below).

The major Union prison at Elmira, New York, was called "Hellmira" and is a fine example. An observation platform was constructed, and visitors could view Rebel prisoners for ten cents each. Meanwhile, the Southerners starved and froze. The prison was on the Chemung River, and there was only enough barracks space for five thousand prisoners, even though more than twelve thousand were assigned there. Many Confederates were forced to live in tents along the Chemung, even in the severe Northern winters, to which they were unaccustomed.

Rats were a problem, so the Yankees employed a medium-sized black dog to kill them. Rat meat was sold to the POWs at a rate of five cents per pound, but few could afford it. Meanwhile, two Rebels were sent to the guardhouse for killing and cooking the dog.

Because of inadequate rations and lack of medical care, dysentery, typhoid fever, pneumonia, smallpox, the brutality of the guards, and the flooding of the Chemung River, 2,963 Southerners died—a 25 percent mortality rate. This was about equal to Andersonville. But the North (which stopped the exchange of prisoners) had plenty of food and resources.

In September 1864, Phoebe Pember, the head of the Chimborazo Hospital in Richmond, recalled receiving a shipment of exchanged Southern

---

[341] Andrews, pp. 57–58.

prisoners. "Living and dead were taken from the flag-of-truce boat, not distinguishable save from the difference of care exercised in moving them. The Federal prisoners we had released were in many instances in a like state, our ports had been blockaded, our harvests burned, our cattle stolen, our country wasted. Even had we felt the desire to succor, where could the wherewithal have been found? But the foe,—the ports of the world were open to him. He could have fed his prisoners upon milk and honey, and not have missed either."[342]

"...The Federal prisoners may have starved at the South, we cannot deny the truth of the charge, in many instances; but we starved with them..."[343]

J. S. Stroud of Alabama rode with Nathan Bedford Forrest, so "you know that I had something to do." He fought in the Battle of Harrisburg, Mississippi, where his brigade lost 984 men out of eighteen hundred engaged. Stroud was among the wounded. He was captured on August 4, 1864, and sent to Ship Island. "There is no way to tell what we had to go through with in those awful, awful days," he recalled. "We had one cup of soup and some hard crackers [per meal]. We had only two meals a day. After awhile we all had smallpox, and men died by the hundreds, as we had very little medical attention. They would haul men off to the pest camp, and it was live or die."[344]

J. F. Smith of the 6th Missouri Infantry was captured at Port Gibson on May 1, 1863. He was sent to the prison camp at Alton, Illinois, "where many a poor fellow went out a corpse," Smith recalled. "This hideous prison had been condemned as unfit for their own prisoners but was good

---

[342] Pember, p. 121.

[343] Pember, p. 122.

[344] Yeary, II, p. 734.

enough for us. Over a thousand prisoners were confined in this horrible place,[345] which swarmed with vermin of every description, and as hard as the Yankees were to contend with, these were worse. There was no chance to whip them nor to retreat. As bad as was our fare, we told the Yankees we would rot before we would take the oath."[346]

There were many Copperheads in Alton, and they helped the Rebels all they could.

Not all inmates at Alton were as lucky as Smith. My own great-great-grandfather, Private Mark Meeks, was a small farmer (and not a slave holder) in Union County. He enlisted in the 37th Arkansas and was captured, along with most of his regiment, during the Battle of Helena on July 4, 1863. He died of maltreatment in February 1864. He had one child, who was born when he was in prison. He never saw his son.

O. P. Scott of the 18th Texas Cavalry was captured at Arkansas Post. "... we were crowded on boats with a regiment of guards who had smallpox. The first night on board a big snow fell. We were eighteen days on the Mississippi River. We were crowded on deck like stock and suffered a great deal from cold. In fact, I got so cold at one time that I got under the blanket with a dead man, but soon found that I could find no warmth there; got out and slipped into the guard room ... but when the first relief came I was discovered and barely escaped the point of a bayonet. We landed at Alton, Ill., and was sent to Camp Douglas and within six weeks fourteen of my company died of exposure, one of whom was my brother."[347]

---

[345] About twelve thousand prisoners were held at Alton during the war. At least 1,534 died.
[346] Yeary II, p.699.
[347] Yeary, II, p. 670. Scott was eventually exchanged and sent to the Army of Tennessee. He was captured again during the Battle of Atlanta (July 22, 1864).

B. E. Masters of the 65th Georgia Infantry regiment was captured at Missionary Ridge on November 25, 1863. He was sent to the prison camp at Rock Island, Illinois, "where we were glad to get a dog to eat."[348]

J. H. Arish of the 2nd Mississippi was shot in the foot at Gettysburg and captured on July 3. After being in the hospital for fifteen to twenty days, he was sent to the prison camp at Fort Delaware. Here, he and his comrades were given the "opportunity" of taking the Oath of Allegiance. When they refused, the Federals took their rations and most of their clothing away from them. "I would prefer two years in the front ranks to spending the same length of time in [a Union] prison," he recalled. He was discharged at the end of May 1865.[349]

Captain James H. Polk of the 1st Tennessee Cavalry of Forrest's Cavalry Corps was captured on January 3, 1864. Initially imprisoned in the penitentiary at Nashville, he was sent to Camp Chase, Ohio, and Fort Delaware. On August 17, he became one of the "Immortal Six Hundred" officers. They were placed on a filthy cattle ship, in which four men were given a space four by six feet. They were on this "floating purgatory" for nineteen days before landing on Morris Island, South Carolina, where they became human shields for Union guns. He was under fire from Confederate batteries for forty-two days. Their rations consisted of ten ounces of rotten corn meal and a pint of salt pickle per day. The death rate was extreme.[350]

---

[348]   Yeary, II, p. 469.
[349]   Yeary, II, pp. 588–589.
[350]   Yeary, II, pp. 614–615.

Freeman W. Jones was a private in Company E of the 56th Virginia, Hunton's brigade, Pickett's division. On Friday, March 31, 1865, he was captured near Five Forks, Virginia, and on April 2, entered Point Lookout. "Oh! How my heart did ache, when those heavy portals, with a loud crash, closed behind us!" he wrote later. "Then I thought of the loved ones at home, that quiet Sabbath morning, wending their way to the old country church in Brunswick county, where from childhood we had been accustomed to worship in peace and quiet. I now realized for the first time that I was indeed a prisoner of war, and all the horrors of a prison life rose up before me. But a soldier must be brave."

Rations deteriorated considerably since the start of the war. They attended roll call early every morning and then marched to the cook house for breakfast, which on alternating days consisted of a small piece of pickled pork or salt beef. Occasionally, they were given a small piece of raw codfish, instead of pork or beef. They took their meat back to their tents, and about 9 a.m. or 10 a.m., the bread wagons arrived. Each man received half a loaf of baker's bread. They used a thin slice of this and the pork or beef, and that was breakfast.

About 1 p.m., the guards marched them to the cook house for dinner, which always consisted of what was called "bean soup."

"It was rare indeed to find any beans, but you seldom failed to find one or more well cooked flies in your so-called 'soup,'" Young Jones recalled. There was never any supper, unless the prisoner saved a small piece of bread from breakfast.

Jones praised the commandant, Major Brady, who he believed did all he could for the prisoners. He would visit the prisoners on horseback with pockets full of chewing tobacco and toss small pieces, about one inch square, to the POWs, until they almost crushed the major and his horse. "The men seemed to be wild for tobacco," Jones declared.

The worst problem was water. The camp had four or five wells, but only two produced water fit to drink. Naturally, the prisoners crowded around these wells and drank them almost dry, so demand exceeded supply. The other wells were contaminated by copperas and Jones recalled, "after standing a while there was always a deposit upon its surface upon which you could almost write your name." It caused a great deal of sickness.

Sometimes the men would get "bread-crust coffee"—a liquid made from parched or burnt bread.

The Rebels spent their days sun bathing or playing games, of which there were many. There were religious services of some kind every day, usually carried on by other prisoners. They were never without rumors, called "grapevine dispatches," and they varied from "we will be paroled tomorrow" to "two thousand prisoners will be shot tomorrow." They were almost always false. Some things haven't changed for 160 years.

Finally, paroling actually began. Brady decided to parole those under age eighteen first. One young man who was apparently over eighteen tried to pass, but the men grabbed him by the beard and dragged him back. Seeing this, Jones returned to this tent and got a buddy to shave him as close as possible. He returned and met Major Brady. "I am only eighteen years of age," he truthfully declared, "and would be glad to go on with the boys."

"Go ahead," the major snapped.

Jones was a tall man, so when he took his position in the ranks, he bent down slightly, so as not to attract attention. He was afraid he might lose his place if he did. That night, a boat carried him to City Point, Virginia. "I bade adieu to Point Lookout," he recalled, "and only hope I may never have to look out again from that point."[351]

On July 5, 1863, Lieutenant John H. Lewis was a prisoner of war aboard a Union train in Baltimore. He spotted two young ladies, about twenty years old, who appeared to be Southern sympathizers. They came as near to Lewis's boxcar as they dared. The lieutenant, whose wife was behind Union lines, wrote her name and address on a piece of paper, along with

---

[351] Bernard, pp. 83–86.

a request that they write her and tell her he was alright and unhurt. When the guards weren't looking, he tossed the message at the feet of one of the young ladies. Without words, she understood what Lewis wanted. There were too many guards around for her to pick up the epistle, so she placed her foot over it. She remained in the hot July sun for more than two hours before it was safe to retrieve it.

A day or two later, Mrs. Lewis received an unsigned letter from Baltimore, telling her that her husband was well but a prisoner of war. "I have blessed that lady from that day, and classed her as near the angels as any mortal ever can get in this world."[352]

T. N. Stewart of the 3rd Georgia and about five hundred other men were captured at Front Royal in 1864. They were sent to Elmira, New York, but first had to march through the streets of Washington, D.C., where they were reviewed by Lincoln and his cabinet. Then they marched through the snow at Baltimore, a pro-Southern town. The Union officials posted extra police to keep the people back. They "would have been glad to give us food and clothing, but they were not allowed to," Stewart remembered. Some of them went upstairs and tossed food to the Rebels on the street.

There were about nine thousand prisoners in a fifteen-acre fenced enclosure at Elmira. The fence was fifteen feet high. They posted a Negro regiment there as guards, which enraged Stewart and his colleagues. The Rebels began to knock them off the catwalks with rocks. Some of the Southerners went to Major Colt, the commander, and asked that a Pennsylvania recruiting company replace the guards. He consented and the trouble ended.[353]

"My prison comrades considered Major Colt one of the best men they ever knew, even if he was a Union soldier," Stewart wrote in 1909. "He certainly had a Christian heart in him, and showed it by his consideration for the prisoners under him. If he is still living I want him to know that

---

[352] Lewis, p. 409.
[353] Yeary, II, p. 721.

this rebel soldier, as well as many others, still cherishes the memory of his many good deeds; and if he has passed on to his reward I don't believe there is a man living who was at Elmira prison who would not gladly contribute to a monument to his memory."[354]

Nineteen-year-old Private Simon Seward of the 12th Virginia Cavalry was captured near Rockville, Maryland, on June 28, 1863. He was carried to the Old Capitol Prison in Washington, D.C., where he remained for about six weeks. He was then transferred to Point Lookout, Maryland, located at the junction of the Potomac River and Chesapeake Bay. Only one thousand prisoners were present at the time, and rations were initially very good. "Just imagine a Confederate soldier eating fresh loaf bread, good coffee with sugar in it, and beef and pork in abundance," Seward recalled. A short time later, the cook house was built. "Then the stealing and short rations commenced." The rations continued to grow smaller and smaller, which contributed to the thousands of deaths among the prisoners—as did the overcrowding. Eventually, Point Lookout (ten acres in size) housed up to twenty thousand men.

The guards closed the main gate at sundown every day. December 1, 1863, was a cold and rainy day. Seward crept out the main gate just before sunset. He hid behind a post underneath a guard tower while the outside guards (a squad) passed within thirty yards of him. He went to the other side of the post, and the guards came back and passed within twenty feet of him. He expected to be recaptured, but the guards were focused on a pile of sand. The prisoners dug a hole (which looked like a grave) that day, and the guards evidently thought there might be Rebels hiding in the pile. They immediately started sticking it with their bayonets. Seward thus escaped detection.

About 9 p.m., when all was quiet, Seward made his move. He had two choices: swim the icy Chesapeake or go through the 5th New Hampshire

---

[354] Yeary, II, pp. 721–722.

regiment, which was camped on the only ground available. He exercised the latter option. He tried to steal a horse, but the soldiers spotted him. He was about one hundred yards from the bay and made a run for it. The New Englanders chased him and fired at him, but the darkness saved him. He jumped into the water and swam for his life with bullets flying all around. Soldiers were camped all along the shore for more than a mile. "When I found I could go no further I gave up to drown, bidding farewell to this world, when I found myself in water only three feet deep." He thought he found a whale, but he was on a sandbar. He rested and continued again, going another six miles. He then went ashore.

It was so cold that Seward's teeth chattered loudly. He put his finger between them to stifle the noise. Thoroughly chilled, he went into the woods, where he found a path. About midnight, he came to a house, rang the doorbell, and a woman in her night dress came to the door. "I know who you are," she said. "Don't speak or our servants will hear you; I will send for my husband."

Seward was fortunate: the family was pro-Southern, even though the husband was a Union naval officer. He gave the escaped prisoner a piece of beef, a bottle of whiskey, a coat, and several dollars. After a short nap, Seward walked most of the rest of the night until he came to a road. He started to cross it when he ran into a man who said: "If you go up this road, you are caught, for the sheriff is coming." Sure enough, Seward looked up the road, and there was the sheriff, riding a horse and carrying a double-barreled shotgun, with a prisoner walking beside him. Seward walked right past him and then quickly ducked into the woods and ran a mile. He crawled into a thicket, where he spent the rest of the night.

After daylight, he continued on to a small house. He got a drink at the well, and the lady of the house said, "You are the man they are looking for. The soldiers on horses have just left here." Seward moved on until he heard them coming back. He then jumped a fence and hid.

By nightfall, Seward was still crossing fields and woods until he was practically exhausted. He traveled twenty-five or thirty miles with nothing to eat. He decided to go to the next house he saw to beg for some food.

The lady of the house would not help him because her husband was not present, but she said he could rest in the yard until he returned.

When the husband—a slave owner—arrived, he allowed Seward to come in, fed him a good meal, and gave him a place to sleep. About 2 a.m., he woke up the Confederate. "The soldiers are here, asking for you, and I have told them that you are not here, but they are going to search. So run!"

Seward ran out the back door, through a gate, and into the garden. Before long, his host called out: "They are gone. Where are you?" Seward came out of hiding, and the man gave him a bucket full of meat and bread. He then showed the Rebel a hiding place in the woods, where he remained for two days. The benefactor arrived again that night with a good supper. He hired a man to take Seward across the river for two barrels of corn. The next morning, Seward "borrowed" a little log canoe. It was about eight feet in length and so narrow that he had to place his feet outside the boat. It was so old that one end had rotted off. A plank was nailed to it to make it serviceable. The river was six miles wide at this point, and the water was rough. Although assured that he would not make it, Seward was determined to try. In deep water, he was hit by a large wave and came so near to sinking "that I commenced to do what my mother taught me at her knee, which had of late been much neglected—I prayed for deliverance." It worked. "The water seemed to jump out of the boat," Seward recalled. "The winds calmed and the waves ceased to roll." Although a Federal gunboat approached him, he was in shallow water by this time, and he reached Virginia's shore.

Simon Seward spent the next day walking through woods and fields without food. That night, he stayed at the home of a true Virginia gentleman, who fed him. In the morning, Seward continued cross-country until he reached the Rappahannock, which he crossed by holding the tail of a large ox as the animal traversed the river. He stayed in a hotel in Tappahannock, but there were no rooms, so he slept on the floor. The next day, he stopped at another house, but the owner said he had no food to give him. When he asked where he was coming from, Seward said: "Point Lookout." The man immediately brightened. He had a son in Point Lookout. It so happened that Seward knew him. The homeowner immediately became the perfect host. The man and his wife shared a good supper with Seward, and he finally reached Richmond. He could not leave the city, however, without a pass.

The next day, Seward went to see Brigadier General John H. Winder, the provost marshal, to request a pass to go home. Winder, however, did not believe his story and arrested him. Meanwhile, a captain from Mosby's rangers passed the office. He recognized Seward from their stay together in the Old Capitol Prison and ordered his immediate release. Seward was given a ten-day pass. He later rejoined his unit and survived the war.[355]

---

[355] Bernard, pp. 77–83.

CHAPTER XX

TRANS-MISSISSIPPI

Α nd what was happening further west?

Realizing that they could molest Southern civilians and could get away with pretty much anything without being punished by their officers, some of the white trash elements of the Federal army continually ran amok. In the spring of 1864, they raided Mr. Worthey's place near Jackson, Louisiana. They took their swords and ran them along the shelves, so the dishes all fell to the floor and were smashed. They took the silverware, threw it into the fields, and trampled it with their horses. The family recovered three knives, four spoons (more or less intact), and four forks, one of which was undamaged. Worthey had a large family. For the rest of the war, they had to eat on the remnants of plates. They did have a wooden paddle and carved rough forks out of tree limbs. They used gourds for cups and glasses.[356]

George A. Watford was a native of North Carolina but was a twenty-nine-year-old school teacher in Tyler, Texas, when the war began. His boys wanted to join the fray and, "as I could not hold them, I decided to go along" and was elected captain and company commander. By 1864, he

---

[356] Sullivan, pp. 192–194.

was the major of the 1st Texas Partisan Rangers, which was part of Walter P. Lane's cavalry brigade. He fought in Missouri, Arkansas, and Indian Territory. After several engagements, his brigade was posted to barracks in Houston. Then they were ordered to make a hasty march to Mansfield, Louisiana. As they rode through the streets, they passed General Richard Taylor, the commander of the Army of Western Louisiana, who declared: "Boys, I am glad to see you." He immediately sent them to the front. Taylor needed every man he could get. U.S. General Nathaniel P. Banks's Army of the Gulf outnumbered him thirty-two thousand to eight thousand eight hundred. Taylor attacked it at Mansfield on April 8, 1864, and crushed it in one of the most incredible routs of the war. He then pursued it for two hundred miles—all the way across Louisiana.

At Mansfield, "We were sent as pickets in front of the enemy," Watford recalled, "and when we got in sight of them we were ordered to tie our horses in the brush and advance as infantry. We beat them back about half a mile, when we saw that we were about to run into Banks's army. We were ordered to retreat to our infantry line. We had to retreat through a field and slightly up hill. We were ordered to dismount and take our places on the left of our infantry. My position on the left was in the timber, but the infantry was through the field. The crossing of that field was awful. The bullets were flying like hail and the shells were bursting, yet the infantry were marching bravely right into the jaws of certain death. As we approached the eastern side of the field our instructions were to keep going till the enemy was found, and when they proved too strong for us to fall back to the main line. We at last reached a fence; I stepped over it and took refuge behind a small post oak tree about the size of a stovepipe. The Yanks spied me and commenced to shoot at me, and bullets came pretty thick. One ball struck the tree and glanced onto my knee. This did not hurt, and it was the only ball that hit me during the war. I heard someone call, and looking around saw it was my nearest left-hand skirmisher; as he started to me he was shot down. His name was John Cranfield. I looked around and not a man was in sight. All had been killed or had retired to the main line. I soon decided that that was no place far [for] Watford, and as I started back to the line I passed Cranfield and he said: 'For God's sake, Major, don't leave me here.'...I could not resist his appeal, so I lay facedown beside him and told him to take me around the neck and pull himself on my back, which he did, and I rose with him and carried him from under fire. In a few minutes our men raised the yell and charged the fence, and the Yankees left in a hurry. We pressed them, and took about six miles of their train. That night we had lots of good things to eat and coffee galore."

George Watford was later promoted to lieutenant colonel. After Banks escaped across the Atchafalaya, Watford remained in camp until May 20, 1865, when he learned that General Lee had surrendered. His brother, R. A. Watford, "was killed at Spanish Fort, Ala., after sundown on the 8th of April, 1865."[357]

General Taylor continued his pursuit of the beaten Yankees on April 10. It was the second time in two weeks that Banks's army crossed over this part of Louisiana, and they took what they could carry and destroyed the rest. The Confederate supply wagons could not keep up, which didn't leave much for the combat units. Private John T. Poe of the 4th Texas Cavalry recalled: "Have lain for four days and nights in the line of battle on one meal a day..." and he used the bark of trees in lieu of plates.[358]

"...for thirty days, we had practically nothing to eat," Private W. R. Smith of the 12th Texas Cavalry recalled. "I remember that one of our mess[mates] slipped off to find something to eat and I gave five dollars and he paid it for a pone of corn bread, and it had a thin white crust on it but nevertheless it was good." Because Smith was in the cavalry, he and his comrades had no tents. "We had to take the weather just as it came, sleep on the cold wet ground. It was rather hard but we stood it pretty well."[359]

---

[357] Yeary, II, 780–781.

[358] Yeary, II, pp. 612–613.

[359] Yeary, II, pp. 708–709. Smith was born in Aberdeen, Mississippi, in 1845 and enlisted in the Confederate army in Bastrop, Texas, in 1863. He fought in every battle from Pleasant Hill to Yellow Bayou, the last battle in the Red River campaign.

In a secondary part of the Red River Campaign, U.S. General Steele's VII Corps, operating out of Little Rock, drove on the town of Washington, the Confederate capital of Arkansas. After Banks was defeated, Confederate General Edmund Kirby Smith attempted to destroy Steele, but the latter sensed a trap and retreated back to Little Rock. Kirby Smith attempted to cut him off but was checked in the Battle of Jenkins Ferry, Arkansas, on April 30.

Sergeant J. J. Stovall of the 8th Texas Infantry recalled that five men were shot down beside him—three on one side, two on the other—"and I tell you I felt as big as a bale of cotton."[360]

Private John Q. Thompson of the 26th Arkansas also fought at Jenkins Ferry. He enlisted in 1861 and recalled: "My first weapon of war was a spear with a handle on it about eight feet long. My next was an old-fashioned bored hunting rifle, for which I had to make or run my own bullets and make my cartridges. My next was an Enfield rifle, which was won on the battlefield." The Enfield was a modern weapon.

At Jenkins Ferry, Thompson's regiment charged and gained some ground, but was ordered to retreat. Thompson and four other men did not hear the order, however. They took shelter behind a large oak tree, and "All were shot down except myself." His gun jammed, so he picked up a comrade's gun and kept firing until the enemy charged his position. "I took deliberate aim at a group of the enemy, fired and then retreated in double quick time" (i.e., he ran back to friendly lines).[361]

Two Yankees arrested Mary Robinson near Clover Bend, Arkansas. (Mrs. Robinson was about twenty-one years old and a widow. Her husband, Clay, died of measles while in the Confederate army.) They accused her of being

---

[360] Yeary, II, p. 730.
[361] Yeary, II, p. 748

a spy—which she was. They took her to their colonel, who announced that he intended to take her to Jacksonport and try her. The only evidence he had, however, was that she was too far from home. Mrs. Robinson replied that she was in the area to recover her brother's horse, which was stolen by Yankees. She said she wouldn't go to Jacksonport because she didn't know anyone there; if she were to be tried, it would have to be near home, where she was known. The only way she would go to Jacksonport would be if he bound her hand and foot and carried her there. The colonel did not want to do this.

He asked her if she would take the oath not to assist the Confederacy.

"If that is the only way of release, I will," she replied.

"Will you be true to the oath?" he asked.

"No, sir," she responded, "I would not consider it worth the snap of my finger after you are out of sight."

The colonel, however, was convinced he did not have enough evidence to obtain a conviction, so when the regiment reached her home, he let her go.[362]

After the Red River Campaign was over, Confederate Major General John A. Wharton, now the Confederate cavalry commander for the Army of Western Louisiana, issued General Order No. 7. Dated May 24, 1864, it read: "Soldiers—For forty-six days you have daily engaged the enemy, always superior to you in numbers. When the beaten foe, four army corps of infantry and 5,000 cavalry, began his retreat, you were formed in battle array in his front and hung upon his flank and rear only to destroy. In his retreat from Grand Ecore to Atchafalaya, you killed, wounded and captured 4,000 men, destroyed five transports and three gunboats. All this was accomplished with a loss to you of 400 men, two-thirds of whom will report for duty again in forty days. The history of no other campaign will

---

[362] CWA, p. 115–116. Mrs. Robinson (nee Scanlan) smuggled dispatches for General Dandridge McRae. She married Captain Dr. B. F. Austin, a former company commander in Confederate infantry, in 1869. She died in 1902.

present the spectacle of a cavalry force capturing and killing more on the enemy than their own numbers. This you have done, and in so doing have immortalized yourselves and added new lustre to Texas, the gallantry of whose sons has been illustrated on every battlefield from Gettysburg to Glorietta."[363]

After the bluecoats retreated to Little Rock, Confederate General Sterling Price led a disastrous invasion into Missouri. J. M. "Mat" Rice of the 10th Missouri regiment served in Marmaduke's brigade and fought throughout the war. He recalled: "As to what Southern soldiers suffered, you can read the history of Washington at Valley Forge and you will have some idea of what we went through. I have stood on picket duty for two hours at a time with ice on the ground without shoes on my feet. We generally had food enough but clothing was scarce, though I once went seven days without food. This was on the 'Lone Jack' raid. We marched two and three weeks at a time when our blankets and clothing would never dry."[364]

Private J. H. Knox was part of Davies' battalion of Price's command during his Missouri Raid. When it began, the battalion had five hundred men. Fifteen were left at the end. "We retreated fighting day and night," he recalled, "without anything to eat, and no rest. Many of my comrades were lost and have never been heard from till this day. Then we marched back through the Indian Nation into Texas, and crossed the Red River. We almost starved to death."

At one point, Knox, Colonel Davies, and about five others went ahead of the command to find food. They came across an old, broken-down army mule. They used it to carry one of their comrades, but when it could go no further, they shot it, cut out its hams, and dined heartily on "mule ham."

---

[363] Yeary, II, p. 682.
[364] Yeary, II, p. 639.

They were saved by "the good women" of Fannin County. "They kept their tables set all day, their servants cooking, and all we had to do was go in, sit down, eat and move on."[365]

Sergeant Thomas J. Stirman of the 4th Missouri Cavalry took part in Price's Raid into Missouri in 1864. Near Newtonia, he was wounded three times and left for dead. He lay in the woods for four days and never heard a human voice. It snowed during the second night and Stirman had nothing to eat, so he killed a raccoon and ate it raw. Eventually, he rejoined his old command.[366]

Private John S. Kritser of the 2nd Missouri Cavalry fought with Shelby in New Mexico and Marmaduke in the Trans-Mississippi, including Price's Missouri raid. He had three horses shot out from under him but was never seriously wounded, although "[I] heard the Yankee bullets going too close to my head to be comfortable. Could have been captured several times, but had a holy horror of Yankee prisons, so I always outrode them. We could always whip them when our numbers were near equal, and if there were too many of them we outran them."[367]

New Mexico was one of the hardest campaigns of the war. Private Charles Robert Scott of the 7th Texas Cavalry was not as fortunate as John Kritser.[368] "While on a forced march in Navajo Indian country in New Mexico, about sixty-five or seventy miles from Albuquerque, N.M., my horse gave out and I had the fun and pleasure of footing it back to San Antonio, about 1,200 miles," he recalled.[369]

---

[365] Yeary, II, pp. 410–411.

[366] Yeary, II, p. 723.

[367] Yeary, II, p. 413.

[368] Scott was part of Colonel Steele's regiment of Tom Green's cavalry brigade.

[369] Yeary, II, p. 667.

Following Price's defeat in Missouri in the fall of 1864, there were no more major battles in the Trans-Mississippi or southeastern Louisiana, although occasional small operations continued. On August 3, 1864, a minor battle was fought at Jackson, Louisiana, in East Feliciana Parish, east of the Mississippi River. The Yankees, who were defeated, lost eighty-nine killed, of which seven were white and eighty-two were U.S. Colored Troops.[370] The Rebels lost at least one killed and 10 wounded.

The Fremaux family (mother and children) were up at 5 a.m. the following morning to salvage what they could from the battlefield. They found several unexploded shells. They unscrewed the caps and emptied the powder into dozens of preserving jars. (They had an old rifle that they used for hunting.) They did not have shoes and had not for some time. They found many cartridge boxes and belts; the top flaps of the boxes made fine leather for shoe soles for the women and children, who had smaller feet than the men. They did, however, wear out quickly, so the family wore them only to church on Sunday. Everywhere else, they went barefoot, but they always carried a cloth to clean their feet when visiting.[371]

"It would be hard to tell of all the hardships we went through during the four long years of fighting and marching day and night," Private W. J. Rutledge of Dallas, Texas, recalled in 1909. "I have walked till my feet were blistered, and then on other occasions I would freeze, and then starve, and if it was not one thing it was something else and more of it...parched corn is good for a lunch after supper around the fire on a cold night, but when it comes to eating parched corn for three days at a time, and then only get about one ear a day, it ceases to be funny. Then to lie down at night with dead and wounded, it was simply heart-rending to listen to the groans of

---

[370] Sullivan, p. 210. Celine Fremaux recorded in her diary that no Rebels died, but Sergeant Willis W. Davis was killed while leading a charge.

[371] Sullivan, pp. 210–211.

the dying soldiers who had given up their lives for their country, but still we kept on and kept up courage and fought on till our army was exhausted. I am thankful to the Supreme Being that I was spared. Not a scratch of a bullet did I receive in all those battles and skirmishes, sometimes lasting more than a day. It hardly seems possible that one could escape. I hope there will never be another war."[372]

---

[372] Yeary, p. 660.

CHAPTER XXI

WESTERN FRONT

Meanwhile, in northern Mississippi and western Tennessee, Nathan Bedford Forrest—"the Wizard of the Saddle"—continued to smash Northern legions at an astonishing rate. One Union brigade commander called the entire region a giant "Forrest Mill" that ground up Yankees at a fearful pace, and no one seemed to be able to stop it. One of his most impressive victories occurred in the heavily wooded territory around Brices Cross Roads, Mississippi, where he routed a Union corps of more than ten thousand men. Forrest had only three thousand two hundred men at the time. Here Private J. J. Vernon of the 21st Tennessee Cavalry recorded later, "is where we fought our first negroes. The Yankees were behind a rock fence, and we came through a thicket of post oak runners. Billy Trice was right in front of me, and he came up to an old tree, and he was trying to look around it he was shot in the head. He never knew what hit him; he was killed instantly. We were lying down, and Gen. Forrest came along talking to us. He said: 'Now I want you boys to show these Yankees that you are Forrest's men.' Then he ordered a charge and we went right over the fence, and I never saw so many Yankees killed at one time in all my battles. We found from one to three dead in every fence corner. They charged us while he were at the fence with a regiment of negroes. I will never forget how those negroes looked; they looked like a big black cloud coming. Our officers gave us orders not to fire until the order was given. They came to within forty or fifty yards of us, and we were ordered to fire and charge at the same time. They broke to run, and if you ever heard of a n_____ running, now they ran. We pulled our pistols and started after them, but did not catch them. In the meantime the white [Northern] men had formed a reserve line at the other side of the hill, but the negroes ran over them, and before they could get straight we were on them and captured the most of them with empty pistols, for most of us had shot out all of our cartridges. It was a hard fight. They tried to get to the wagon train so as to save their cannon, but some of our men went down the road and passed the wagons and shot a horse down in each of the teams. We got seventy-five wagons and so many prisoners that it was a hard matter for us to guard them. The white men were nice men, and they were brave men. One of them told me after we had captured them that if they had not tried to stop those negroes that we would not have captured the whites. They certainly cursed those negroes."[373]

The decisive campaign of 1864—and probably the deciding campaign of the whole war—occurred in north Georgia, where Union General William T. Sherman's army group struggled to take Atlanta. Between May 7 and September 2, there were battles or large skirmishes almost every day.

Alcohol was the cause of many casualties during the Civil War. During the Atlanta Campaign, Captain William H. Ledbetter of the 9th Texas Infantry led 462 men in an attack against a Union regiment that had recently captured a distillery. All the bluecoats were drunk as lords and unable to offer effective resistance. Ledbetter's men killed ninety-six and wounded and captured 123. The Texans lost one killed and one wounded.[374] Most battles, however, did not have such a favorable outcome for the South. By the third year of the war, many Rebels were immune to the shock of death. Confederate veteran F. J. Mason recalled the fighting around Atlanta. Four or five members of Company H, 5th Mississippi

---

[373] Yeary, II, pp. 767.
[374] Bernard, p. 427. Ledbetter was later disabled at Franklin, where his horse was killed and fell on him. That ended his active service.

Infantry Regiment, were lying in the trenches, and there was a lull in the shelling and fighting. The company managed to acquire a sizable number of biscuits, and the infantrymen sat Turk style on a blanket, ready to enjoy the unusually large repass. Old Tommie stretched out his arm to pick up the biggest biscuit when a minie ball blew off a large part of his head, and he fell on the biscuits.

George H. jerked him off the pile and shouted: "Damn it, boys, don't let the old man bleed on the biscuits."[375]

From December 16, 1863 to July 17, 1864, Joseph E. Johnston commanded the Army of Tennessee. Although his record as a general was mixed at best, he did have a talent for inspiring his troops. On May 19, 1864, he issued a general order to his men. It read: "Soldiers of the Army of Tennessee, you have displayed the highest quality of the soldier—firmness in combat, patience under toil. By your courage and skill you have repulsed every assault of the enemy. By marches by day and by marches at night, you have defeated every attempt upon your communications. Your communications are secure.

"You will now turn and march to meet his advancing columns. Fully confiding in the conduct of the officers, the courage of the soldiers, I lead you to battle. We may confidently trust that the Almighty Father will still reward the patriot's toils and bless the patriot's banners. Cheered by the success of our brothers in Virginia and beyond the Mississippi, our efforts will be crowned with the like glories."

Sergeant Major Robert W. Banks of the 37th Mississippi recalled that "all were inspired by confidence, and there was little doubt as to which side the victory would fall."[376]

---

[375] CWA, p. 41.

[376] Robert W. Banks, *The Battle of Franklin* (New York: 1908), pp. 12–13 (hereafter cited as "Banks"). Banks later was a captain and company commander in the 37th Mississippi. As a lieutenant colonel in the U.S. army, he commanded the 3rd Mississippi Infantry during the Spanish-American War.

Sergeant W. S. McShan of the 3rd Mississippi Infantry Battalion served four years on the western front, except for four months as a prisoner of war. (He was wounded and captured at Murfreesboro.) McShan was promoted to second lieutenant in 1863. He was in combat for sixty straight days or more during the Atlanta Campaign.

"We underwent hardships that no one can tell," Lieutenant McShan recalled. "We got for rations a small pone of cornbread and a smaller piece of 'Jerked' beef and three little cakes of bread as a full day's rations. It was no uncommon thing for us to eat it all at once, and do without the remainder of the day. We were only half clad and barefooted, but always went where we were ordered, faced death or anything else that was in the line of duty."[377]

During the Battle of Resaca (May 13–15), General Johnston retreated, burning his bridges behind him. J. W. Wynn and his company (Company F, 11th Tennessee) were on forward picket duty and were forgotten about, or at least were overlooked when the order to retreat was issued. When dawn broke, they found themselves on the wrong side of the river with three burning bridges at their backs. Two of the bridges were down and the other was wet with turpentine every few feet and on fire. Wynn and his comrades succeeded in jumping the flames and reached the main army at noon.[378]

Private B. M. Thompson enlisted in the 10th Texas Infantry Regiment in March 1862 and fought in thirty-five skirmishes and major engagements,

[377] Yeary, II, pp. 506–507.
[378] Yeary, II, p. 827.

mostly in the Army of Tennessee. He fought in the Battle of Atlanta (July 22, 1864), and took part in the surprise attack in which U.S. General James McPherson, the commander of the Army of the Tennessee, was killed. He recounted how they initially routing the Federals, but Confederate General W. H. T. Walker's division failed to attack, and the Yankees were able to rally and throw in one line after another. "The last gun I fired the Federal was not more than six feet from me," he recalled. "I reached for another cartridge and there were three soldiers at my back..." He was brought to the Union rear, where the Northern enlisted men told their officers that the captured Texans ought to be shot because they had killed two hundred bluecoats and the Union men had killed only thirty Texans. Cooler heads prevailed, however. "We were taken to Camp Chase, Ohio. Congress passed the retaliation act and put us on one-fourth rations," Thompson noted. He was released on May 15, 1865 and returned home in July, having been absent more than three years.[379]

Despite the constant hammering by the Union army, Rebel morale remained quite high. John Loughridge was a private in Selden's artillery battery, part of Shelby's brigade, Walthall's division, on the western front. He recalled in the 1890s: "When you speak of the war today to most of the rising generation, you are thought to be romancing; that the scenes, incidents, and events through which we claim to have passed with a jest were impossible—and it does seem so. But it was the fun, the laugh, the humor in spite of what fate had in store for us, that kept the strain from 'snapping the cord,' and at night around the campfire someone would start a song—a song of home, 'with cadence sweet and strong,' and soon we were peacefully wrapped in slumber, regardless of the fact that at daylight we would be in a hail of death-dealing lead."[380]

---

[379] Yeary, II, p. 746.
[380] Yeary, II, p. 450.

M. D. Smith enlisted in the Confederate army in the fall of 1861 at the age of sixteen. He was not sent to a combat unit until 1864, when he joined the 1st Alabama Cavalry of the Army of Tennessee. Not accustomed to military life, he was slow to saddle and mount on his first day and so was left behind. He hurried to catch up with his unit. "I was not aware of what was up, or I might have gone a different direction," he recalled, "but as I had been looking for trouble, I now found it." When he rejoined his company, it was forming a line of battle, facing east. "Just across the river it seemed that the whole earth was blue and the battle was opened from both sides" with artillery and small arms. "At the sight of so many soldiers I felt as if I had rather have gone the other way," Smith said later. "We yelled once and awhile and held the Yankees back for some time. Finally we received orders to fall back. I did not like that, as I did not like to turn my back on the enemy…but of course had to do like the rest of the crowd."[381]

Private Smith was part of Wheeler's command when it opposed Sherman's March to the Sea. He also fought in South and North Carolina. He had some close calls "as most every soldier had," and was twice involved in hand-to-hand fighting. He survived the war, however, without being seriously wounded.

M. D.'s brother, M. M. Smith, was a corporal in the 10th Confederate Cavalry. He was also in the Atlanta Campaign. During the Battle of Marietta, a shell burst over his head and cut a soldier beside him almost in two. Smith helped carry him off the field. "…he told us to inform his wife and family of his fate and that he died at his post fighting for his rights."[382]

General Johnston refused to assure Richmond that he would not abandon Atlanta without a fight and at times would not even communicate with

---

[381] Yeary, II, p. 703.

[382] Yeary, II, pp. 703–704.

Jefferson Davis. A frustrated president sacked him on July 17. Unfortunately for the Confederacy, Davis replaced Johnston with John Bell Hood. The new full general was one of the least capable of the Rebel commanders at the army level. He launched a series of futile counterattacks, most notably in the Battles of Peachtree Creek (July 20), Atlanta (July 22), and Ezra Church (July 28). The Army of Tennessee suffered such high casualty rates that it was unable hold Atlanta, which fell on September 2.

"For nine or ten weeks the order of business seemed to be fortifying by day and falling back by night," Robert W. Banks wrote later.[383]

General Hood recalled: "The men…were ceasing to be soldiers by disuse of military duty. Thus for seventy-four days and nights that noble army, which, if ordered to resist, no force that the enemy could assemble could dislodge from a battlefield, continued to abandon their country, to see their strength departing, and their flag waving only in retreat or in partial engagements."[384] The army, according to Robert Webb Banks, grew weaker in both numbers and spirit.

Hood took charge of the army on July 17 and defended Atlanta for six weeks, fighting four major battles and many skirmishes and cavalry clashes in the process.

On September 26, 1864, President Davis visited the army at Palmetto, Georgia. That same day, Hood started offensive operations against Sherman's line of communications.

From September 26 to November 30, the Army of Tennessee marched more than five hundred miles. They often were issued only three ears of corn a day to eat, and occasionally nothing.[385]

---

[383] Banks, pp. 16–17.
[384] Banks, p. 17.
[385] Banks, p. 24.

Private John D. Shipp of the 6th Alabama [Cavalry] battalion was scouting in northern Alabama when he was captured by Tennessee Tories, homegrown Yankees. He thought they would kill him, but they decided a duel would be more fun. They had an African American cook with them and, thinking he was a great shot, offered to let Shipp shoot it out with him. Shipp agreed, provided they would give him his own pistol and let him load it. They consented, so Shipp and the cook lined up back-to-back. They took the traditional ten paces, wheeled around, and fired. The cook's bullet barely missed Shipp's head. His bullet struck the cook between the nose and the mouth. The surprised Tories kept their word, gave Shipp his pistols, and let him rejoin his company.[386]

"Elm Springs," near Columbia, Tennessee, was a two-story brick house, built in the Greek Revival style in 1837. In 1864, it was owned by Abraham M. Looney, a prominent local attorney and state senator who was now a lieutenant colonel in the 1st Tennessee Infantry. It now produced swine and cattle instead of cash crops.

As the Yankees retreated toward Franklin, they decided to burn it. Two of them set a broom on fire and tossed it and some kindling into a central closet. The home was saved by a servant named Sampson, who pulled the broom out of the closet. Meanwhile, the Yankees went out the front door to obtain more kindling and spread the fire while Rebel Brigadier General Frank Armstrong entered via the back door with a squad of his men. They had a gunfight inside the house and one Northerner was killed—possibly by General Armstrong. Another Federal who was collecting kindling was shot dead near the house.[387] Elm Springs was saved and became the headquarters of the Sons of Confederate Veterans and the Military Order of the Stars and Bars in 1992. The HQ

---

[386] Yeary, II, p. 685.

[387] Adam Southern, executive director of the Sons of Confederate Veterans, personal communication, 2021.

was moved to a nearby museum, but Elm Springs is still extant and hosts events for the SCV.

On the morning of November 30, 1864, the 15th Mississippi arrived near Franklin and was sent to the right flank, near the Harpeth River. They sat around for two hours or so, waiting for more troops to arrive. During that time, a young man arrived. He was the brother of Lieutenant Charles H. Campbell of Company E, whose father lived at nearby Thompson's Station and had sent provisions to the officer. Seeing that he had an abundance, he invited Colonel Mike Farrell (the regimental commander) and Captain Smith and Lieutenant Allen of Company E to join him. Realizing that there was more than enough, Farrell invited Lieutenant Colonel Walter A. Rorer of the 20th Mississippi and Major Crumpton of the 14th Mississippi to join them, with Campbell's permission, of course. Campbell also invited Captain Roland Jones of Rayburn's battalion and Major Brunner of the 12th Louisiana to join the little party. While they enjoyed the feast, the eight officers freely discussed the military situation. The mood was somber. Two were optimistic, or at least pretended to be. The other six believed the upcoming battle would probably be the last chapter in their lives, and this would be their last meal.

They were right. Colonel Rorer, Major Crumpton, and Major Brunner were all killed or mortally wounded. Captain Smith was killed, and Lieutenant Allen fell over his body less than thirty seconds later, also dead. Both of young Colonel Michael Farrell's legs were shattered. He spent an agonizing night on the field and the next morning was carried to the McGavock House. Both of his legs were amputated. He failed to rally from the operation and died on December 25.

Of the remaining two, Roland Jones and Charles Campbell were crippled for life. Jones died shortly after the war. Campbell was still alive in 1908, but he walked with a permanent limp after Franklin.[388]

---

[388] Banks, pp. 60–64; Allardice, *Colonels*, p. 144.

"At Franklin we marched two miles, without any protection, in view of the Yankees," Corporal Thomas J. Wilson of Company G, 45th Alabama recalled. "We fought right up to the breastworks, and stayed there until nearly all our men were killed. When the battle was over there were six men in my company, and we started into the fight with twenty-six. Could give you instances like these that would cover pages, that happened in every battle. As to food and clothing, we got to where we could almost live without either."[389]

"From the battle of Chickamauga to the close of the war it was all hard," B. F. Williams of the 7th Texas remembered. "…The Tennessee campaign of 1864, I think, was the hardest part of the war for our little army. The weather was very cold and we were poorly clothed and on short rations most of the time. I think the battle of Franklin, Tenn., was the most desperate struggle of the whole war. Our boys seemed to think that if we were defeated here there would be but little chance for our cause and every man seemed to think that the victory depended on his energy. I never saw such bravery and heroism displayed. Our Company B of the Seventh Texas went into the charge with eleven men and had five killed, one badly wounded, two slightly wounded, one captured, and two escaped injury."[390]

Edward Russell was a color-bearer in the "High Pressure Brigade" from Mississippi. At age sixteen, he enlisted as a private in Company E, 41st Mississippi and became a color-bearer in the Battle of Jonesboro. At Franklin, the regiment's commander, Colonel Byrd Williams, was killed,

---

[389] Yeary, II, pp. 809–810.
[390] Yeary, II, p. 797.

and the other field-grade officers were wounded. All the captains were killed or wounded and command of the regiment devolved on a lieutenant. Leading the way, Russell planted his flag on the Union fortifications. He and some of his comrades fought hand-to-hand in the forward Yankee trench, which they captured. For a time, they were not able to advance or retreat. They managed to escape during a lull in the fighting.[391]

Elsewhere, Lieutenant H. C. Shaw of Company K, 33rd Mississippi, picked up the regimental flag fifteen paces from the Union works. He was in the act of planting it when he was shot dead. He fell into the Federal trench, and the regiment lost its colors. Shaw was the fourth color-bearer to be cut down that day.

The colors of the 15th Mississippi were initially carried by Charles Frierson, but he was severely wounded several hundred yards from the Union fortifications. The flag was picked up by another soldier, who carried it a short distance and was killed. Another man picked it up and carried it to the Union bois d'arc hedge, where he was shot down. Private McMath of Company E grabbed the flag and made an opening in the obstruction. He rushed forward and attempted to cross the Union works, but he was shot and seriously wounded. The Northerners pulled him over the line, and he and the colors were captured.[392]

Private W. P. Peacock of the 15th Mississippi was a recently exchanged prisoner of war who reached his command on November 30. He had no gun when the battle began, so he grabbed an axe. When the command reached the Union bois d'arc hedge, it was stopped by the obstruction. Seeing the problem instantly, Peacock went to work and cleared holes in the hedge. Remarkably, despite a "galling fire," he was not killed or wounded.[393]

---

[391] Banks, pp. 44–47. After the war, Russell later became vice president of the Mobile and Ohio Railroad.

[392] Banks, pp. 57–58.

[393] Banks, p. 59.

The 37th Mississippi reached the ditch in front of the Union fortifications, where they faced an enfilade fire, which was terribly effective. "So thick were the dead and wounded in the ditch there, it became a sort of out-door 'chamber of honors,'" Sergeant Banks recalled later. "When night came down, the groans and frenzied cries of wounded on both sides of the earth-works were awe-inspiring. The ravings of the maimed and mangled victims were heart-rending. Crazed by pain, many knew not what they did or said. Some pleadingly cried out, 'Cease firing! Cease firing!' while others agonizingly were shouting, 'We surrender! We surrender.'"[394]

"In regard to hardships I will say we starved many times during the struggle," Private Tidwell of the 27th Alabama wrote after the war. "Bare footed, feet bleeding, nearly without clothing and still with all this suffering and destitution, Gen. Cleburne swept everything before him with his destitute boys until he fell at Franklin, Tenn."[395]

Cleburne, arguably the best division commander on either side, died instantly from a single bullet through the heart. His fiancée in Mobile learned of his death from a newspaper boy who was hawking his product.

U.S. Colonel Henry Stone of General Thomas's staff later wrote: "It is impossible to exaggerate the fierce energy with which the Confederate soldiers that short November afternoon threw themselves against the works, fighting with what seemed the madness of despair."[396]

---

394 Banks, p. 76.
395 Yeary, II, p. 751.
396 Henry Stone, "Repelling Hood's Invasion of Tennessee" in Robert U. Johnson and Clarence C. Buel, eds, *Battles and Leaders of the Civil War* (New York: 1884–1886), Vol. IV, p. 446.

"What do you want to do?" some of the Rebel infantrymen yelled at their comrades. "Live forever?"

"At the battle of Franklin we fought the hardest battle I was in during the war," Sergeant J. W. Wynn of the 11th Tennessee recalled. "The enemy was entrenched and we charged their breastworks and fought them hand-to-hand for six hours. In this contest I discharged my gun and the man in front of it fell and the man behind him pointed his gun at me and at one lean I sprang past the muzzle of his gun, grasping it with the left hand. Raising my gun as a club with my right, I ordered him to surrender, which he did, and I took him and his gun out of line of battle to prison." Wynn's own gun was struck by a ball and bent slightly, so we used the captured weapon for the rest of the battle. "The two men on each side of me and the one behind me were shot dead. We would drop and load and rise and fire. The second man on my right while I was down was shot through the head and fell dead across my body. The destruction was so great at this time that Gen. Cheatham, who commanded Gen. Hardee's Corps, sat on his horse and wept as he viewed the dead and dying of his old division."[397]

After he enlisted in the 8th Kentucky Cavalry in 1863, J. M. Slayden rode with Nathan Bedford Forrest for the rest of the war. He recalled that Franklin was "the hardest battle [fought] by the Army of Tennessee and Forrest's cavalry. The infantry and cavalry lost about 5,000 as brave men as ever went into battle. We marched, fought and nearly froze until we drove the Yanks into Nashville. Then it began to rain and sleet. Hood's army was defeated, and began the retreat. We fought every day while we were in Tennessee. On the retreat from Nashville we formed line of battle, and as one of the boys was riding off the field his finger was shot off. He held up

---

[397] Yeary, II, pp. 827–828.

his hand and said: 'Boys, this is good for a ninety days' furlough.' He got his furlough, all right, and went to Kentucky, and the Yanks caught him, and they thought so much of him that they kept him until the end of war."[398]

"The simple fact of my having been a private soldier during that fearful struggle covers the whole ground as effectually as if I should write a volume," Francis A. Taulman of the 32nd Texas Cavalry (Dismounted) commented later. "My life, like that of thousands of others, during that period was a continuous succession of hard, wearisome marches with blistered feet; with scant clothing and food; exposed to all kinds of weather practically unsheltered, and to conflicts with the enemy in which it was the duty of the private soldier to kill—and, perchance, ere the termination of the struggle, to get killed."

After fighting in the Battle of Pea Ridge, Taulman served on the western front until after the Battle of Nashville. In 1865, he fought in the Siege of Mobile. "While many of my comrades fell around me I was mercifully spared," the Texan recalled, "and when my mind wanders back, as it frequently does, to those perilous times when bullets buzzed like a swarm of bees I marvel that so many of us were permitted to survive the ordeal."[399]

---

[398] Yeary, II, p. 691.
[399] Yeary, II, p. 740.

CHAPTER XXII

DESOLATION

"Things now began to look dark," Sergeant Major Johnston recalled. "General Sherman was marching through Georgia to the sea; Hood's army had been defeated at Nashville. The situation was grave in the extreme. With all this came strange presentiments. The dark clouds that had been for some time overhanging us were settling down. The patriotism, enthusiasm and untold sacrifices of the past four years seemed all for naught, and our men could not be required to shoulder a heavier cross than was now the lot of the Confederate soldiers. But a patriotic people and a valiant soldiery might yet accomplish success, looking as we were, but in vain, for foreign intervention, or something else to turn up. If to satisfy the Northern people and gain our separate existence meant to give up slavery, the army was ready to see it abolished. In fact, the great bulk of the army was ready to make almost any sacrifice required for independent and separate government. Our forefathers had resisted British tyranny, we were resisting Northern aggression upon the sovereignty and reserved rights of the States of the Confederacy."

"Dark and discouraging as were these days, the spirit of the army was yet unbroken, and the men were willing to fight it out, although it appeared but a question of time when we should all go down."[400]

---

[400] Johnston, n.p.

In October 1864, the government seized the railroads for military use, putting an end to private travel.[401]

Phoebe Pember recalled the ordeal of returning to Richmond after a thirty-day furlough in Georgia. It included a twelve-hour layover in West Point, Georgia. There were no bedrooms available, no candles, and the female passengers had to sit at a little bar in a tavern, as the hotel was closed. They could only eat what they carried and the room was lighted only by a burning pine knot.

The next day, they traveled two hours to Opelika and had another six-hour layover. Mrs. Pember and some friends she ran into managed to secure four seats reserved for General Beauregard and his staff when those men were detained by business in Macon. After another stop, she talked her way into a mail room, which had neither a window nor a light. She finally arrived in Augusta. She had only two biscuits to eat in twenty-four hours.[402]

Mrs. Pember had no vehicle to convey her from the railroad depot to the hotel, and it was raining. She accepted a ride on the mail wagon and, sitting on top of bags of mail, reached the hotel in time for breakfast.

She finally got on the train to Richmond, which often did not have wood for the stoves, and the nights were chilly. There were no longer any lamps, which did not matter because there was no oil. They stopped about every hour to repair some part of the train or the railway. Sometimes, they had to exit the train and walk one to five miles. The entire trip from Georgia to Richmond took ten days. [403]

The situation had one fringe benefit for the Confederacy, however. By the winter of 1864–1865, the soldiers who came into the hospitals were almost all wounded. The army had become inured to pneumonia and typhoid.

---

[401]   Pember, p. 138.

[402]   Pember, pp. 141–147.

[403]   Pember, pp. 147–156.

By the winter of 1864–1865, the Confederate economy had basically col-lapsed. In Richmond, for example, tea and coffee disappeared and were replaced by corn flour. (The cost of wheat was too high.) Then butter van-ished, and brown sugar disappeared when the price reached twenty dollars per pound. As late as November 1864, however, the people retained faith in the ultimate success of the Southern cause.[404]

Mary Jones, her daughter Mary Mallard, Kate King (an adult friend) and five children were at Montevideo, not far from Savannah, when Sherman's legions arrived. Jones was a widow; Mallard and King had husbands in the Confederate army.

About 4 p.m. on December 7, 1864, about forty or fifty thugs from Kilpatrick's cavalry arrived. They smashed crockery and broke into the safe. They took all the food they could steal. They even took locks of chil-dren's hair Mrs. Jones had cut half a century before and trampled them underfoot, just for meanness. They stole knives, spoons, forks, tin cups, and coffeepots. They were extremely foul-mouthed and some of them hoped aloud that the women and children starved.[405]

On December 17, another detachment of cavalry arrived. It frightened the ladies, who feared they would be raped. Fortunately, an officer with another detachment arrived. He wanted only provisions. He took all the chickens, turkeys, and ducks they could catch, the family's only pig, and all the syrup from the smokehouse. They appropriated the family carriage to carry the chickens and the family horses to move it. Later, they broke the carriage into pieces and left it. They rounded up seven of the slaves and took them as well, despite the fact they did not want to go.

---

[404] Pember, pp. 156–157.
[405] Sullivan, pp. 233–234.

Three days later another group arrived and found the family's last yoke of oxen. They stole the family's wagon and used the chain from the well to yoke them. Mrs. Jones pled with them to leave the chain, as they needed it to draw water. They replied that the family had no right to wood or water.[406]

The Federals also shot all twelve of the family's sheep and left them dead in the field.

The nearby plantation of South Hampton was also looted by 150 men. They found a three-month supply of corn had been given to each African American, as well as all the syrup and sugar the planter had. The bluecoats took it all, killed forty or fifty hogs and seven beeves, and took all of the syrup and sugar.[407]

Celine Fremaux, who was fourteen years old in 1864, wore a bag underneath her skirts for the purpose of hiding things from Yankees. When Northerners arrived, they hid silverware and jewelry. Similar devices were placed under the clothes of children because they were less likely to be searched. Women—who wore hooped skirts in those days—were often searched.[408]

Once, the Yankees arrived too quickly. Miss Jane Pond attempted to hide silverware in her hoopskirt, but everything fell out. Three Yankee officers laughed at her and picked everything up while she cried with vexation. But they were gentleman and kept nothing.[409]

Southern hospitality extended even to Yankees. In the fall of 1864, as Sherman's cavalry came within striking distance of Andersonville, thousands

---

[406] Sullivan, pp. 236–238.
[407] Sullivan, pp. 241–243.
[408] Sullivan, pp. 191–192.
[409] Sullivan, p. 192.

of prisoners were evacuated to Camp Lawton near Millen, Georgia; Camp Sorghum, near Columbia, South Carolina; and smaller prisons. Because of the deterioration and partial destruction of the Southern rail system, it was not possible to send them exclusively by rail. The malnourished Yankees had to march much of the way. The planters along their route of march furnished them with food and drink. Mrs. Troup Butler (nee Andrews) gave them her last drop of milk and clabber. She begged the officer in charge to let them wait until she could cook food for them. After the officer told her this was not possible, she gave them what food she could spare that could be eaten raw, including potatoes and turnips. Several of Mrs. Butler's neighbors behaved in a similar manner. One of the grateful prisoners, S. S. Andrews of the 64th Ohio, wrote Mrs. Butler after the war and expressed his gratitude. "I still feel thankful for the help we got that day."[410]

In December 1864, Sherman captured Savannah. He issued orders expelling the wives of Confederate soldiers from the city. While they were packing, he sent soldiers to watch them. One of the ladies sent him a letter, castigating him for this. He responded: "You [Southern] women are the toughest set I ever knew. The men would have given up long ago but for you. I believe you would keep this war up for thirty years."[411]

In December 1864, Sara Pryor decided to make a Christmas dinner for her family. She bought a piece of corned beef for fifty dollars and boiled it with some peas. Her servant John made a "perfectly satisfactory" pie out of sorghum molasses, a little flour, and some walnuts.

It was snowing heavily, and just as they sat down, an exhausted company of soldiers trudged past their door. Her boys elected to give their beef

---

[410] Andrews, pp. 59–60.
[411] CWA, p. 114.

and peas to the soldiers, who praised the children to the roof tops. "They were full of it for days," Mrs. Pryor recalled.[412]

Both sides had a problem with lice from the winter of 1861–1862 until after the war. "Here it was that we formed our first acquaintance with 'gray-backs,'" one private recalled. They "filled our clothing and blankets, much to our discomfort. Oh! the digging under the shirt collar, under the arm pits, and every point where the cruel pest found the flesh of the poor soldier. It was a difficult matter to rid ourselves of them—they seemed over anxious to remain with us. Nothing short of boiling them hard in water got rid of them. The next Summer [1862] on the peninsula, in the swamps of the Chickahominy, and around Richmond, we had them in abundance, the boys often saying that they had stamped upon their backs the letters, 'I.F.W.,' which, interpreted, meant 'In for the war.'"[413] The problem was even worse during active campaigning. During the Red River campaign of 1864, for example, the 32nd Texas Cavalry was not able to wash or change clothes for more than thirty days. They blamed the lice on the Yankees, although exactly how Lincoln's men caused a lice infestation in a Texas cavalry unit was never explained. One unusually filthy man in Company E refused to bathe. The men of the 32nd stripped him, threw him into the bayou, burned his clothes, and left him there.[414] How the naked private got out of his fix is not recorded.

Private David Johnston of the 7th Virginia recalled going out onto the battlefield near Malvern Hill "to help gather up the wounded, and to get me a pair of trousers and shoes, both of which I had need of, and which I procured, selecting a dead Union soldier about my size. His shoes I could not wear, as they were too small, and I gave them to a comrade; and I almost regretted having put on his trousers, for they were inhabited by the same sort of graybacks common to the Confederate and Union soldiers.

---

[412] Pryor, p. 319.
[413] Johnston, n.p.
[414] Duaine, p. 83.

After more than 50 years the thought of this wretched parasite makes my flesh itch. But these pests were unavoidable to soldiers continually on the march through mud, mire, and over dusty roads, without opportunity to cleanse their clothes or make a change thereof, and this was particularly so with the Confederate soldier, who seldom had, or could procure a change of raiment."[415]

In December 1864, Miss Eliza Andrews reached the town of Gordon, Georgia, on the Georgia Central Railroad, three weeks after Sherman passed by. "…the desolation was more complete than anything we had yet seen," she recorded in her diary. "There was nothing left of the poor little village but ruins, charred and black as Yankee hearts. The pretty little depot presented only a shapeless pile of bricks…The R.R. track was torn up and the iron twisted into every conceivable shape." She was particularly outraged that some of them were wrapped around the trunks of trees, killing them.[416]

In Fayetteville, Arkansas, the Federals stationed troops at all the grist mills, and no Southern woman was allowed to enter. Every country store outside the town was burned, and the ladies were not allowed to buy or trade at stores in Fayetteville. The women had to produce everything they ate by themselves. This included salt. They learned to beat corn and wheat on the tops of hard stumps to process flour for bread or cornbread. Mrs. W. D. Wasson later stated that they made the best bread she ever ate. "We had splendid appetites," she added. "In fact, that was about all that we did have at times."[417]

---

[415] Johnston, n.p.

[416] Andrews, pp. 47–48.

[417] CWA, p. 161

Food was always scarce, especially in areas looted by the U.S. army. One landlady rented a room to a pair of sisters. She greeted them like a pair of long-lost relatives, but had nothing to serve them for supper except a jar of pickles she had hidden in the fireplace.[418]

In late December 1864, Eliza Frances Andrews and her younger sister Metta were living in Washington, Georgia. They decided to go to another sister's plantation in southwest Georgia, which they correctly believed would not be disturbed by the war.

Metta Andrews, 1872

They took the Georgia Railroad for eleven miles. It once ran from Atlanta to Augusta, but then only sixteen miles of track were intact. The ladies were accompanied part of the way by their brother Fred, the commandant of the Camp of Instruction at Macon. So overloaded was the

---

[418] Andrews, p. 40.

train and so badly maintained was the railroad that it took them two hours to travel eleven miles. Then the two ladies proceeded by hired wagon, which was full of other passengers.

One of the men, Sam Weller, talked about the things "Sherman's robbers" did, and Fanny recalled, "it made my blood boil." A captain asked him if some of the rascals, such as stragglers, weren't caught. "Yes," he replied with a wink, "our folks took lots of prisoners; more'n'll ever be heard of agin." When questioned, he said they "Just took 'em out in the woods and *lost* 'em." He turned to Ms. Andrews and asked: "Ever heerd ko' *losin'* men, lady?"

"Yes, I had heard of it, but thought it a horrible thing." She later wrote that this conversation "made my flesh creep—for after all, even Yankees are human beings, though they don't always behave like it."

"I don't b'lieve in losin' 'em, neither, as a gener'l thing," he replied. "I don't think it's right principal, and I wouldn't lose one myself, but when I see what they have done to these people round here, I can't blame 'em for *losin'* every devil of 'em they kin git their hands on."

A captain asked what was the process of losing a prisoner. Did they use firearms?

Only when they were in a hurry, Weller replied, but usually they were hanged by gravevines and danced "on nothin' till they died." He asked Fanny if she had ever heard of "dancin' on nothin.'"

She said he ought to be ashamed of himself for telling it: "even a Yankee was entitled to protection when a prisoner of war."

"But these fellows wasn't regular prisoners of war, lady," a sick soldier replied. "They were thieves and houseburners." Fanny recalled that "I couldn't but feel there was something in that view of it."

"In justice to both sides," she wrote later, "it must be understood that the class of prisoners here referred to were stragglers and freebooters who had wandered off in search of plunder, and probably got no worse than they deserved when they fell into the hands of the enraged country people, who were naturally not inclined to regard the propriation [sic] of their family plate and household goods and burning of their homes as part of legitimate warfare." She believed there were "many brave and honorable men" in Sherman's army who would not resort to plunder, but this kind of man was unlikely to get "lost."[419]

As they crossed through what the locals called "Burnt Country," through which Sherman passed, she saw many lone chimney-stacks, called "Sherman's Sentinels"—all that was left of someone's home. The fields were trampled down and the road was lined with the rotting carcasses of hogs, horses, mules, and cattle, which the invaders could not carry with them, so they shot them in order to starve civilians and prevent them from making their crops. In places, the stench was unbearable. Hay ricks and fodder stacks were destroyed, corn cribs were empty or burned, and cotton bales were torched. People were eating raw turnips, parched corn, and even loose grains Sherman's horses left behind. "I could better understand the wrath and desperation of these poor people," she wrote. "I almost felt as if I should like to hang a Yankee myself."[420]

As a result of these depredations, many people starved to death immediately after the war. A minimum estimate of those who starved was one hundred thirty thousand; eighty thousand of these were African Americans. The Union army made next to no effort to save them.[421]

En route to Washington, Georgia, Eliza Andrews's party came across a "galvanized Yankee:" a Union mercenary/deserter or prisoner-of-war who defected to the Confederacy. This one was sick and shaking with fever and terror. Andrews looked upon him with distaste. She favored bona fide Yankees who remained true to their own cause. (Lincoln recruited 489,920 foreign mercenaries from fifteen different countries, mostly Germany and Ireland. Robert E. Lee's Army of Northern Virginia never had one hundred thousand men in its history.) The people in the wagon, however, couldn't help but feel sorry for him and took him in because the country people would certainly hang him if they caught him. He turned out to be one of Lincoln's foreign mercenaries named Hans, and he only knew a few

---

[419] Andrews, pp. 30–32.

[420] Andrews, p. 32.

[421] For the story of African American starvation during and after the war, see James Downs, *Sick from Freedom: African-American Death and Suffering During the Civil War and Reconstruction* (Oxford, U.K.: 2012).

English words.[422] They fed him, protected him, and Sam gave him a wad of Confederate money. The man moved off with Weller but first delivered a speech to the "laties unt shentlemansh," thanking them for saving him.

"Now, don't lose the poor wretch," Miss Andrews remarked to Weller.

"No, no, miss, I won't do that," he assured her.

"I felt Hans was safe in the care of this strange, contradictory being, who could talk so like a savage, and yet be capable of such real kindness," she wrote in her diary.[423]

---

[422] Andrews called him a Dutchman, although it is more likely that he was German
[423] Andrews, pp. 34–37.

CHAPTER XXIII

RATTLING DOWNHILL

In Richmond and Petersburg, ball followed ball in quick succession during the winter of 1864–1865. "The soldier danced with the lady of his love at night, and on the morrow danced the dance of death in the deadly trench on the line," Mrs. Pryor recalled.

"I think all who remember the dark days of the winter of 1864–1865 will bear witness to the unwritten law enforcing cheerfulness. It was tacitly understood that we must make no moan, yield to no outward expression of despondency or despair."[424]

Forced optimism was, indeed, the order of the day, both in the trenches and on the home front. "The more misfortunes overwhelm my poor country, the more I love it," Eliza Andrews wrote. "The more the Yankees triumph, the worse I hate them, wretches! I would rather be wrong with men like Lee and Davis, than right with a lot of miserable oppressors like Stanton and Thad Stevens. The wrong of disrupting the old Union was nothing to the wrongs that are being done for its restoration."[425]

Not everybody felt as Miss Andrews did. Sara Pryor recalled: "The month of January brought us sleet and storm. Our famine grew sterner every day...The days were so dark and cheerless, the news from the armies at a distance so discouraging, it was hard to preserve a cheerful demeanor for the sake of the family. And now began the alarming tidings, every

---

[424]   Pryor, p. 327.
[425]   Andrews, pp. 188–189.

morning, of the desertions during the night. General Wilcox wondered how long his brigade would hold together at the rate of fifty desertions every twenty-four hours.

"The common soldier had enlisted, not to establish the right of secession, not for the love of the slave,—he had no slaves,—but simply to resist the invasion of the South by the North, simply to prevent subjugation. The soldier of the rank and file was not always intellectual or cultivated. He cared little for politics, less for slavery. He did care, however, for his own soil, his own little farm, his own humble home; and he was willing to fight to drive the invader from it. Lincoln's Emancipation Proclamation did not stimulate him in the least. The negro, free or slave, was of no consequence to him. His quarrel was sectional one, and he fought for his section...Now, in January, 1865, the common soldier perceived that the cause was lost. He could read its doom in the famine around him, in the faces of his officers, in tidings from abroad. His wife and children were suffering. His duty was now to them; so he stole away in the darkness, and, in infinite danger and difficulty, found his way back to his own fireside. He deserted, but not to the enemy.

"But what can we say of the soldier who remained unflinchingly at his post *knowing* the cause was lost for which he was called to meet death? Heroism can attain no loftier height than this."[426]

Prices, meanwhile, skyrocketed. In February 1865, flour sold for $1,500 a barrel; bacon, twenty dollars a pound; beef, fifteen dollars per pound; butter twenty dollars a pound. One chicken cost fifty dollars. Two shad cost fifty dollars (as opposed to between ten and fifteen cents before the war). One dollar in gold brought one hundred dollars in paper money.[427] The Confederate private was paid eighteen dollars a month.

Some people tried to obtain food by fishing. There was not a fishhook for sale in Richmond or Petersburg. In any case, the fishing was not good. Many of the fish were driven downstream by the firing.

---

[426] Pryor, pp. 320–321.
[427] Pryor, p. 329.

Sherman cut a path through South Carolina eighty miles wide. He burned Hardeeville, Grahamville, Gillisonville, McPhersonville, Barnwell, Blackville, Midway, Orangeburg, Lexington, Winnsboro, Camden, Cheraw, and others. "Indignities and outrages [rapes] were perpetrated upon the persons of the inhabitants. The implements of agriculture were broken; dwellings, barns, mills, gin-houses, were consumed; provisions of every description appropriated or destroyed; horses and mules carried away; and sheep, cattle and hogs were either taken for actual use, or shot down and left behind."[428]

On February 16, 1865, the Federals reached the west bank of the Congaree River[429] across from the capital city of Columbia, which contained forty thousand to fifty thousand people. Without demanding that it surrender, they simply started shelling the place, without giving the women, children, or elderly a chance to evacuate. The shelling continued off and on throughout the day. The Confederate rearguard under General M. C. Butler withdrew on February 17, and Mayor Dr. T. J. Goodwyn and city aldermen surrendered the city to the first Union general they could find. By 11 a.m., the Yankees were in full possession of the city. The Yankee soldiers immediately began breaking into stores and sacking the city. What they did not steal they threw into the streets. Thousands of bluecoats—many of them drinking and carousing—robbed civilians, broke into private homes, robbed bank vaults, and stole anything of value. Citizens appealed to the provost marshal for protection, but he responded, "I cannot undertake to protect private property."

Sherman himself arrived at 3 p.m. and met with the mayor. He promised to protect the city and asked Dr. Goodwyn to take him to a woman of his acquaintance. As they were going there, a shot was fired. Yankee soldiers had killed an African American man for no particular reason. Sherman demanded to know why he had been shot. The troops answered that the black man had been insolent to them. Sherman stepped over the

---

[428] Brooks, *Stories*, p. 331.
[429] The Congaree is the headwater of navigation for the Santee and Cooper Rivers navigation system.

dead body and told his men to stop shooting people, but no arrests were made. He clearly did not care that the black man was dead or who murdered him.[430]

Despite Sherman's assurances and promises, many houses were burned that afternoon, including those of General Hampton and that of his sisters. One Union lieutenant with friends and relatives in the South sent a written warning to Mrs. L. S. McCord, saying: "Ladies, I pity you. Leave this town— go anywhere to be safer than here." This warning was issued in the morning. The lieutenant obviously knew what was about to happen.

About 7 p.m., a squad of soldiers looted the home of William H. Orchard, a highly respected citizen. He apparently impressed the squad leader, who asked to speak with him privately. The Yankee whispered: "You seem to be a clever sort of a man, and have a large family, so I will give you some advice: if you have anything you wish to save, take care of it at once, for before morning this d____d town will be in ashes—every house in it."

Orchard asked if this could be true.

"Yes," the squad leader replied, "and if you don't believe me, you will be the sufferer; if you watch, you will see three rockets go up soon, and, if you do not take my advice, you will see hell."

The signal rockets were fired shortly after. They were the signal for a general conflagration. Columbia fire engines raced to the scenes of some of the blazes, but Yankee soldiers disabled them and cut their hoses with axes and bayonets. The wind was high, and the fires spread rapidly. Women attempted to escape with bundles of clothes. Federals stopped them, took what they wanted, and threw the rest in the fire. Some were subjected to "personal indignities and outrages." Men were threatened with death by gun-toting Yankees if they did not reveal where their gold or silver was hidden. They robbed churches and took communion plates, candlesticks, and anything else of value.

By 3 a.m. on February 18, more than two-thirds of Columbia was reduced to ashes, including the entire business district. It was a cold

---

[430]   Brooks, *Stories*, p. 334

winter's night in Columbia, and thousands of people were without shelter. Sherman blamed Confederate Governor Andrew G. Magrath for the destruction. He failed to burn dozens of barrels of whiskey in the city because it was private property. Later, he changed his story and blamed Mayor Goodwyn. Sherman admitted his men were drunk and "beyond my control." A great many survivors, however, later testified that most of the bluecoats were, in fact, sober. Mayor Goodwyn recalled: "I saw very few drunken soldiers that night; many who appeared to sympathize with our people told me that the fate and doom of Columbia had been common talk around their camp-fires ever since they left Savannah."[431]

Sherman later lied and said the city burned because Wade Hampton set some cotton on fire as he retreated. Hampton denied it; he, in fact, ordered the cotton not be burned because the winds were too high and the fires might endanger Columbia. His orders were passed to his entire corps. General Butler signed a deposition confirming this fact, as did Dr. Goodwyn and Rev. A. Toomer Porter, who were also present, made similar depositions. Edwin J. Scott testified that he saw the Federals burning the cotton. Sherman later admitted that his story was not true.

For the next three months, the U.S. army provided up to eight thousand people with food, which generally consisted of a pint of meal and a small amount of poor beef.

In March 1865, the Yankees burned every mill in Marlboro County, South Carolina, except for one. On the 10th, they reached the home of Captain L. L. McLaurin. They were met by his daughter, Mary McLaurin, a schoolgirl, who saw them coming with their torches. The "bummers" told her they had orders to burn the mill, and they intended to carry them out. She told them that they were infamous cowards and "You shall never do it." They kindled a fire, and she poured water on it. This established a pattern. After several failed attempts, the Yankees threw up their hands, declared

---

[431] Brooks, *Stories*, pp. 335–338.

that Mary was the bravest woman they had ever seen, and abandoned the attempt.[432]

Without the McLaurin Mill, the people of the area would have no place to grind their corn into meal. Miss Mary's courage helped them survive.

In "Slave Narratives," Ida Adkins related a story to the Federal Writers about how she, a small, African American child, ingeniously routed a detachment of Union cavalry and saved her master's plantation house.[433]

"I was born before the war. I was about eight years old when the Yankee soldiers came through. My mother and father were Hattie and Jim Jeffries and they belonged to Marse Frank Jeffries. Marse Frank come from Mississippi, but when I was born he and Miss Mary Jane were living down here near Louisburg in North Carolina where they had a big plantation with I-don't-know how many slaves. Marse Frank was very good to his slaves—maybe excepting that they never got enough to eat. He worked 'em hard on half rations but he didn't believe in all the time beating or selling his slaves.

"My father worked at the stables, he was a good horseman, but my mother worked at the big house helping Miss Mary Jane. Mother worked in the weaving room. I can see her now sitting at the weaving machine and hear the pedals going 'plop, plop,' as she treaded them with her feet. She was a good weaver. I stayed around the big house too, picking up chips, sweeping the yard and such as that. Miss Mary Jane was quick as a whippo-will. She had black eyes that snapped, and they saw everything. She could turn her head so quick that she'd catch you every time if you tried to steal a lump of sugar. I liked Marse Frank better than I did Miss Mary Jane. All of us little children called him 'Big Pappy.' He'd go to Raleigh about twice a year and every time he would come back he brought all of us children some candy. Raleigh was a far ways from the plantation—near about

---

[432] Brooks, *Stories*, p. 62. Mary McLaurin married Captain John R. Parker in 1866 but died three or four years later.

[433] This anecdote was provided by Mr. Ted Brode, who corrected the language for clarity.

sixty miles. It always took Marse Frank about three days to make the trip. A day to go, a day to stay in town, and a day to come back. He would always get back at night unless he rode the horse back instead of the carriage—and then he would get back about sun-down.

"Marse Frank did not go to the war, he was too old. So when the Yankees come through they found him at home. When Marse Frank saw the Yankees coming down the road, he ran and got his gun. The Yankees were on horses. I ain't never seen so many men. They was thick as hornets coming down the road in a cloud of dust. They come up to the house and tied the horses to the pailin's of the fence. There were so many they were all around the yard. When they saw Marse Frank standing on the porch with a gun leveled on them they got mad. Marse Frank shot one time and a big bully Yankee snatched the gun away and told Marse Frank to hold his hands behind his back. Then they tied his hands and pushed him down on the floor beside the house and told him that if he moved an inch they would shoot him. Then they went into the house.

"I was scared near about to death, but I ran into the kitchen and got a butcher knife, and when the Yankees were not looking, I tried to cut the rope and set Marse Frank free. But one of them blue devils saw me and come a running. He said: '*What you doin' you black brat*[434]—*you stinking little alligator bait!*' He snatched the knife from my hand and told me to *stick out my tongue*, that he was gonna *cut it off*. I let out a yell and run behind the house.

"Some of the Yankees was in the smoke house getting [stealing] the meat, some of them was at the stables getting [stealing] the horses, and some of them was in the house getting [stealing] the silver and things. I saw them put the big silver pitcher and tea pot in a bag. Then they took the knives and forks and all the candle sticks and platters off the side board and they went in the parlor and got the gold clock that was Miss Mary Jane's grandmother's clock. Then they got all the jewelry out of Miss Mary Jane's box. And they even went up to Miss Mary Jane and while she looked at them with those black eyes snapping, they took the rings off her fingers,

---

[434] Not his exact words.

and the gold bracelet off her hand, they even took the ruby earrings off of her ears and the gold comb out of her hair.

"By that time I was done peeping in the window and was standing beside the house when the Yankees come out in the yard with all the stuff they was toting off. Masre Frank was still on the porch floor with his hands tied and couldn't do nothing. About that time I saw all those bee gums [boxes] in the side yard. They was a whole line of the gums. Little as I was I had a notion. I run and got me a long stick and turned over every one of them gums. Then I stirred them bees up with the stick till they was so mad I could smell the poison. And bees!! You ain't never seen the like of it— bees everywhere!! They was swarming all over the place. They sailed into them Yankees like bullets—each one madder than the other. They lit on the Yankees' horses till the horses looked like they were alive with the var- mints. The horses broke they bridles and tore down the pailings and lit out down the road. That running wasn't nothing—to what the Yankees done. They bust out cussing—but what did a bee care about cuss words! They lit on them bluecoats and every time they lit they stuck in a poison sting. The Yankees forgot all about the meat and things they done stole; they took off down the road on a run, *passing the horses*. The bees were right after them in a long line. They'd *zoom and zip* and *zoom and zip* and every time they *zip* a Yankee would yell.

"When they were all gone, Miss Mary Jane untied Marse Frank and then they took all the silver and meat and things the Yankees left behind and buried and hid it so if they came back they couldn't find it. Then they called me and said:

"Ida Lee, if you hadn't turned over the bee gums the Yankees would have toted off near about everything fine that we have. We want to give you something you can keep so you'll always remember this day and how you ran the Yankees away. Then Miss Mary Jane took a plain gold ring off her finger and put it on mine. And I've been wearing that ring ever since."

This was a unique incident in the Civil War—an eight-year-old African American girl single-handedly routing a large detachment of Union cavalry.

After serving ten months in the cavalry, Sergeant James H. Kimball was given the task of running the blockade on the Mississippi River. He crossed the river every week in a canoe, often carrying important officials from the eastern Confederacy to the Trans-Mississippi and vice versa. Two of them were Admiral Semmes and his son, an army major. The Yankees were anxious to capture him and offered a reward of $10,000 in gold for him but were never successful. His last scheduled passenger was Jefferson Davis, but the president never arrived.

"I tried to do the duty of a soldier, and was faithful to the trust assigned me," Sergeant Kimball recalled.[435]

Jim Canada of the 8th Kentucky Cavalry was not lucky. He was with Forrest's Cavalry at Harrisburg, Mississippi, where he was captured. After months in a Union prison, he was exchanged and rejoined Forrest on April 2, 1865—just in time for the Battle of Selma. Here, Forrest's elite cavalry corps was finally overwhelmed and defeated. Canada was captured again. "Jim said that was pretty tough on him," a comrade recalled, "but such was war."[436]

Aron Wilburn fought from Shiloh to the Atlanta Campaign, where he fell ill. He was sent back to Mobile, Alabama, where he fought his last battles at Fort Blakely from April 2–9, 1865. They called out every available boy over the age of fourteen to defend the city and placed six boys on picket duty for every veteran soldier. Wilburn was given six inexperienced youths. Writing in 1909, he remembered telling them that if the enemy charged,

---

[435] Yeary, Vol. II, pp. 402–403.
[436] Yeary, II, p. 690.

they were to break for the breastworks as quickly as possible. One little fellow replied: "I will not leave the rifle pit till you do."

About 3 p.m. on April 9, the Federals attacked with three lines of battle. Wilburn told the boys to run for the breastworks. The little fellow had to be told twice. Wilburn took a shot and reloaded, but the Yankees were almost on top of him, "...with shells and bullets flying thick I struck out for the breastworks and when I had run about forty yards I jumped over the little boy with the top of his head shot off. I have no doubt that his parents never heard from him again or ever saw his corpse...one of the Federals followed me from the picket line and hit me between the shoulders with the butt of his gun as I ran up over the breast works and from this blow I have suffered more or less to the present time."[437]

---

[437] Yeary, II, pp. 793–794.

CHAPTER XXIV

THE DEATH OF LEE'S ARMY

"No such army ever trod this earth," one author wrote, "as the Army of Northern Virginia, composed of the best body of fighting men that ever shouldered a musket." President Theodore Roosevelt said of them: "The world has never seen better soldiers than those who followed Lee."[438]

U.S. General "Fighting Joe" Hooker agreed. Testifying before the congressional committee, he said of the Army of Northern Virginia: "That army had by discipline alone a character for steadiness and efficiency unsurpassed, in my judgment, in ancient or modern times. We have not been able to rival it."

By the spring of 1865, however, it was at last on its last legs.

The final struggle for Richmond began on April 1, 1865, with the Battle of Five Forks, on the extreme right of the Confederate line, where Pickett's division suffered a decisive defeat. They were outnumbered twenty-six thousand to eight thousand (which included nine hundred of Fitz Lee's cavalry), were poorly led, and were simply overwhelmed. David Johnston wrote later: "In the woods where we were fighting it was getting dark, the moon beginning to shine. My position as Sergeant-Major was on the left of the regiment, which I occupied during the fierce contest. Seeing the regiment move rapidly by the right flank and to the rear, but in good

---

[438] Johnston, n.p.

order, I stood for a moment reflecting whether I should leave or take the chances of death or becoming a prisoner. Choosing the former, and passing the road over which we had fought our way a few minutes before, I found myself with two Confederates, who were a little in advance of me, and proceeding but a short distance we found ourselves plump up against the lines of Federal cavalry. A Sergeant demanded our surrender, the Confederate nearest him threw down his gun; the one next to me turned and said, 'What shall we do?' I still had the carbine I had picked up the day before in the battle near Dinwiddie, but no ammunition, and without replying to the question or dropping my gun, but keeping my eyes fixed on the sergeant, who was separated by a small space from his comrades as well as from me, I observed that his cap had been knocked off by the limb of a pine bush under which he had ridden, and that his attention was fixed upon an effort to get his cap. Just then seeing an opening where the Federal regiments joined, I darted through, amidst a shower of bullets, the wind and heat of some of them being felt distinctly in my face. The reader may easily imagine the speed made just then by a Confederate Sergeant-Major. In less than two hundred yards beyond, I overtook my command forming across the road."

The fighting was fierce—sometimes hand-to-hand—but the Confederates were defeated. Rebels lost 450 killed, 750 wounded, 3,244 missing or captured, and lost four guns. Union losses were 124 killed and 706 wounded.[439]

The next day, Lee's lines were finally broken. Richmond was evacuated on April 2–3, and Grant occupied the former Confederate capital during the morning of April 3.

Constance Cary went to church on the morning Lee's line finally collapsed. She recalled: "On the morning of April 2, a perfect Sunday of the Southern spring, a large congregation assembled as usual at St. Paul's. I happened to sit in the rear of the President's pew, so near that I plainly saw the sort of gray pallor that came upon his face as he read a scrap of paper thrust into his hand by a messenger hurrying up the middle aisle. With stern set

---

[439] Johnston, n.p.

lips and his usual quick military tread, he left the church, a number of other people rising in their seats and hastening after him, those who were left swept by a universal tremor of alarm. The rector, accustomed as he was to these frequent scenes in church, came down to the altar rail and tenderly begged his people to remain and finish the service, which was done.

"Before dismissing his congregation the rector announced to them that General Ewell had summoned the local forces to meet for defense of the city at three in the afternoon. We knew then that Longstreet's regulars must have been suddenly called away, and a sick apprehension filled all hearts.

"On the sidewalk outside the church we plunged at once into the great stir of evacuation, preluding the beginning of a new era. As if by a flash of electricity, Richmond knew that on the morrow her streets would be crowded with her captors, her rulers fled, her government dispersed into thin air, her high hopes crushed to earth. There was little discussion of events. People meeting each other would exchange silent hand grasps and pass on. I saw many pale faces, some trembling lips, but in all that day I heard no expression of a weakling fear. Movement was everywhere, nowhere panic. Begarlanded Franklin Street, sending up perfume from her many gardens, was the general rendezvous of people who wanted to see the last of their friends. All over town citizens were aiding the departure of the male members of their family who could in any way serve the dispossessed government. In the houses we knew, there was everywhere somebody to be helped to go; somebody for whose sake tears were squeezed back, scant food prepared, words of love and cheer spoken. Those good, dear women of Richmond, who had been long tried as by fire, might bend but would not break.

"Between two and three in the afternoon formal announcement was made to the public that the government would vacate Richmond that evening. By nightfall all the flitting shadows of a Lost Cause had passed away under a heaven studded by bright stars. The doomed city lay face to face with what it knew not..."[440]

---

[440] Harrison, pp. 207–208.

As Lee's army retreated, its logistical infrastructure failed completely.

T. N. Skeen of the 7th Georgia fought in all the battles on the eastern front from the First Manassas to Appomattox. He also fought in the attack on Knoxville, Tennessee, where he was wounded four times by minie balls in less than a minute. His regiment, which had thirteen hundred men when the war began, had only ninety at the surrender.

Skeen recalled that they did not draw a pound of rations from the fall of Petersburg on April 3, 1865, until Lee capitulated. He said: "I do not think Gen. Sherman was mistaken in his definition of war."[441]

From April 1 to 6, 1865, the remnants of the 7th Virginia were engaged in more or less constant skirmishing. The end came in the Battle of Sayler's Creek, which was sometimes incorrectly called the Battle of Sailor's Creek. Sergeant Johnston recalled: "In the afternoon, probably 2:30 or a little later, a heavy force of the enemy's cavalry made a charge on a battalion of Confederate artillery in advance of us on the same road. To check this cavalry charge, we were hurried across Sailor's Creek, reaching the guns of Colonel [Frank] Huger's battalion in time to see most of the artillerists, including Colonel Huger, taken away as prisoners. The enemy not being able to take these guns away, as we were now at their heels, they hurriedly chopped with an axe the spokes out of the wheels, disabling them for present use, then retreated, we following in line of battle and going forward through an open field, meeting no resistance, and halting on a piece of high ground. A squadron of Federal cavalry, spying General Pickett with his staff riding up in our rear, made a dash for him; about the same time he discovered the object of these bold riders, and galloped quickly to the lines of the brigade to our left, which was in a body of scattering timber. These reckless troopers pushed up after the General until close to our men, who

---

[441] Yeary, II, p. 691.

fired upon them, emptying every saddle. This incident is given to show the reader how desperate was this prolonged game of death.

"On the brow of the hill where our brigade halted on the road on which we had been marching, there was intersection with another road leading directly west. Here we hurriedly tore away an old worm fence, piling up the rails to make some protection against rifle balls. On the left rear of Pickett's and part of Bushrod Johnson's divisions on Sailor's Creek were Custis Lee's and Kershaw's 3,000 men under General Ewell, with whom we had no connection, nor with Mahone's division and other troops ahead of us, leaving gaps through which the Federal cavalry passed, enabling them to get on our flanks and rear. The enemy's troops in this engagement—one army corps with three cavalry divisions—numbered 25,000 or more men, while the Confederates did not have 7,500 all told. The fighting was desperate. Along our front and fully five hundred yards away we could see passing to our right heavy bodies of the enemy, evidently bent upon getting ahead of us. Moreover, this must have been manifest to our commanding officers, who permitted us to remain idle for several hours and until the enemy made full preparations to attack us. That somebody blundered, there is no doubt, as any enlisted man in the ranks could clearly see. We should have moved on. The attack came between 3 and 4 o'clock P.M. by an assault on [Colonel T. T.] Munford's dismounted cavalry in a skirt of woods to our right. This attack, as were others on our right front, was repulsed.

"General Terry, our brigade commander, had given the order to move to the right, when he discovered another advance upon us, this time in heavy force. We were ordered to remain where we were and not to fire until the enemy were close enough to see the whites of their eyes, then fire and charge with the bayonet. We were behind the rails, close to the ground. The enemy, armed with repeating rifles, when within seventy-five yards or so opened upon us, filling the air with balls, and coming at us. Every man who raised his head above the rails gave his life for the venture. Captain Harris, the adjutant general of the brigade, raised his head to look and fell back dead; a sandy haired man of my regiment at my elbow met the same fate. He was from Orange County and never knew what hit him. Then came a lull in the firing in front, and I heard a noise behind us; looking around, I saw a column of Federal cavalry close behind us, one of whom had boldly dashed up behind our regiment, seized the colors, and with drawn saber compelled Torbett, the color bearer, to surrender the same. Such was the character and bravery of the men we had to fight. Some one just then cried, 'Fire!' and a portion of our regiment delivered its fire into the faces of the enemy in front. In a moment began an indiscriminate fight with clubbed muskets, flagstaffs, pistols and sabers. In a few moments all was over. We had met the enemy and we were theirs. This final struggle was most tragic. We were now marched out and surrounded by a cordon of cavalry."[442]

Johnston was complimentary of the victors, who, although poorly supplied themselves, shared their rations with the captured Southerners. He recalled of his fellow prisoners: "Gloom was depicted on every countenance, and sorrow was in every face. These men had seen their comrades go down day by day, by which they were impressed that if the war continued it was only a question of time when they too would bite the dust. They, however, had this consolation regarding their fallen comrades: that they had gone down in the conscientious belief in the justness of their cause, in the hope of victory, and had not lived to see their flag furled in defeat, and were saved the humiliation of tasting the bitter cup of submission, of which we were to drink to its very dregs. Maybe these after all were the lucky men—who knows? The gallantry and devotion of our soldiers in the unequal struggle proved how thorough were their convictions of the righteousness of their cause. Their devotion to that cause and their kindness and humanity to those whom the fate of war placed in their power, proved them worthy sons of noble ancestry. These men viewed the attempt at coercion on the part of the Northern people as aggression, and their action in defense of their country, homes and firesides, as an inherent, inalienable right—a defense of constitutional liberty."

General Lee finally surrendered at Appomattox on April 9, 1865. Ben Hill of Georgia eulogized him as follows: "When the future historian

---

[442] Johnston, n.p.

comes to survey the character of Robert E. Lee he will find it rising like a great mountain above the undulating plain of humanity, and will be compelled to lift his eyes heavenward to catch a glimpse of its summit. He possessed every virtue of the other great commanders of history, without any of their vices. He was a foe without hate, a friend without treachery, a private citizen without wrong, a neighbor without reproach, a Christian without hypocrisy, and a man without guile. He was a Caesar without his ambition, a Frederick without his tyranny, a Washington without his reward. He was as obedient to authority as a servant, and as loyal to authority as a true king. He was as gentle as a woman, modest and pure as a virgin, watchful as a Roman vestal on duty, and grand in battle as Achilles."[443]

In Germany, Colonel Heros von Borcke concurred. "Lee's glorious army," he wrote, "is no longer in existence: the brave men who formed it have, after innumerable sufferings and privations, bowed to the enemy's power and numbers...But those who have survived the fearful struggle for independence, can look back upon a series of battles and victories unequalled in history; and every one of us will forever speak with pride of the time when he was a soldier of the Army of Northern Virginia. I myself am still an invalid. The ball which I carry in my lungs gives me frequent sufferings, and has broken my once so robust health; but as every renewal of my pains reminds me of the past, they are alleviated and almost effaced by the pleasure with which I revert to the time when I fought side by side with those brave men; and I shall ever rejoice that I drew my sword for the gallant people of the late Confederacy."[444]

One by one, the Rebel units signed off. "The population of the North was so numerous, and her resources were so vast and immense, that the South was finally overwhelmed; but it was only by numbers that those brave spirits were forced at last to sheathe their swords, and the seared and veteran legions to lay down their arms: they had fought with courage that

---

[443] Bowman, p. 44.

[444] Borcke, pp. 437–438.

never faltered to the close," Private Ephraim Anderson of the 1st Missouri Brigade wrote after the war.[445]

"The weak, as a rule, are borne down by the strong," Carlton McCarthy wrote, "but that does not prove that the strong are also right. The weak suffer wrong, learn the bitterness of it, and finally, by resisting it, become the defenders of right and justice."[446]

Major General Fitzhugh Lee, the commander of the cavalry of the Army of Northern Virginia, surrendered with his uncle, Robert E. Lee, at Appomattox on April 9, 1865. As he rode away from Appomattox, he met an old soldier from North Carolina.

"Ho, there, where are you going?" Fitz Lee asked.

"I've been off on furlough and am now going back to join General Bob Lee," the veteran replied.

"You needn't go back, but can throw your gun away and return home, for Lee's surrendered," Fitz replied.

"Lee's surrendered?"

"That's what I said," the cavalry general retorted.

"It must have been that damned Fitz Lee, then," the infantryman replied. "Rob Lee would never surrender." He gave the cavalryman a look of contempt and walked on.[447]

---

[445] Anderson, *Missouri*, p. 9.
[446] McCarthy, p. 3.
[447] CWA, p. 34.

CHAPTER XXV

CHAOS

The end—as is usually the case when a nation dies—was chaotic. There were many Southern refugees in 1865. Columbus, Georgia, fell on April 16. Hundreds of refugees fled into what was left of Confederate Georgia and Alabama. Eliza Andrews noted that the railroad cars "were filled with refugees and their goods. It was pitiful to see them, especially the poor little children, driven from their homes by the frozen-hearted Northern Vandals, but they were all brave and cheerful, laughing good-naturedly instead of grumbling over their hardships. People have gotten so used to these sort of things that they have learned to bear them with philosophy."[448]

Among those wounded in the struggle for Columbus was Dr. John Stith Pemberton (1831–1888), a former surgeon and chemist who became a pharmacist. He was a lieutenant colonel commanding a cavalry battalion on April 16 when a Yankee saber cut him across the chest. He suffered from this wound for the rest of his life. To alleviate the pain, he invented several medicines, as well as a popular soft drink: Coca Cola. He initially advertised it as a brain tonic, but sales were poor. In 1888, he sold the formula for $1,750.

---

448   Andrews, p. 146.

The Rebels were good at inventing soft drinks. Although several stories exist concerning the origin of the soft drink "Dr. Pepper," it is said to be named after Dr. Charles T. Pepper (1830–1903), a Confederate surgeon. He spent most of the war at Emory and Henry College, which the Confederacy commandeered as a hospital.

In several localities, the fighting continued after Appomattox. Mobile did not fall until April 12. Another pitched battle took place in West Point, Georgia.

C. D. W. McNeil was a sergeant in Company H of the 4th Georgia Infantry. He was sent to West Point, Georgia, where he reported to Brigadier General Robert C. Tyler on April 15, 1865. Tyler was eating what turned out to be his last supper on earth. The next morning, Tyler knew the Yankees were advancing and that he would be badly outnumbered in the subsequent battle. He ordered McNeil to go into town and get all the volunteers he could to help defend his main position, an earthwork ambitiously dubbed Fort Tyler.

Most of the men of West Point had already joined the army, but McNeil found three enthusiastic volunteers, William Austin, Thomas Cherry, and Willie Morris, ages eleven to thirteen. They fought like tigers and proudly "threw [fired] leaden pellets in the Federal ranks," the sergeant recalled.

Tyler's command repulsed charge after charge. The battle lasted seven and three-quarters hours, and at times, the fighting was heavy. When the garrison finally surrendered, the boys' faces were black with burned powder. The boys capitulated with the rest of the command, "and stood the hardships [of prison] without a murmur…True heroes of the Southern cause."

Seizing an opportunity to escape, Sergeant McNeil ordered the boys to take to the woods. The four of them spent the night in an old Confederate camp near Reid's Fish Pond. The next morning, they returned to Fort Tyler, which the Yankees overran and then abandoned, and saw the refuse of war: smashed Enfield rifles, dismounted cannon, and so forth. They sat on the parapets and watched the Federals leave town. They returned to West Point, where civilians fed them. Sergeant McNeil did not see the boys again until the first of May, when they all surrendered and were paroled.[449]

In April 1861, the able-bodied men of Troup County, Georgia, formed the LaGrange Light Guard, the cavalry unit of the 4th Georgia Infantry, and went off to war. By 1863, the women of the town felt their town might be threatened by the Yankees, so they formed the Nancy Harts, which were named after a Revolutionary War hero who successfully defended her home against the British.[450] These women were the forerunners of the WACs (Women's Army Corps) of World War II fame. They drilled as an infantry unit and trained themselves in the use of firearms, as well as in infantry tactics. They were led by Nancy Colquitt Hill Morgan (a twenty-one-year-old bride of six months) and Mrs. Mary Cade Heard, who was twenty-seven years old. Mrs. Heard managed two plantations and directed one hundred slaves. Morgan became the captain, and Heard was the first lieutenant. Most of the women in the ranks were students or graduates of LaGrange Female College. They were assisted by Dr. H. C. Ware, a veteran who was no longer able to perform field service.

The Nancy Harts drilled and engaged in target practice twice a week. They wore their regular dresses—some of them with hoops. Most of them initially had the bad habit of closing their eyes just before pulling the trigger, missing the target entirely. One day, one of them closed her eyes and turned her head before firing. Her bullet struck a hornets' nest. The insects counterattacked and routed the ladies, but they rallied and finished the

---

449 Yeary, pp. 505–506.

450 Nancy Morgan Hart was born in North Carolina around 1735. She stood six feet tall and was known for her physical and emotional strength. Five or six intoxicated British soldiers killed her prize turkey and entered her home. She invited them to have an alcoholic beverage, so they carelessly stacked their muskets where Nancy could reach them. She shot and killed one of the intruders, wounded another, and held the rest at gun point until help arrived. They were eventually hanged from an oak tree in Hart's front yard. They may have been Tories.

drill. On another occasion, one of their errant bullets killed a local bull. Before long, however, they learned how to use their muskets properly.

LaGrange was on a major rail line, and in 1863, every train seemed to bring in wounded from Mississippi, Tennessee, or Virginia. The women became nurses, but they continued drilling and engaging in target practice.

In April 1865, General Robert Tyler needed all able-bodied men, including the walking wounded at LaGrange, for the defense of West Point, Georgia (see above). There were no men left in LaGrange. U.S. Colonel Oscar LaGrange (who had no connection to the town) crossed the Chattahoochee River and captured West Point and Fort Tyler, killed the general, and destroyed the railroad facilities there, including nineteen locomotives and 340 cars loaded with supplies. He then turned on LaGrange. On April 18, he was met by the Nancy Harts, who were in battle formation.

Colonel LaGrange was no doubt surprised to see a forty-woman combat unit blocking his path. He had been in the town before. In the spring of 1864, he had been seriously wounded and captured by Confederate forces. He was sent to LaGrange, where the hospitals were full, so a local belle volunteered to take him in. (She was a niece of Benjamin Harvey Hill, a Confederate senator.) Colonel LaGrange was transported to "Bellevue," a plantation house near the town, where he was nursed back to health by the niece and other Southern women. He was later exchanged.[451]

The colonel did not want to fight women or lose any more casualties, so he asked a prisoner to introduce him to Captain Morgan. She told him that they intended to defend their homes and families. The colonel compromised. If the ladies would disarm, he would not harm any private homes. Given this option, they dispersed, but armed women continued to guard private homes that night.

---

[451] Bellevue was the home of Confederate (and former U.S.) Senator Benjamin Harvey Hill. LaGrange did not allow his men to burn Hill's home. After the war, Hill returned to Congress and was again elected to the Senate in 1877. He served until his death in 1882. Hill opposed secession in 1861. Bellevue, a fine example of Greek Revival architecture, became a National Historic Landmark in 1973. It is now owned by the LaGrange Women's Club and is a museum.

Meanwhile, one of the Nancy Harts invited Colonel LaGrange to dinner. He accepted and temporarily paroled several local men (who were captured at Fort Tyler) so they could attend. Union troops burned the local places which had military value (the tannery, the cotton warehouses, the train depot, and a few other buildings) and they did loot a few local stores, but LaGrange was spared the desolation many Georgia towns incurred.

The local men were marched to Macon, Georgia, and were supposed to be sent to a Northern prison camp, but when Colonel LaGrange learned that Lee had surrendered, he released them on parole.

Meanwhile, refugees continued to pour into Washington, Georgia. One of them was an African American man, "Little Johnny Nightingale," the servant of Captain John Nightingale. (Some people, suffering from Noble Cause Delusion Disorder—a common malady in some places—swell up with moral self-righteousness and declare vehemently there were no black Confederate soldiers—as if they knew anything about it. There were, in fact, between eighty thousand and ninety-six thousand of them.) Little Johnny had served years with the Confederate army and had been captured. He managed to steal a horse and escape. He had absolutely no use for Yankees and was in Washington, looking for his master, Captain John Nightingale. Judge Andrews put him up in the Negro quarters of his plantation, in hopes that the captain would also turn up at Haywood, the Andrewses' plantation.[452]

On April 24, 1865, the remnants of the Army of Northern Virginia began arriving in Washington, on their way home. They arrived in large numbers and strained the local populace's resources nearly to the breaking point. "Emily is kept busy cooking rations for them, and pinched as we are ourselves for supplies, it is impossible to refuse anything to the men that have been fighting for us," one resident recalled.[453]

---

[452] Andrews, p. 183.
[453] Andrews, p. 182.

As the remnants of the armies passed through Georgia, one lady travelling in a buggy met "the weary and ragged and travel-stained" veterans in gray. "I felt ashamed of myself for riding when they had to walk. These are the straggling remnants of those splendid armies that have been for four years a terror to the North, the glory of the South, and the wonder of the world. Alas, alas!"[454]

During the afternoon of May 1, 1865, law and order broke down in Washington, Georgia. The Confederate government had basically broken up, people were demoralized, and chaos was the result. A Texas regiment rioted over rations and was joined by soldiers and civilians, as well as African Americans and children. They plundered the commissary and quartermaster's departments and stole everything, including pens, paper, buttons, tape, and cloth, as well as all the food (especially bacon) they could carry. The provost guards refused to intervene; they would not fire on their colleagues. The looters also confiscated horses and mules. Even General Elzey lost nine mules. The plunderers allowed how it was better for them to take these things than the Yankees, who should arrive within a few days. They were right about that.

Eliza Andrews recalled that the stragglers were very generous and gave away pens, paper, and other supplies, to anyone they happened to meet. Judge Andrews collected a great many reams of paper and intended to return them to the authorities but soon learned the headquarters had dissolved and there was no longer anyone in authority.[455]

Confederate money was now useless. People traded gunpowder, lead, cartridges, and even buttons for currency. Everywhere "ragged, starving, hopeless, reckless [soldiers] are roaming about without orders or leaders," making their way home as best they can. "The props that held society up are broken. Everything is in a state of disorganization and tumult … no law save the primitive code that might makes right."[456]

---

[454] Andrews, p. 186.
[455] Andrews, pp. 194–195.
[456] Andrews, p. 198.

Jefferson Davis and the remnants of the Confederate government were also on the road, hoping to somehow escape west of the Mississippi. Burton Harrison, the private secretary to the president, recalled how the presidential party fled through North Carolina. "During all this march," he wrote, "Mr. Davis was singularly equable and cheerful. He seemed to have had a great load taken from his mind, to feel relieved of responsibilities, and his conversation was very bright and agreeable. He talked of men and of books, particularly of Walter Scott and Byron; of horses and dogs and sports; of the woods and the fields; of roads and how to make them; of the habits of birds and of a variety of other topics. His familiarity with and correct taste in the English literature of the last generation, his varied experiences in life, his habits of close observation, and his extraordinary memory made him a charming companion when disposed to talk. Indeed, like Mark Tapley, we were all in good spirits under adverse circumstances, and I particularly remember the entertaining conversation of Mr. Mallory, the Secretary of the Navy."[457]

---

[457] Harrison, p. 223.

CHAPTER XXVI

RETURNING HOME

A nd so the Confederate States of America faded into history. Those who survived returned to their homes—if they still had them. Here, their experiences varied widely. Richard Kerry was a private in the 38th Alabama Infantry Regiment and fought on the western front from Fishing Creek, Kentucky (January 1861) to Nashville. He surrendered at Decatur, Alabama, and headed home.

His wife died during the war. When he passed his mother-in-law's house, he saw some children playing in the woodpile. They were his. He asked the girl if she knew him. "No!" she answered. He told her he was her father. She did not believe him but went into the house and told her grandmother that there was an old, ragged soldier outside claiming to be her papa. Mrs. Hughes went out to investigate and, sure enough, it was true. She gave him dinner and a chance to clean up so he looked better.[458]

After two years of war, seventeen-year-old S. W. Thompson surrendered with the Army of Tennessee on April 26, 1865. "Got home [to Lynnville, Tennessee] and found everything gone. Not a good horse in the country except those brought from the army. But we went to work to build up the waste places, and strange to say, in three years you could not tell that we had been to war except now and then an empty sleeve or a one-legged

---

[458] Yeary, II, pp. 401–402.

man. The men who were great in war have proved themselves the yeomen of the South in peace."[459]

Private John Q. Thompson of Monticello, Arkansas, who fought from June 1862, wrote about 1909: "I lost everything I had during the war, and was owing between $3,000 and $4,000. I went to work, paid it all up, kept striving, and I now have a good home and plenty to live on." [460]

Burton Harrison was captured with President and Mrs. Davis on May 10 and imprisoned at Fort Delaware, where he continued his legal studies. He was released in 1866, established a law practice, and married Constance Cary in 1867. He remained active in politics and was an envoy to the Dominican Republic in 1872. He was later offered an ambassadorship to Italy and the post of assistant secretary of state but declined both. He died in 1904.

Constance Cary Harrison became a highly successful novelist, writer, and playwright. Her pen name was "Refugitta," apparently after General Fitz Lee's horse. She died in 1920.

The Cary family was luckier than most. They lived in Vaucluse, the estate of Constance Cary's maternal grandfather, in Alexandria, Virginia. When the war began, they decided to flee to safety in the Confederacy. They placed all of their silver in two large traveling trunks. Aided by a "faithful old negro gardener" and a young nephew, they worked half the night burying them in the cellar.[461]

They returned four years later and discovered the house had been destroyed by incendiaries. The site had been used by the U.S. army and

---

[459] Yeary, II, p. 749.

[460] Yeary, II, p. 748.

[461] Constance Cary (later Mrs. Burton Harrison) (1843–1920) was a descendant of Thomas Jefferson's nephew and a cousin of Robert E. Lee. She lived at Vaucluse, the Alexandria, Virginia, estate of her maternal grandfather, prior to the war. Later she became a famous and prolific writer. She created an early Confederate battle flag at the request of a Confederate congressional committee. She and her cousins, Hetty and Jennie Cary, each sewed Confederate battle flags. In 1867, she married Burton N. Harrison, who was formerly the private secretary to President Davis. One of her sons, Francis B. Harrison, was a U.S. congressman from New York and governor-general of the Philippines.

all of the trees cut down and used to form breastworks and probably firewood. They identified the probable location of the cellar only by a slight depression in the ground. The family hired several laborers who worked for hours trying to find the boxes. One of the ladies cried, apparently, because she was sure the Yankees had discovered the silver. Finally, just as they were about to give up, a worker shouted and held up a teaspoon, which was jet black. Soon they discovered that the boxes had rotted and everywhere there was candelabras, tea-sets, tankards, and complete silver services.

Constance Cary Harrison
(Virginia Museum of History and Culture)

"Any idle soldier prodding the ground might have struck the boxes," Mrs. Burton Harrison (then Miss Constance Cary) wrote later, but everything was there. "…not even a salt-spoon missing," she declared.[462]

Matthew Calbraith Butler was not so fortunate. He lost all his material possessions during the war. "I was twenty-nine years old, with one leg gone, a wife and three children to support, with seventy slaves emancipated, a debt of $15,000, and in my pocket, $1.75," he recalled. He nevertheless refused to give in to depression. He resumed his law practice, was elected to the legislature in 1866, and ran unsuccessfully for lieutenant

---

[462] Harrison, pp. 44–45.

governor in 1870. He worked for a return to home rule in South Carolina, which occurred when the Federal troops withdrew in early 1877. The legislature promptly elected him to the United States senate, a seat he held until 1895. Later he served as a major general of U.S. volunteers during the Spanish-American War.

As soon as they were financially able, the survivors, widows, and orphans began erecting monuments to their lost loved ones. In 1908, Confederate veteran J. D. Hogan declared: "When in the course of coming events the true history of a glorious South is written by men free from prejudice, from malice and from hatred then will the heroes of the Lost Cause stand out in bold relief and generations yet unborn will point with pride to the names emblazoned on monuments erected to the soldier statesmen of the old South."[463]

And so it was for more than a century. An unofficial truce evolved between North and South, which lasted until early in the 21st century. The North admitted that the South was fighting for liberty and independence, while the South accepted that the North was fighting to preserve the Union and because Old Glory had been fired upon. The two great heroes of the conflict became Abraham Lincoln and Robert E. Lee, while the South admitted that slavery was wrong but refused to concede that it was cruel, at least as it was practiced in Dixie. Northern historian John Fiske wrote: "For my own part, I have sympathized with so many of the rebellions in history, from the revolt of the Ionian cities against Darius Hystaspes down to the uprising in Cuba, that I am quite unable to conceive of 'rebel' as a term of reproach. In England, to this day, Cromwell's admirers do not hesitate to speak with pride of the Great Rebellion. While my own sympathies are thoroughly Northern, as befits a Connecticut Yankee, I could still take off my hat to the statue of Robert E. Lee when I passed it in New Orleans. His was devotion to self-government, which seemed in mortal peril."[464]

---

[463] *Confederate Veteran*, Vol XVI (1908).

[464] Bankston, pp. 10–11.

David Johnston—perhaps the youngest sergeant major in the Confederate army—emigrated to Oregon, where he became a judge and a highly respected member of his community. He wrote: "I believe the world has never produced a body of men superior in courage, patriotism and endurance to the private soldiers of the Confederate armies. I have repeatedly seen these soldiers submit with cheerfulness to privations and hardships which would appear to be almost incredible; and the wild cheers of our brave men, when their lines sent back opposing hosts of Federal troops, staggering, reeling and flying, have often thrilled every fiber in my heart. I have seen with my own eyes ragged, barefooted and hungry Confederate soldiers perform deeds which, if performed in days of yore by mailed warriors in glittering armor, would have inspired the harp of the minstrel and the pen of the poet."[465]

Thomas R. Murray of the 14th Arkansas would have agreed with the judge. He recalled: "The sons of today look back on their four years' college course as the brightest and best years of their lives, and I, despite the horrors of war, found the same inspiring comradeship in my four years' course. But time has not graduated me into an ex-Confederate yet; I am only an ex-soldier."[466]

J. M. "Coot" Pyle echoed Johnston and Murray. Pyle joined the 3rd Texas Cavalry of Ross's brigade and fought at Wilson Creek, Pea Ridge, Shiloh, Iuka, both battles of Corinth, Van Dorn's Holly Springs Raid, Thompson's Station, and the Second Battle of Jackson, Mississippi. He was transferred to the Trans-Mississippi, and was present with Rip Ford at Palmetto Ranch, the last battle of the Civil War. He served in the Confederate army from June 1861 until May 1865. He recalled: "I have no regrets and nothing to take back. I feel that it was a very great favor that I had been permitted to help in the Confederate service."[467]

---

[465] Johnston, n.p.

[466] Yeary, II, p. 557. Murray fought in the Vicksburg Campaigns and was captured at Big Black River. Later, he served with Sterling Price in the Trans-Mississippi.

[467] Yeary, II, p. 624.

Thomas H. Bowman, who was captured at Fallen Timbers, was exchanged in 1862 and fought at Iuka and the Second Corinth. Later, he joined a horse artillery battery and rose to the rank of lieutenant. Eventually, his health failed and forced him to leave the service in the summer of 1864. Antebellum, he became Texas secretary of state and the superintendent of the State Orphan Home.

After three months in Federal hospitals, Sergeant Major David Johnston was released from Union prison. After the war, he resided in Giles County, Virginia, and studied law. He was admitted to the bar in 1867 and practiced in Petersburg, Virginia. Later, he moved to Pearisburg, Virginia, and Mercer County, West Virginia, where he was prosecuting attorney from 1872 to 1876. (There was a law against former Confederates practicing law in West Virginia, but Johnston was somehow able to skirt it.) He was elected state senator in 1878 and was a judge on the 9th Judicial Circuit Court from 1880 to 1888. He was elected to Congress as a Democrat in 1898 and served from March 4, 1899 to March 3, 1901. Defeated for reelection in 1900, he moved to Portland, Oregon, in 1908, and again became a judge. During this period, he wrote his war memories, *The Story of a Confederate Boy in the Civil War*, which was published in 1914. He ended it thusly: "I doubt not, had the South at any time during the contest agreed to return to the Union, that the Federal soldier would have thrown down his musket and gone home, for he was not fighting for the destruction of slavery, but for the preservation and restoration of the Union. I attach no blame to the brave Union soldier. He was as sincere and conscientious in the fight he made as was I in the one I made. We were both right from our respective viewpoints. With charity for all and malice toward none, this narrative is closed."[468] He died in Portland on July 7, 1917, at age seventy-two. He is buried in Lincoln Memorial Park.

---

[468] Johnston, n.p.

Sergeant Major David E. Johnston married Sarah Elizabeth Pearis in 1867. They had at least one child, a daughter. Mrs. Johnston, who was born in 1842 and died in 1924.

Mrs. Phoebe Levy Pember was matron and head of the Chimborazo Hospital from November 1862 until April 4, 1865, when the Union army took over. She remained on duty, however, until all of her patients had convalesced or been removed. When she departed, all she had was a ten-cent silver piece and a box of Confederate money, which was useless. After the war, she wrote *A Southern Woman's Story*, which was published in 1879. She also wrote articles for the *Atlantic Monthly* and *Harpers*. She eventually returned to Georgia and spent much of her time travelling. She died in 1913 and is buried in Laurel Grove Cemetery, Savannah. She was honored on a U.S. postal stamp in 1995.

One of Chimborazo's buildings currently houses the Confederate Medical Museum.

Phoebe Pember died at age eighty-nine. She is buried beside her husband. Her sister Eugenia, the Confederate spy, died in 1902 at the age of eighty-two. She is also buried in Laurel Grove Cemetery, Savannah.

Lieutenant Colonel Heros von Borcke suffered from his wounds for the rest of his life . He returned to Prussia and wrote his memoirs on the Army of Northern Virginia, which were published in 1867. He served on the staff of Prince Friedrich Karl in the Austro-Prussian War. Afterward, he retired to his family estate at Giesenbruegge, Germany (now Gizyn, Poland). He died in 1895 of sepsis caused by the Union shrapnel that was still in his body. His gravestone was destroyed by the Soviet army in 1945 but was restored by the Sons of Confederate Veterans in 2008.

Fletcher Archer, whose alarm battalion saved Petersburg in June 1864, was personally commended by General Beauregard and promoted to lieutenant colonel for his brilliant performance. He remained in the siege line south of Petersburg for the next nine and a half months, except for when he was recovering from a wound to the arm. He was wounded again during the retreat to Appomattox but was with the army when it surrendered.

Archer resumed the practice of law after the war and later served on the Petersburg City Council. He was briefly mayor of the city (1882–1883). He died in 1902.[469]

---

[469] Calkins, 2021; Bernard, pp. 123–127.

EPILOGUE

As the South gradually recovered economically, the surviving veterans, widows, and orphans naturally began erecting monuments to their dead loved ones, who left a legacy of valor and self-sacrifice worthy of anyone to emulate.

In 1890 John F. Harris, a black Confederate veteran, was serving in the Mississippi House of Representatives. A bill came before the house to erect a monument to the Confederate soldiers of Mississippi, but times were hard in the Magnolia State, and the younger, white legislators were blocking any bill which they considered fiscally unnecessary or superfluous. Mr. Harris was ill and could have stayed at home, but that was not in his nature. He could have remained silent and coasted along the easy road of the "political correctness" of his day, but his innate courage wouldn't allow him to do that. He dragged himself to the session and rose to speak:

"Mr. Speaker! I have risen here in my place to offer a few words on the bill. I have come from a sick bed…perhaps it was not prudent for me to come. But, sir, I could not rest quietly in my room without…contributing…a few remarks of my own. I was sorry to hear the speech of the young gentleman from Marshall County. I am sorry that any son of a soldier should go on record as opposed to the erection of a monument in honor of the brave dead. And, sir, I am convinced that had he seen what I saw at Seven Pines and in the Seven Days fighting around Richmond, the battlefield covered with the mangled forms of those who fought for their country and for their country's honor, he would not have made that speech….

When the news came that the South had been invaded, those men went forth to fight for what they believed, and they made no requests for monuments...But they died, and their virtues should be remembered. Sir, I went with them. I too wore the gray, the same color my master wore. We stayed four long years, and if that war had gone on till now I would have been there yet...I want to honor those brave men who died for their convictions. When my mother died I was a boy. Who, Sir, then acted the part of a mother to an orphaned slave boy, but my old missus? Were she living now, or could speak to me from those high realms where are gathered the sainted dead, she would tell me to vote for this bill. And, Sir, I shall vote for it. I want it known to all the world that my voice is given in favor of the bill to erect a monument in honor of the Confederate dead."

Harris's address helped convince all six African American representatives to unanimously vote in favor of the monument bill. It passed and the monument was erected.[470]

---

[470] Reprint from the Jackson *Daily Clarion Ledger*, February 23, 1890, found in the Old City Courthouse Museum, Vicksburg, Mississippi.

BIBLIOGRAPHY

Allan, William. *The Army of Northern Virginia in 1862*. Boston: 1892.

Allardice, Bruce S. *Confederate Colonels*. Columbia, Missouri: 2008.

Anderson, Ephraim McD. *Memoirs, Including the Campaigns of the First Missouri Confederate Brigade*. St. Louis: 1868.

Andrews, Eliza Frances. *The War-Time Journal of a Georgia Girl, 1864–1865*. New York: 1908.

Arkansas Division, United Confederate Veterans. *Confederate Women of Arkansas*. Little Rock: 1907.

Banks, Robert W. *The Battle of Franklin*. New York: 1908.

Bankston, Marie Louise Benton. *Camp-Fire Stories of the Mississippi Valley Campaign*. New Orleans: 1914.

Beale, R. L. T. *History of the Ninth Virginia Cavalry*. Richmond: 1899.

Bernard, George S., comp. and ed. *War Talks of Confederate Veterans*. Petersburg, Virginia: 1892.

Borcke, Heros von. *Memoirs of the Confederate War for Independence*. Philadelphia: 1867.

Bowman, Thornton H. *Reminiscences of an Ex-Confederate Soldier or Forty Years on Crutches*. Austin, Texas: 1904.

Branch, Mary Polk. *Memoirs of a Southern Woman "Within the Lines."* Chicago: 1912.

Brode, Ted. "Black Confederates." Presentation to the McGuire Camp #1714, Sons of Confederate Veterans. West Monroe, Louisiana: February 9, 2018.

Brooks, U. R. [Ulysses Robert]. *Stories of the Confederacy*. Columbia, S.C.: 1912).

Christopher M. Calkins, "Archer, Fletcher H. (1817-1902)," *Encyclopedia of Virginia*, https://encyclopediavirginia.org/entries/archer-fletcher-h-1817-1902/, accessed 2021.

Collins, Donald E. "War Crime or Justice? General George Pickett and the Mass Execution of Deserters in Civil War Kinton, North Carolina," in Steven E. Woodworth, ed., The Art of Command in the Civil War: 1998, http://homepages.rootsweb.com/~ncuv/kinston1.htm, accessed 2021.

Confederate Veteran. Various issues.

Cooke, John Esten. *Wearing of the Gray*. New York: 1867.

Davis, Burke. *Jeb Stuart, the Last Cavalier*. New York: 1957.

Douglass, Frederick. *Douglass' Monthly*. Vol. IV (September 1861).

Dowdey, Clifford. *Lee*. New York: 1955.

Downs, James. *Sick from Freedom: African-American Death and Suffering During the Civil War and Reconstruction*. Oxford, U.K.: 2012.

Duaine, Carl L. *The Dead Men Wore Boots: An Account of the 32nd Texas Volunteer Cavalry, C.S.A.* Austin, Texas: 1966.

Dufour, Charles L. *The Night the War Was Lost*. New York: 1960. Reprint ed., New Orleans: 1990.

Early, Jubal A. *A Memoir of the Last Year of the War for Independence in the Confederate States of America*. Lynchburg, Virginia: 1867.

Eicher, David J. *The Longest Night*. New York: 2002.

Eicher, John H. and David J. Eicher. *Civil War High Commands*. Stanford, California: 2001.

Freeman, Douglas S. *R. E. Lee*. New York: 1933–1935. Four volumes.

Gilmor, Harry. *Four Years in the Saddle*. New York: 1866.

Harrison, Mrs. Burton (nee Miss Constance Cary). *Recollections Grave and Gay*. New York: 1911.

Johnson, Robert U. and Clarence C. Buel, eds, *Battles and Leaders of the Civil War*. New York: 1884–1886.

Johnston, David E. *Confederate Boy in the Civil War.* Portland, Oregon: 1914, from Project Gutenberg, https://www.gutenberg.org/files/44889/44889-h/44889-h.htm.

Kennedy, James Ronald and Walter Donald Kennedy. *The South Was Right!* 3rd ed. Columbia, South Carolina: 2021.

King, William C., and W. P. Derby, comp. *Camp-Fire Sketches and Battle-Field Echoes.* Springfield, Massachusetts: 1886.

Lankford, Nelson. "Virginia Convention of 1861," Encyclopedia Virginia, February 1, 2021. https://encyclopediavirginia.org/entries/virginia-convention-of-1861.

Lewis, John H. *A Rebel in Pickett's Charge at Gettysburg.* 1895.

Livermore, Thomas L. *Numbers and Losses in the Civil War in America.* Boston and New York: 1900.

Long, E. B. *The Civil War Day by Day.* New York: 1971.

McCarthy, Carlton. *Detailed Minutiae of Soldier Life in the Army of Northern Virginia, 1861–1865.* Richmond, Virginia: 1899.

McGuire, Hunter H., *The Confederate Cause and Conduct in the War Between the States.* Richmond, Virginia: 1907.

Mendes, Thomas C. "Blacks, Jews Fight on the Side of the South. *Washington Times.* June 15, 2002.

Mitcham, Samuel W. Jr. *Vicksburg.* Washington, D.C.: 2018.

Moore, Frank. *The Civil War in Song and Story.* New York: 1865.

"Papers." Old City Courthouse Museum, Vicksburg, Mississippi.

Pember, Phoebe Yates Levy. *A Southern Woman's Story.* New York: 1879.

Pryor, Mrs. Roger A. [Sara Agnes Rice Pryor]. *Reminiscences of Peace and War.* New York: 1905.

Rollins, Richard, ed. *Black Southerners in Gray: Essays on Afro-Americans in Confederate Armies.* Murfreesboro, Tennessee: 1994.

Ropes, John C. *Story of the Civil War.* New York: 1894. Two volumes.

Segars, J. H. and Charles K. Barrow. *Black Southerners in the Confederate Army.* Gretna, Louisiana: 2001.

Southern, Adam. Personal communications, 2021.

Southern Literary Messenger. January 1861.

Stone, Henry. "Repelling Hood's Invasion of Tennessee" in Robert U. Johnson and Clarence C. Buel, eds, *Battles and Leaders of the Civil War* (New York: 1884–1886), Vol. IV.

Sullivan, Walter, ed. *The War the Women Lived: Female Voices from the Confederate South.* Nashville, Tennessee: 1995.

Trisler, Walter. "The CSS Arkansas." Lecture delivered to Camp 1714, Sons of Confederate Veterans, West Monroe, Louisiana, July 13, 2021.

Trisler, Walter. "The Rebel Terror from Yazoo." *Southern Defender,* November 2019.

Tunnard, W. H. *A Southern Record: The History of the Third Louisiana.* Baton Rouge: 1866.

United Confederate Veterans. *Confederate Women of Arkansas in the Civil War, 1861–1865.* Little Rock: 1907.

United States War Department. *The War of the Rebellion: A Compilation of the Official Records of the Union and Confederate Armies.* Series 1. Robert N. Scott, comp. Washington, D.C.: 1880–1901.

United States War Department. *The War of the Rebellion: A Compilation of the Official Records of the Union and Confederate Armies.* Series 3. Fred C. Ainsworth and Joseph W. Kirkley, comp. Washington, D.C.: 1900. www.jewishworldreview.com. Accessed 2012.

"Virginia County Vote on the Secession Ordinance, May 23, 1861," New River Notes, https://www.newrivernotes.com/historical_antebellum_1861_virginia_voteforsecession.htm, accessed 2012.

Yeary, Mamie. *Reminiscences of the Boys in Gray, 1861–1865.* Dallas: 1912. Two volumes.